REA's Books Are The Best...
They have rescued lots of grades and more!

SO-AHP-136

(a sample of the <u>hundreds of letters</u> REA receives each year)

" Your books are great! They are very helpful, and have upped my grade in every class. Thank you for such a great product. "

Student, Seattle, WA

" Your book has really helped me sharpen my skills and improve my weak areas. Definitely will buy more. "

Student, Buffalo, NY

" Compared to the other books that my fellow students had, your book was the most useful in helping me get a great score. "

Student, North Hollywood, CA

" I really appreciate the help from your excellent book. Please keep up your great work. "

Student, Albuquerque, NM

" Your book was such a better value and was so much more complete than anything your competition has produced (and I have them all)! "

Teacher, Virginia Beach, VA

(more on next page)

(continued from previous page)

"Your books have saved my GPA, and quite possibly my sanity. My course grade is now an 'A', and I couldn't be happier."

Student, Winchester, IN

"These books are the best review books on the market. They are fantastic!"

Student, New Orleans, LA

"Your book was responsible for my success on the exam. . . I will look for REA the next time I need help."

Student, Chesterfield, MO

"I think it is the greatest study guide I have ever used!"

Student, Anchorage, AK

"I encourage others to buy REA because of their superiority. Please continue to produce the best quality books on the market."

Student, San Jose, CA

"Just a short note to say thanks for the great support your book gave me in helping me pass the test . . . I'm on my way to a B.S. degree because of you!"

Student, Orlando, FL

Super Review®

All You Need to Know!

ITALIAN

C.H. Grandgent, Ph.D.
Professor of Romance Languages

E.H. Wilkins, Ph.D.
Professor of Romance Languages

**and the staff of
Research & Education Association
Carl Fuchs, Language Program Director**

Research & Education Association
Visit our website at
www.rea.com

Research & Education Association
61 Ethel Road West
Piscataway, New Jersey 08854
E-mail: info@rea.com

SUPER REVIEW®
OF ITALIAN

Year 2007 Printing

Copyright © 2002 by Research & Education Association, Inc. All rights reserved. No part of this book may be reproduced in any form without permission of the publisher.

Printed in the United States of America

Library of Congress Control Number 2001093916

International Standard Book Number 0-87891-389-0

 SUPER REVIEW® and REA® are registered trademarks of Research & Education Association, Inc.

What this Super Review® Will Do for You

REA's **Super Review** provides **all you need to know** to excel in class and succeed on midterms, finals, and even pop quizzes.

Think of this book as giving you access to your own private tutor. Here, right at your fingertips, is a brisk review to help you not only understand your textbook but also pick up where even some of the best lectures leave off.

Outstanding **Super Review** features include...

- Comprehensive yet concise coverage
- Targeted preparation for subject tests
- Easy-to-follow **Q** & **A** format that helps you master the subject matter
- End-of-chapter quizzes that provide pretest tune-up

We think you'll agree that, whether you're prepping for your next test or want to be a stronger contributor in class, REA's **Super Review** truly provides **all you need to know**!

Larry B. Kling
Chief Editor

ITALY

Aosta

Bolzano

Udine

Venice

Milan Verona

Turin

Bologna

San Marino

Genoa

Pisa

Florence

Ancona

Elba

Pescara

Rome

Taranto

Sassari

Naples

SARDINIA

Cagliari

Palermo

Messina

SICILY

Catania

Pantelleria

CONTENTS

Chapter   **Page**

1   PRONUNCIATION **1**
    Sounds, Spelling, Accent, and Syllabication 1
    Additional Notes on Pronunciation 6
    Inflections of the Voice 9

2   ARTICLES **11**
    The Definite Article 11
    The Indefinite Article 14

3   NOUNS **16**
    Gender 16
    Number 18

4   ADJECTIVES **21**
    Gender and Number 21
    Comparison 23

5   AUGMENTATIVES, DIMINUTIVES, AND
    NUMERALS **26**
    Augmentative and Diminutive Endings 26
    Numerals 28

6   DEMONSTRATIVE, INTERROGATIVE,
    RELATIVE, AND POSSESSIVE PRONOUNS **32**
    Demonstrative Pronouns 32
    Interrogative Pronouns 33
    Relative Pronouns 34
    Possessive Pronouns 35

7   PERSONAL PRONOUNS **38**
    Conjunctive Forms 38
    Disjunctive Forms 43
    Forms of Address 46

8   AUXILIARY VERBS **48**
   Auxiliaries of Voice and Tense
       (essere, avere) 48
   Modal Auxiliaries 54

9   REGULAR AND IRREGULAR VERBS **56**
   The Regular Verb 56
   The Irregular Verb 61

10   MOODS AND TENSES **65**
   Infinitive and Participle 65
   Past, Present, and Future 67
   Past, Future, or Conditional 69
   Subjunctive 69

**11   CONJUNCTIONS, PREPOSITIONS, AND
     ADVERBS** **73**
   Conjunctions 73
   Prepositions 75
   Adverbs.. 78

12   INDEFINITE PRONOUNS **82**

13   LIST OF IRREGULAR VERBS **86**
   First Conjugation............................... 88
   Second Conjugation......................... 89
   Third Conjugation 92
   Fourth Conjugation........................... 97

**14   ALPHABETICAL LIST OF IRREGULAR AND
     DEFECTIVE VERBS** **100**

15   LESSONS AND EXERCISES **105**

─────────

ITALIAN–ENGLISH VOCABULARY **163**

ENGLISH–ITALIAN VOCABULARY **179**

CHAPTER 1

Pronunciation

SOUNDS, SPELLING, ACCENT, AND SYLLABICATION

1. The Italian alphabet has the same letters as the English, except that **k**, **w**, **x**, and **y** do not occur in native words in modern Italian.

2. The Italians distinguish seven vowels: **a**, close **e**, open **e**, **i**, close **o**, open **o**, **u**; to these may be added an intermediate **e** and **o**, used in unaccented syllables. Every vowel has a clear sound, no matter what may be its position in the word. It is never obscured; and it never tends, as do the English long vowels, to become a diphthong.

Italian vowels are all pronounced rather quickly; hence there is but little difference in quantity between accented and unaccented sounds. English-speaking students must carefully avoid drawling the accented and slighting the unaccented syllables; they should try to give to every Italian vowel about the length of **i** in 'bitter.'

a is nearly like *a* in 'father': as fava, canna, cassa, palla.

e close is nearly like *a* in 'fate': as beve, vere, stelle, messe.

e open may be formed by trying to pronounce *e* in 'bell' with the mouth very wide open: as bella, amena, fera, pensa.

i is nearly like *ee* in 'feet': as miri, vini, fissi, spilli.

o close is nearly like *o* in 'mope': as dopo, dove, bollo, sotto.

o open is nearly like *aw* in 'saw' pronounced with the mouth wide open: as no, odi, poi, donna.

u is nearly like *oo* in 'boot': as una, cura, nulla, ruppi.

(*a*) The letters **i** and **u** are sometimes used to represent consonant sounds (see **4**); but in formulating rules they are always counted as vowels.

3. As close and open vowels are not distinguished in spelling, some rules are necessary:

1. Unaccented **e** and **o** are intermediate between close and open: as mare, *sea;* amo, *I love.*

2. **e** and **o** are close in all monosyllables[1] ending in a consonant: as con, *with;* non, *not;* per, *for.*

3. In monosyllables[1] and oxytones[2] ending in a vowel, final **e** is close, final **o** is open: as che, *what;* me, *me;* re, *king;* credè, *he believed;* perchè, *why;* do, *I give;* Po, *Po;* sarò, *I shall be;* andò, *he went.*

EXCEPTIONS: (*a*) Final **e** is open in è=*is*, re=*re*, interjections (as aimè, *alas;* chè, *nonsense*), proper names (as Noè, *Noah*), and foreign words (as caffè, *coffee*). (*b*) Final **o** is close in lo and o.

4. Accented **e** and **o** are always open in the groups **ie** and **uo**: as piede, *foot;* fuoco, *fire.* **e** and **o** standing for **ie** and **uo** are open: as ven=viene, *he comes;* cor=cuore, *heart.*

5. In words that have always formed a part of the spoken language, accented **e** is nearly always close when it represents Latin *ē* or *ĭ*, open when it represents Latin *ĕ* or *ae;* accented **o** is nearly always close when it represents Latin *ō* or *ŭ*, open when it represents Latin *ŏ* or *au*. In book words accented **e** and **o** are usually open.

4. B, f, m, p, q, v are pronounced as in English.

c, before **e** or **i**, sounds like *ch* in 'chin'; elsewhere it is always like English *k*: as cima, *top;* come, *how;* dolce, *sweet.*

---

[1] Not including shortened forms of words that regularly have more than one syllable. [2] Words accented on the last syllable.

g, before **e** or **i**, sounds like *g* in 'gem'; elsewhere it is always like *g* in 'go': as ga**tt**o, *cat;* **g**ente, *people;* spin**g**i, *push.*

(*a*) A **cc** or a **gg** before **e** or **i** has merely the sound of *ch* in 'chin' or *g* in 'gem' prolonged: as fa**cc**e, *faces;* le**gg**e, *law.*

d, l, n, t are pronounced farther forward in the mouth than in English; the tip of the tongue should touch the back of the upper front teeth: as a**l**to, *high;* **d**ato, *given;* **l**u**n**a, *moon;* **n**u**d**o, *naked;* **t**uo**n**o, *thunder.*

h is always silent: as a**h**i, *oh!* **h**a, *he has.*

i, unaccented, before a vowel, sounds like English *y*: as **i**eri, *yesterday;* pa**i**o, *pair;* p**i**ù, *more.* In the groups **cia, cio, ciu, gia, gio, giu**, an unaccented **i** serves only to show that the **c** or **g** is soft: as fa**ci**a, *face;* guan**ci**a, *cheek;* **ci**ò, *that;* **gi**ù, *down;* man**gi**a, *eat;* ra**gi**o, *ray.*

j is merely another way of writing **i**.

n before a **q** or a hard **c** or **g** has the sound of English *ng*: as ba**n**ca (bang-ka), *bank;* du**n**que (dung-kwe), *therefore;* lu**n**go (lung-go), *long.*

r is always rolled, the point of the tongue vibrating against the teeth: as ca**r**o, *dear;* **r**osso, *red;* pe**r**, *for.* When **r** is double or followed by a consonant, the trill is prolonged: as ca**rr**o, *cart;* bu**rr**o, *butter;* ma**rr**one, *chestnut;* ca**r**ne, *meat;* po**r**ta, *door.*

s is generally pronounced nearly like English *s* in 'see,' but with a somewhat sharper sound: as **s**o, *I know;* **s**pillo, *pin.*

Initial **s** before a sonant (**b, d, g, l, m, n, r, v**) has a sound intermediate between **s** and English *z*: as **s**drucciolare, *to slip;* **s**litta, *sleigh.*

A single **s** between vowels has, in most words, the sound of English *z*: as ca**s**o, *case;* cau**s**a, *cause;* vi**s**o, *face.* But in the following cases it is pronounced like *s* in 'see,' 'mason':

(*a*) In annu**s**are, a**s**ino, ca**s**a, Chiu**s**i, co**s**a, co**s**ì, de**s**iderio, na**s**o, para**s**ito, pe**s**o, Pi**s**a, pi**s**ello, po**s**a, ripo**s**o, ri**s**o, su**s**ina, and their derivatives, and in some uncommon words.

(*b*) After the prefixes **de–**, **di–**,[1] **pre–**, **pro–**, **re–**, **ri–**, **tra–**[1]: as desistere, disegno, presumere, proseguire, reservare, risolvere, trasudare.

(*c*) In the adjective ending **–oso** and the adjective and substantive ending **–ese**: as noi**o**so, *troublesome;* ingl**e**se, *English;* m**e**se, *month.* But in cort**e**se, franc**e**se, lucch**e**se, march**e**se, pa**e**se, pal**e**se, the **s** is like English *z.*

(*d*) In the past absolute and past participle of **chiedere, chiudere, nascondere, porre, radere, ridere, rimanere, rispondere, rodere**, and all verbs in **–endere**; and in their compounds and derivatives: as chie**s**i, socchiu**s**o, nasco**s**e, rispo**s**ero, ra**s**oio, rima**s**e, corrispo**s**i, ro**s**ero, acce**s**i, re**s**o, sce**s**a.

EXCEPTIONS to this rule are **deridere**, verbs in **–cludere**, and derivatives of **rodere**.

u, unaccented, before a vowel, sounds like English *w*: as b**u**ono, *good;* g**u**ardare, *to look;* p**u**ò, *he can.*

z and **zz** are generally pronounced like a long and vigorous *ts*: as al**z**are, *to lift;* a**z**ione, *action;* pre**zz**o, *price;* **z**io, *uncle.*

In the following cases, however, **z** and **zz** sound like a prolonged *dz*:

(*a*) In a**zz**urro, do**zz**ina, me**zz**o, pran**z**o, ribre**zz**o, roman**z**o, **z**elo, and many less common words.

(*b*) In verbs in **–izzare** (as utili**zz**are, *to utilize*); except atti**zz**are, diri**zz**are, gui**zz**are, ri**zz**are, sti**zz**are, and their compounds, and a few uncommon words.

5. The following combinations are to be noted:

ch (used only before **e** and **i**) is always like English *k*: as fi**ch**i (plural of **fico**, *fig*). **sch** is like *sk*: as **sch**erzo, *sport.*

gh (used only before **e** and **i**) is always like English *g* in 'go': as a**gh**i (plural of **ago**, *needle*).

---

[1] Not to be confused with **dis–**, **tras–**: disonore, trasandare.

gli (written **gl** if the following vowel be **i**) is nearly like English *lli* in 'million': as figlio, *son;* figli, *sons.*

But in Anglia, geroglifico, glicerina, negligere and its derivatives, and a few uncommon words borrowed from the Greek or Latin, gl is like English *gl.*

gn is nearly like *ni* in 'onion': as ogni, *every.*

qu is always like *kw*: as questo, *this.*

sc before **e** and **i** is nearly like *sh* in 'ship': as uscire, *to go out.*

Before all other letters it is pronounced *sk*: as scuola, *school;* scherno, *contempt.*

6. Every letter in Italian is distinctly and separately sounded; the only exceptions are **h**, silent **i** (see **4**), and the combinations mentioned in **5.**

arte, *art.*	andai, *I went.*	paura, *fear.*
firma, *signature.*	aura, *breeze.*	sentii, *I felt.*
furto, *theft.*	bugie, *lies.*	noi, *we.*
giorno, *day.*	Europa, *Europe.*	poi, *then.*
verso, *toward.*	miei, *my.*	suoi, *his.*

Where a double consonant is written, both letters must be sounded, the first at the end of the preceding, the second at the beginning of the following syllable:

anno, *year.*	babbo, *father.*	fatto, *done.*
messo, *put.*	quello, *that.*	bocca, *mouth.*

For **rr**, **zz**, and soft **cc** and **gg**, see **4.**

l, **m**, **n**, and **r**, when preceded by an accented vowel and followed by another consonant, are prolonged:

alto (all-to), *high.*	tanto (tann-to), *so much.*
sempre (semm-pre), *always.*	parte (parr-te), *part.*

7. The grave (ˋ) accent is placed on the last syllable of oxytones and on some monosyllables.

8. Italian words are divided in such a way that, if possible, every syllable shall begin with a consonant:

ta-vo-li-no, *table.*	mez-zo, *half.*
frat-tan-to, *meanwhile.*	cac-cia, *hunt.*
al-l' uo-mo, *to the man.*	og-gi, *to-day.*
nar-ra-re, *to relate.*	po-e-ta, *poet.*

In the groups **s**+consonant, consonant+**r**, those mentioned in **5**, and **cl, fl, gl, pl**, both consonants belong to the following syllable. **i**=y and **u**=w go with the following vowel; **ai, au, ei, eu, oi** are not separated.

fe-sta	ca-sti-ghi	ri-flet-te-re
te-a-tro	del-l' ac-qua	miei
a-vro	in-chio-stro	al-l' au-ra
bi-so-gno	mi-glio-re	tuoi

ADDITIONAL NOTES ON PRONUNCIATION

[The numbers prefixed to the following notes refer to the paragraphs of the foregoing chapter.]

1. The Tuscan names of the letters are:

a	e	i	enne	erre	vu or vi
bi	effe	je or i lungo	o	esse	zeta (with z pro-
ci	gi	elle	pi	ti	nounced *dz*)
di	acca	emme	cu	u	

They do not change in the plural. Their gender is not fixed; in general those ending in −**a** or −**e** are considered as feminine, the others as masculine. **K, x, y** are *cappa, iccase, ipsilon,* all masculine.

2. (*a*) The sounds **a, e, o,** followed by a single consonant, are somewhat longer than the other vowels: for instance, in d**a**to, f**e**ro, **o**vo the accented **a, e, o** are longer than in d**a**ttero, v**e**ro, **o**ve. Final accented vowels sound particularly short: as in am**ò**, belt**à**, caff**è**.

(*b*) In forming **i** the mouth should be made as broad as possible from side to side. For **u** and **o** the lips should be puckered. For **a** and **e** the mouth should be opened very wide.

3. (*a*) If an adverb in –**mente** is formed from an adjective containing **e** or **o**, this vowel has, in the adverb, a secondary accent, and retains its open sound: as (breve) brevemente, *briefly;* (nobile) nobilmente, *nobly.* Furthermore, **e** and **o** retain their quality in seeming compounds that consist, in reality, of two or more separate words: as **tostochè** = tostoche = tosto che, *as soon as.*

(*b*) Past absolute forms and past participles in –**esi**, –**eso**, –**osi**, –**oso** have a close **e** or **o**; except chiesi (also chiesi), esplosi, esploso, leso.

(*c*) In the suffixes –**eccio** (–a), –**esco** (–a), –**ese**, –**essa**, –**etto** (–a), –**ezzo** (–a), –**mente**, and –**mento** the **e** is always close; while in the diminutive suffix –**ello** (–a), and in the endings –**ente**, –**enza**, –**erio** (or –**ero**), and –**esimo** (–a) it is open: as inglese, *English;* probabilmente, *probably;* prudente, *prudent;* ventesimo, *twentieth.*

(*d*) In the endings –**oio**, –**one**, –**ore**, and in the suffix –**oso** (–a) the **o** is close; while in the ending –**orio**, and in –**occio** (–a), –**otto** (–a), and –**ozzo** (–a), used as suffixes to nouns or adjectives, it is open: as vassoio, *tray;* amore, *love;* romitorio, *hermitage;* casotta, *good-sized house.*

(*e*) In the following cases accented **e** or **o** may have either the close or the open sound: in Giorgio, maestra, maestro, nego (from **negare**), neve, organo, scendere, senza, siete and sono (from **essere**), spegnere, Stefano, vendere; and in the past future endings –**esti**, –**emmo**, –**este**. The present subjunctive forms dieno, sieno, stieno are pronounced also dieno, sieno, stieno.

(*f*) In poetry we often find **e** for **ie**, **o** for **uo**: as **ven** = **viene**, *he comes;* **cor** = **cuore**, *heart.* Simple **o** for **uo** is very common in modern spoken Tuscan: as **bono** = **buono**, *good;* **novo** = **nuovo**, *new.*

4. **c.** (*a*) Between two vowels, of which the second is **e** or **i**, single **c** and single **g** are, in ordinary Tuscan speech, pronounced respectively like *sh* in 'ship' and *si* in 'vision': as pace, *peace;* stagione, *season.*

(*b*) Between two vowels, of which the second is **a**, **o**, or **u**, a single **c** or a **q** is, in popular Tuscan speech, sounded nearly like English *h*: as poco (poho), *little;* di questa cosa (di hwesta hosa), *of this thing.* This pronunciation is regarded as inelegant.

j. Some writers use **j**, except after a consonant, for the **i** that is pronounced **y**: as **j**eri for ieri, *yesterday;* pajo for paio, *pair.* It is sometimes used also for final **i** in the plural of words in unaccented **–io**: as specch**j** (also specchi and occasionally specchii) for specchi, *mirrors,* plural of specch**i**o.

z. Aside from verbs in **–izzare, z** and **zz** have the value *dz* in the following words and their derivatives:

arzillo	frizzo	magazzino	romanzo	zelo
azzurro	garzone	manzo	ronzio	zenit
barzelletta	gazzella	mezzo	rozzo	zero
bizza	gazzetta	orizzonte	zaffiro	zeta
brezza	gonzo	orzo	zaffrone	zinco
bronzo	Lazzaro	penzolo	zanzara	zodiaco
donzella	lazzeretto	pranzo	zebra	zolla
dozzina	lazzo	ribrezzo	zeffiro	zona

also in all derivatives of the Greek *zoos,* and in many uncommon words.

5. In pronouncing **gli** and **gn** the point of the tongue should remain behind the lower teeth: as fi**gli**o, *son;* o**gn**i, *every.*

6. If one of the words mentioned below, or any oxytone ending in a vowel, is closely followed by a word beginning with a consonant, this consonant is, in Tuscany, generally pronounced double. The words are:[1]

a	dì, *day*	giù	o[4]	sopra
che	di', *say*	ha	più	sta[2]
chi	e	ho	qua	sto
cio	è	infra	qualche	su
come	fa[2]	intra	qui	te[3]
contra	fè, *faith*	là	re	tra
da	fe'=fece	li	sa	tre
da, *gives*	fo	ma	se, *if*	tu
da', *give*	fra	me[3]	sè	va[2]
do	fu	mo'=môdo	si	vo=vado
dove	già	nè	so	vo'=voglio

---

[1] The materials for this list were taken from D'Ovidio's article in Gröber's *Grund riß der romanischen Philologie,* I, p. 496 (2d ed., p. 644).

[2] Both the imperative sing. and the pres. ind. third sing.

[3] The disjunctive form.

[4] Both the conjunction *or* and the interrogative particle.

verrà da me domani (verraddammeddomani), *he will come to my house tomorrow.* In such cases **c** is, of course, never pronounced like *h* (see 4, **c**, (*b*).

INFLECTIONS OF THE VOICE

1. Italian speech is at once smoother and less monotonous than American: it is less interrupted by breathings, and it has far greater variations of pitch. In order to speak or read Italian well, an American must learn to breathe in speaking as he does in singing; he must inhale deeply at the beginning of the clause, and not stop again until he reaches the end of it. The following directions may be of use; they are based on the Tuscan pronunciation, and particularly on that of Siena.

2. (*a*) The simplest inflection in a declarative sentence is as follows: at the beginning the voice is pitched low; it rises in the middle (in earnest conversation often to a falsetto), and falls again at the end. The most emphatic word generally receives the highest tone; if there are no words after it to complete the cadence, the first words of the phrase are often repeated at the end: as **me lo dicono tutti me lo dicono,** *they all tell me so,* where the **u** of **tutti** is an octave higher than the beginning and the close of the sentence.

(*b*) When there is a pause on some not particularly emphatic word before the main verb, that word has a slight circumflex accent, the voice rising about one semitone and falling about three: as **fuori di città** ∧ **c' è una bellissima villa**\, *outside the city there's a beautiful villa,* where **bellissima** has the high pitch, and the **a** of **città** has the circumflex. This accent is generally heard whenever modifying clauses or phrases precede the main clause.

(*c*) Almost all declarative sentences are made up chiefly of these two inflections, the long rise and fall and the short circumflex. Americans must avoid breaking up their sentences by meaningless falling tones. The fall occurs in Italian, as in English, on a very emphatic word, and at the end of a sentence. It is used, also, with a verb of saying or thinking, followed by a direct quotation;

and with any word or phrase used as a vocative, except in loud calling (see 4, *b*): as **allora chiama Alfredo e gli dice\: Bambino\, dimmi la verità\,** where the syllables **fre, bam,** and **dim** have the highest pitch.

3. (*a*) Questions to which the answer may be 'yes' or 'no' have either one of two circumflex accents: in the first the voice rises about five semitones and falls one; in the second, which is sometimes used in reading and in polite phrases, the voice rises and falls about an octave. Ex.: **l'hai visto?** *have you seen him?* where the pitches of **l' hai, vi,** and **sto** may be represented by the notes *do, fa, mi;* **ha ben dormito?** *did you sleep well?* where **mi** is an octave higher than **dor** and **to.** The former accent may be heard in the Irish pronunciation of English.

(*b*) These inflections are nearly always confined to the last few syllables of the sentence. In some questions, however, they appear twice, generally occurring first on the verb; and occasionally the circumflex on the verb is the only one.

(*c*) Questions that cannot be answered by 'yes' or 'no' usually begin high, the pitch depending on the emphasis. The voice then falls, but generally rises again at the last syllable, going up about three semitones: as **o come\ hai fatto/?** *how did you do it?* This accent is common among the Irish, and may be heard in England. The final rise is, however, often omitted, especially in very short sentences and in polite phrases: as **come sta\?** *how do you do?*

4. (*a*) Exclamations of surprise begin very high, and sink rapidly: as **senti\!** *no!* **un affar di niente\!** *you don't say so!* where **un** has the main stress; **per mio bacco!** *I want to know!* with the accent on **per.**

(*b*) In calling to persons at a distance, the Tuscans sing rather than speak; the usual tune is *do, la, sol,* the accented syllable being highest: as **Agostina!** *Augustine!* **partenza!** *all aboard!*

CHAPTER 2

Articles

9. The article is not declined, but it agrees with its noun in gender and number.

10. Masculine:

(*a*) Sing. **il**, pl. **i**, before a word beginning with any consonant except **s** impure[1] and **z**.

(*b*) Sing. **lo**, pl. **gli**, before a vowel or **s** impure or **z**.[2]

Before a vowel **lo** becomes **l'**; **gli** becomes **gl'** before **i**.

il padre, *the father.*	**i** padri, *the fathers.*
lo stesso padre, *the same father.*	**gli** stessi padri, *the same fathers.*
lo sciame, *the swarm.*	**gli** sciami, *the swarms.*
lo zio, *the uncle.*	**gli** zii, *the uncles.*
l' uomo, *the man.*	**gli** uomini, *the men.*
l' insetto, *the insect.*	**gl'** insetti, *the insects.*

11. Feminine:

Sing. **la**, pl. **le**.

Before a vowel **la** becomes **l'**; **le** becomes **l'** before **e**.

la madre, *the mother.*	**le** madri, *the mothers.*
l' ora, *the hour.*	**le** ore, *the hours.*
l' erba, *the herb.*	**l'** erbe, *the herbs.*

12. When the definite article is preceded by one of the prepositions **di, da, a, in, con, su, per,** the article and prepo-

---

[1] That is, **s** followed by another consonant.

[2] **Li** is sometimes used for **gli**. Some writers use **il, i** before **z** and before **sce-** or **sci-**. In poetry **lo** is often used for **il**.

sition are generally contracted into one word, as shown in the following table (**con, per** are often uncontracted[1]):

	il	i	lo	gli	la	le	l'
di, *of*	del	dei or de'	dello	degli	della	delle	dell'
da, *by*	dal	dai or da'	dallo	dagli	dalla	dalle	dall'
a, *to*	al	ai or a'	allo	agli	alla	alle	all'
in, *in*	nel	nei or ne'	nello	negli	nella	nelle	nell'
con, *with*	col	coi or co'	collo	cogli	colla	colle	coll'
su, *on*	sul	sui or su'	sullo	sugli	sulla	sulle	sull'
per, *for*	pel	pei or pe'	per lo	per gli	per la	per le	per l'

del padre, *of the father.*   **dai** padri, *by the fathers.*
allo specchio, *to the mirror.*   **negli** specchi, *in the mirrors.*
colla madre, *with the mother.*   **colle** madri, *with the mothers.*
sull' uomo, *on the man.*   **per gli** uomini, *for the men.*

(*a*) The word *some* is frequently rendered in Italian by **di** with the definite article. This is called the *partitive* construction.

Datemi **del** vino.   *Give me some wine.*
Delle belle cose.   *Some fine things.*

13. In the following cases the definite article is used in Italian, though not in English:

(*a*) Before the possessive adjectives:

Il nostro giardino.   *Our garden.*
I suoi fratelli.   *His brothers.*

When, however, the possessive qualifies an otherwise unmodified noun in the singular expressing relationship, the article is generally omitted: as **mia madre**, *my mother.* For a fuller statement, see **45**, *a.*

[1] Some writers, especially poets, prefer to keep other prepositions separate from the article.

(b) Before an abstract noun or one denoting a whole class; but not before one designating a part of a class:

L' uomo propone.	*Man proposes (i.e., all mankind).*
I fiori nascono dal seme.	*Flowers spring from the seed (i.e., all flowers).*
La morte è il peggiore **dei** mali.	*Death is the worst of evils (i.e., death in general, and all evils).*

BUT

Il mio giardino è tutto fiorito; rose, gigli, viole mandano un odore soave.	*My garden is all in flower; roses, lilies, violets send forth a sweet fragrance (i.e., some roses, etc.).*

(c) Before a noun and adjective used either in a specific or in a general (but not in a partitive) sense:

L' anno scorso.	*Last year (i.e., the last year).*
Il povero Luigi non viene.	*(The) poor Lewis doesn't come.*
Gli uomini buoni.	*Good men (i.e., all good men).*

BUT

Ho trovato dappertutto uomini buoni.	*I have found (some) good men everywhere.*

(d) Before a title followed by a proper name:

La regina Elizabeth.	*Queen Elisabetta.*
Il signor Bruni.	*Mr. Brown.*

It is not used, however, before **Don**, **Messer**, and **Ser**.

(e) Before family names; often before familiar given names of women; occasionally before familiar given names of men:

Il Bianchi è morto.	*White is dead.*
La Patti canta.	*Patti sings.*
Conosco l' Olivia.	*I know Olivia.*
Viene il Tonio.	*Tony is coming.*

(f) Before names of provinces, countries, and continents:

la Toscana, *Tuscany.*	**all'** Italia, *to Italy.*
la Svizzera, *Switzerland.*	per **l'** Europa, *for Europe.*

But the article is omitted after **in** in phrases that denote going to or dwelling in a country; and often after **di** or **in** when the

Campania, Positano

Leaning Tower of Pisa

preposition with the name of a country is equivalent to an adjective of nationality:

Vado in Germania.	*I go to Germany.*
Rimango in Francia.	*I remain in France.*
La regina d' Inghilterra.	*The queen of England* (*i.e.,* the English queen).
Il vino di Spagna.	*The wine of Spain* (*i.e.,* Spanish wine).
Il teatro in Italia.	*The drama in Italy* (*i.e.,* the Italian drama).

The article is not used regularly with names of cities: as vedremo **Roma**, *we shall see Rome.* **La** Spezia, however, has the article; and so have a few others.

In all the above cases (beginning with **13**, *a*) the article, unless it would be employed in English, is omitted when the noun is used as a vocative or is modified by a numeral or a pronominal adjective. It is often omitted in lists.

Signora Monti, come sta?	*Mrs. Monti, how do you do?*
Italia, ti rivedo.	*Italy, I see thee again.*
Vieni, amico mio.	*Come, my friend.*
Due bellissimi cani.	*Two very fine dogs.*
Questa sua opera.	*This work of his.*
Ha parecchi vizi.	*He has several bad habits.*
Fede, speranza, carita.	*Faith, hope, and charity.*

THE INDEFINITE ARTICLE

14. Masculine:

(*a*) **Un** before a vowel or any consonant except **s** impure and **z.**

(*b*) **Uno** before **s** impure or **z.**[1]

un padre, *a father.*	**un** uomo, *a man.*
un anello, *a ring.*	**uno** specchio, *a mirror.*
uno sciame, *a swarm.*	**uno** zio, *an uncle.*

Note that masculine **un** before a vowel has no apostrophe.

---

[1] Some writers use **un** before **z** and before **sce–** or **sci–**.

15. Feminine:

Una, which becomes **un'** before a vowel.

una madre, *a mother*.   **un'** ora, *an hour*.

16. In the following cases the indefinite article, though expressed in English, is omitted in Italian:

(*a*) Before a predicate noun expressing occupation, condition, rank, or nationality, and not accompanied by an adjective.

Lui è poeta, *he is a poet*.   Sono marchese, *I am a marquis*.
Siete italiano, *you are an Italian*.   È medico, *he is a doctor*.

(*b*) Generally before an antecedent (of a relative clause) used in apposition to a preceding noun modified by a definite article or a demonstrative pronoun.

L' Arno, fiume che traversa   *The Arno, a river which traverses*
Firenze.   *Florence.*

(*c*) After **da** meaning *as, like,* or *for*. See **79**, *g*.

Da uomo.   *Like a man.*

CHAPTER 3

Nouns

Pitti Palace, Florence

17. Italian nouns are not declined. Possession is denoted by the preposition **di**:

Lo specchio **di** mio padre.   *My father's mirror.*

GENDER

18. There are no neuter nouns in Italian.[1]

Nouns denoting males and females keep their natural gender; except **creatura**, *creature;* **guida**, *guide;* **guardia**,

---

[1] Latin neuters become masculine in Italian; masculines and feminines retain their Latin gender. This rule has very few exceptions.

guard; **persona,** *person;* **sentinella,** *sentinel;* **spia,** *spy;* **staffetta,** *courier;* **vedetta,** *scout;* which are feminine.

il fratello, *the brother.*	mia sorella, *my sister.*
il poeta, *the poet.*	la poetessa, *the poetess.*
una spia, *a spy.*	la nostra guida, *our guide.*

19. Of nouns denoting objects without sex some are masculine, some feminine. Their gender can often be determined by the final letter. All Italian nouns end in –a, –e, –i, –o, or –u:[1]

(*a*) Those ending in –a are feminine; except **colera,** *cholera;* **qualcosa,** *something;* Greek neuters in –ma,[2] many geographical names, and a few other words, mostly foreign.

un' ora, *an hour.*	un telegramma, *a telegram.*
il Canadà, *Canada.*	il sofà, *the sofa.*

(*b*) Of those ending in –e and –i some are masculine, some feminine. All ending in –zione, –gione, or –udine are feminine.

il fiume, *the river.*	la pace, *peace.*
un dì, *a day.*	una metropoli, *a metropolis.*
la ragione, *the reason.*	la servitudine, *service.*

(*c*) Those ending in –o are masculine; except **mano,** *hand.*

il ginocchio, *the knee.*	la mano, *the hand.*

(*d*) Those ending in –u are feminine; except **soprappiù,** *surplus,* and a few foreign words.

la virtù, *virtue.*	il bambù, *bamboo.*

20. Any other part of speech (except an adjective[3]) used as a noun must be masculine: as **il viaggiare,** *traveling.*

21. Masculine names of trees in –o or –e have a feminine form in –a or –e respectively, denoting their fruit; but **il dat-**

---

[1] A few foreign nouns used in Italian end in a consonant: as **lapis,** *pencil* (**i lapis,** *the pencils*). Nouns in –o or –e often drop that vowel if the preceding consonant is l, n, or r: as cane = can, *dog.*   [2] Mostly scientific terms.

[3] Adjectives of course have the gender of the nouns they represent. An adjective used as an abstract noun is masculine: **il bello,** *the beautiful* = *beauty.*

tero, *date*, il fico, *fig*, il limone, *lemon*, il pomo, *apple*, are always the same, whether denoting the tree or the fruit.

un susino, *a plum tree.*   una susina, *a plum.*
il noce, *the walnut tree.*   la noce, *the walnut.*
questi fichi, *these fig trees, these figs.*

NUMBER

22. Feminines in unaccented **a** form their plural by changing **a** into **e**.

la strada, *the street.*   le strade, *the streets.*
una bugia, *a lie.*   le bugie, *lies.*

(*a*) Feminines in –**ca** and –**ga** form their plural in –**che** and –**ghe** respectively (the **h** being inserted merely to indicate that the **c** and **g** keep their hard sound).

un' oca, *a goose.*   molte oche, *many geese.*
la bottega, *the shop.*   parecchie botteghe, *several shops.*

(*b*) Nouns in unaccented –**cia** and –**gia** form their plural in –**ce** and –**ge** respectively.[1]

la guancia, *the cheek.*   le guance, *the cheeks.*
una ciliegia, *a cherry.*   tante ciliege, *so many cherries.*

23. Masculines in unaccented –**a** and *all* nouns in unaccented –**o** and –**e** (not –**ie**) form their plural in –**i**.[2]

un poeta, *a poet.*   due poeti, *two poets.*
lo zio, *the uncle.*   gli zii, *the uncles.*
la mano, *the hand.*   le mie mani, *my hands.*
un mese, *a month.*   tre mesi, *three months.*
la cornice, *the frame.*   quattro cornici, *four frames.*

(*a*) Masculines in –**ca** and –**ga** form their plural in –**chi** and –**ghi** respectively.

il monarca, *the monarch.*   i monarchi, *the monarchs.*
il collega, *the colleague.*   i colleghi, *the colleagues.*

---

[1] **Provincia** has **provincie.** In general borrowed words and words whose plural is necessarily very rare keep the **i:** audacia, audacie.

[2] In old Italian and in poetry words in –**ello** and –**ale** often form their plural in –**egli** or –**ei**, –**agli** or –**ai:** capello, capegli; animale, animai.

(*b*) Nouns in unaccented –**io** form their plural by changing –**io** to –**i** (often written **i**, **j**, or **ii**).

lo specch**io**, *the mirror.*	gli specch**i**, *the mirrors.*
il cilieg**io**, *the cherry tree.*	i cilieg**i**, *the cherry trees.*

(*c*) Nouns in –**go** form their plural in –**ghi**. Nouns in –**co** form their plural in –**chi** if the penult is accented, otherwise in –**ci**.

il cast**igo**, *the punishment.*	i cast**ighi**, *the punishments.*
un catal**ogo**, *a catalogue.*	due catal**oghi**, *two catalogues.*
il f**ico**, *the fig.*	cinque f**ichi**, *five figs.*
ant**ico**, *ancient.*	gli ant**ichi**, *the ancients.*
un med**ico**, *a doctor.*	sei med**ici**, *six doctors.*

This rule has a number of exceptions. In the following lists, words whose irregular plural is rare are omitted.

1. Compound nouns in –**logo** denoting persons engaged in the sciences, and all compound nouns in –**fago** form their plural in –**gi**.[1]

il fisio**logo**, *the physiologist.*	i fisio**logi**, *physiologists.*
antropo**fago**, *cannibal.*	antropo**fagi**, *cannibals.*

2. The following words form their plural in –**ci**, although the penult is accented:

amico	*greco*	inimico	nemico	porco[2]

Greco has a regular plural in the expression **vini grechi**.

3. The following words form their plural in –**chi**, although the penult is unaccented:

abbaco	*farmaco*	lastrico	rammarico	strascico
acrostico	indaco	manico	risico	tossico
carico[3]	intonaco	parroco	sciatico	traffico
dimentico[3]	intrinseco	pizzico	stomaco	valico[4]

Acrostico and **farmaco** have also regular plurals.

---

[1] Likewise the rare or obsolete words: flemmagogo, idragogo, metallurgo, sargo (also reg. plur.), sortilego. *Magicians* = **maghi**; *Magi* = **magi**.

[2] Likewise the rare words: aprico, lombrico (also reg.), uvamico, vico.

[3] Likewise its compounds.

[4] Likewise the rare or obsolete words: filaccico, mantaco (also reg.), ostatico, sfilaccico, statico (noun), uncico.

(*d*) The following masculines in –o have an irregular plural in --a which is feminine:

| centinaio, *hundred*. | miglio, *mile*. | uovo, *egg*. |
| migliaio, *thousand*. | paio, *pair*. | |

Many masculines in –o have this irregular feminine plural in –a besides the regular masculine plural in –i. The most common are:

braccio, *arm*.	grido, *shout*.	muro, *wall*.
dito, *finger*.	labbro, *lip*.	orecchio, *ear*.
frutto, *fruit*.	legno, *wood*.	osso, *bone*.
ginocchio, *knee*.	membro, *member*.	

un paio, *a pair*.	sette paia, *seven pairs*.
il mio braccio, *my arm*.	le tue braccia, *thy arms*.
il labbro, *the lip*.	le labbra *or* i labbri, *the lips*.
un osso, *a bone*.	le ossa *or* gli ossi, *the bones*.

Braccio, **ginocchio**, **labbro**, and **orecchio** nearly always have the irregular plural when denoting the two *arms, knees, lips,* or *ears* belonging to the same body.

24. All monosyllables, and all nouns ending in –i, –ie, –u, an accented vowel, or a consonant, are invariable.

il re, *the king*.	i re, *the kings*.
il brindisi, *the toast*.	i brindisi, *the toasts*.
una specie, *a kind*.	otto specie, *eight kinds*
la virtù, *virtue*.	le virtù, *the virtues*.
una città, *a city*.	dieci città, *ten cities*.
l' omnibus, *the omnibus*.	gli omnibus, *the omnibusses*.

25. The following nouns have irregular plurals:

| bue, *ox*, pl. **buoi**. | moglie, *wife*, pl. **mogli**. |
| dio, *god*, pl. **dei**.[1] | uomo, *man*, pl. **uomini**. |

[1] The article used with **dei** is **gli**: **gli dei**.

CHAPTER 4

Adjectives

26. Adjectives agree with their nouns in gender and number. An adjective modifying two nouns of different genders is generally put in the masculine plural.

Il gatto è pulito.	*The cat is neat.*
Stanze pulite.	*Neat rooms.*
Una casa e un giardino bellini.	*A pretty house and garden.*
La ragazza è bellina.	*The girl is pretty.*

27. Numeral and pronominal adjectives, **bello, bravo, buono**, and the commonest adjectives of size and quantity, precede their nouns. Adjectives of nationality, shape, and material follow.

Adjectives whose use is prompted by emotion, and adjectives used in a figurative sense, generally precede.

Otherwise, of the noun and adjective, the one that contains the chief idea comes last.

Due cani.	*Two dogs.*
Troppo pane.	*Too much bread.*
La **buona** madre.	*The good mother.*
Le **grandi** città.	*Great cities.*
Un libro **francese**.	*A French book.*
Questa palla **rotonda**.	*This round ball.*
Pover' uomo!	*Poor man!*
La vostra **gentilissima** lettera.	*Your kind **letter**.*
È un uomo **gentilissimo**.	*He is a **kind** man.*

GENDER AND NUMBER

28. Adjectives ending in –o are masculine, and form their feminine in –a. Adjectives in –e are invariable in the singular.

buono stivaletto, *good boot.*	buona scarpa, *good shoe.*
ragazzo felice, *happy boy.*	ragazza felice, *happy girl.*

29. Adjectives form their plural in the same way as nouns (see **22, 23**): –o, pl. –i; –a, pl. –e; –e, pl. always –i.

sei buoni cassettoni, *six good bureaus.*	otto buone seggiole, *eight good chairs.*
due uomini felici, *two happy men.*	tre donne felici, *three happy women.*

(*a*) **Parecchi,** *several,* has for its feminine **parecchie.**

(*b*) **Qualche,** *some,* is used only in the singular, even when the meaning is plural: as **qualche volta,** *sometimes.*

(*c*) When preceding a noun, **bello,** *beautiful,* has forms similar to those of the definite article; and **Santo,** *Saint,* and **grande,** *great,* have corresponding forms in the singular.[1] **Buono,** *good,* when preceding its noun, has a singular similar to the indefinite article. The masculine of these words (which is the only irregular part) is, therefore, as follows:

Before any consonant except s impure or z: **bel, San, gran, buon;** pl. **bei, Santi, grandi, buoni.**

Before s impure or z: **bello, Santo, grande, buono;** pl. **begli, Santi, grandi, buoni.**

Before a vowel: **bell', Sant', grand', buon;** pl. **begli, Santi, grándi, buoni.**

When used *after* a noun or in the predicate these adjectives have their full forms (**bello, belli, Santo, Santi, grande, grandi, buono, buoni**).

Un **bel** quadro.	*A fine picture.*
Due **bei** letti.	*Two fine beds.*
Un **bello** scaffale.	*A fine bookcase.*
Quattro **begli** stivali.	*Four fine boots.*
Un **bell'** andito.	*A fine hall.*
Molti **begli** orologi.	*Many fine clocks.*
Una **bella** stufa.	*A fine stove.*
Parecchie **belle** tende.	*Several fine curtains.*
Il palazzo è **bello.**	*The palace is fine.*

---

[1] **Gran** is, moreover, often used in the fem. sing. (for **grande**), and sometimes in the plur. (for **grandi**); it is regularly used before fem. sing. nouns in –e, and in the expression **una gran bella** (or **brutta**) **cosa.** **Grande,** on the other hand, is occasionally used for **gran.**

Le sedie son **belle**.	*The chairs are beautiful.*
San Pietro, **Santo** Stefano e **Sant'** Antonio.	*St. Peter, St. Stephen, and St. Anthony.*
Un **gran** fuoco.	*A big fire.*
Grandi camini.	*Big fireplaces.*
Il **grande** scaldino.	*The big foot-warmer.*
Dieci **grandi** spilli.	*Ten big pins.*
Un **grande** sciame.	*A great swarm.*
Il **grande** zipolo.	*The large spigot.*
Un **grand'** armadio.	*A big wardrobe.*
Venti **grandi** alberi.	*Twenty big trees.*
Una **grande** camera.	*A large bedroom.*
Cinque **grandi** finestre.	*Five big windows.*
Il salotto è molto **grande**.	*The parlor is very large.*
Un **buon** lume.	*A good lamp.*
Buoni fiammiferi.	*Good matches.*
Il **buono** sgabello.	*The good stool.*
Nove **buoni** scolari.	*Nine good pupils.*
Il **buon** olio.	*The good oil.*
Parecchi **buoni** aghi.	*Several good needles.*
Una **buona** cucina.	*A good kitchen.*
Le **buone** candele.	*The good candles.*
Il bambino è **buono**.	*The child is good.*

30. Any adjective of either gender or either number may be used as a noun.

I buoni, *the good.*　　　　　　**la bella,** *the beautiful woman.*

COMPARISON

31. All Italian adjectives form their comparative by prefixing **più**, *more*, and their superlative by prefixing the definite article to the comparative.

bello, *beautiful;* **più** bello, *more beautiful;* **il più** bello, *the most beautiful.*

lungo, *long;* **più** lungo, *longer;* **il più** lungo, *the longest.*

When the superlative immediately follows the noun, this article is omitted.

La via **più** corta.　　　　　　*The shortest way.*

(*a*) The following adjectives have an irregular comparison in addition to the regular one:

alto, *high;* più alto *or* superiore; il più alto *or* il superiore.
basso, *low;* più basso *or* inferiore; il più basso *or* l' inferiore.
buono, *good;* più buono *or* migliore[1]; il più buono *or* il migliore.
cattivo, *bad;* più cattivo *or* peggiore[1]; il più cattivo *or* il peggiore.
grande, *big;* più grande *or* maggiore; il più grande *or* il maggiore.
piccolo, *small;* più piccolo *or* minore; il più piccolo *or* il minore.

Higher and *lower* are commonly rendered by **più alto** and **più basso**; **superiore** and **inferiore** generally mean *superior* and *inferior*. **Migliore** and **peggiore** are more used than **più buono** and **più cattivo**, which have the same sense. *Larger* and *smaller* are generally **più grande** and **più piccolo**; **maggiore** and **minore** usually signify *older* and *younger*.

Noi siamo **migliori** di loro.	*We are better than they.*
Questa sala da pranzo è la **più grande**.	*This dining room is the biggest.*
Pietro è il fratello **minore**.	*Peter is the youngest brother.*

32. The adverb *less* is expressed by **meno**, *least* by **il meno**. *As . . . as, so . . . as* are **tanto . . . quanto, tanto . . . come, così . . . come**, or simply **quanto**.

Quella stanza è la **meno** bellina.	*That room is the least pretty.*
Paolo non è **tanto** buono **come** Roberto.	*Paul isn't so good as Robert.*
Giovanni è alto **quanto** Filippo.	*John is as tall as Philip.*

33. *Than* is **che**.

L' albergo è più grande **che** bello.	*The hotel is bigger than it is beautiful.*

But before a noun, a pronoun, or a numeral *than* is rendered by the preposition **di** (see **12**).

Riccardo è peggiore **di** me.	*Richard is worse than I.*
Voi siete più ricchi **del** re.	*You are richer than the king.*
Meno di cinque.	*Less than five.*

---

[1] The adverbs *better* and *worse* are **meglio** and **peggio**.

If, however, this *than* is preceded by a word meaning *rather*, it is translated **che**.

Piuttosto la morte **che** il diso-   *Rather death than dishonor.*
nore.

Before an inflected verb *than* is **che non** or **di quel che** If the verb has a negative subject, *than* is **che**.

Abbaia più **che non** morde.   *He barks more than he bites.*
Prometto meno **di quel che** do.   *I promise less than I give.*
Più lieto **che** nessun figlio lo   *Happier than any son had been.*
era stato.

34. *The more . . . the more, the less . . . the less,* are **più . . . più, meno . . . meno.** *More* and *less* after a number are **di più, di meno.** In speaking of time, *longer* after a negative is **più**.

Più studio, **più** imparo.   *The more I study, the more I learn*
Trenta giorni **di meno.**   *Thirty days less.*
Non lo vediamo **più.**   *We see him no longer.*

Torre de Orologio, Venice

The Ponte Vecchio, Florence

Siena

CHAPTER 5

Augmentatives, Diminutives, and Numerals

AUGMENTATIVE AND DIMINUTIVE ENDINGS

35. Instead of a word expressing size or quality, the Italians often use a suffix. This suffix may be added to a noun, an adjective, or an adverb. When added to an adjective, and generally when added to a noun, it takes the gender of the word to which it is affixed: occasionally, however, a suffix with masculine termination is added to a feminine noun, which thereby becomes masculine. A word loses its final vowel before a suffix; but the preceding consonant, if it be **c** or **g**, must keep its former quality: as Carlo+ino = Carlino, voce+one = vocione, poco+ino = pochino, adagio+ino = adagino.

(*a*) The commonest ending is –issimo (fem. –issima), *very*, which in general is added only to adjectives and adverbs. Adverbs in –**mente** add the –**issima** before the –**mente** (see **85**). Any adjective may take it, and it is very often used in cases where it would be entirely superfluous in English.

largo, *wide.*	larghissimo, *very wide.*
bene, *well.*	benissimo, *very well.*
grande, *big.*	grandissimo, *very big.*
fa un tempo bellissimo, *it's beautiful weather.*	bellissimamente, *very beautifully.*

(*b*) The principal suffix denoting bigness is –**one**; it is always masculine, but has a rare feminine form, –**ona**.

libro, *book.*	un librone, *a big book.*
casa, *house.*	un casone, *a large house.*
boccia, *decanter.*	una bocciona, *a big decanter.*

(c) The most important suffixes denoting smallness are –ino, –cino, –icino, –iccino, –etto, –ello, –cello, –icello, –arello, –erello, –otto, –uccio, –uzzo, –uolo, with their fem. –ina, etc. These endings, especially –uccio, are often used to express affection; some of them may be used to express pity or contempt. **Otto** sometimes means *somewhat large* instead of *small*.

sorella, *sister.*	sorellina, *little sister.*
bello, *beautiful.*	bellino, *pretty.*
brutto, *ugly.*	bruttino, *rather ugly.*
piazza, *square.*	piazzetta, *little square.*
Giorgio, *George.*	Giorgetto, *Georgie.*
campana, *bell.*	campanello, *little bell.*
aquila, *eagle.*	aquilotto, *eaglet.*
casa, *house.*	casotta, *rather large house.*
Giovanni, *John.*	Giovannuccio, *dear little Johnny.*
pazzo, *mad.*	pazzarella, *poor mad woman.*
povero, *poor.*	poverini, *poor things!*

(d) The ending –**accio** denotes worthlessness.

roba, *stuff, goods.*	robaccia, *trash.*
tempo, *weather.*	tempaccio, *nasty weather.*
Alfredo, *Alfred.*	Alfredaccio, *naughty Alfred.*

36. Of the endings added to nouns –**ino** is by far the most common; the only ones that are freely used to form new compounds are –**ino**, *little*, –**one**, *great*, –**uccio**, *dear*, and –**accio**, *bad*. In very many cases, endings lose their character of independent suffixes, and become inseparable parts of certain words, whose meanings they often change: as **scala**, *stairway;* **scalino**, *stair;* **scaletto**, *ladder.* So *brother, sister* are always **fratello, sorella.** Some suffixes (as –**uolo**) are rarely used except in this way. Others (as –**cino**, –**icíno**, –**ello**, –**cello**, –**icello**, –**arello**, –**erello**) cannot be attached to any word at pleasure, their use being determined by precedent or euphony.

37. Sometimes several suffixes are added at once to the same word: as **ladro**, *thief;* **ladrone**, *terrible thief;* **ladroncello**, *terrible little thief*.

NUMERALS

38. The cardinal numerals are:

1, uno.	15, quindici.	28, ventotto or	101, centuno or
2, due.	16, sedici.	vent' otto.	cent' uno.
3, tre.	17, diciassette.	29, ventinove.	105, centocinque.
4, quattro.	18, diciotto.	30, trenta.	115, centoquindici.
5, cinque.	19, diciannove.	31, trentuno or	125, cento venti-
6, sei.	20, venti.	trent' uno.	cinque.
7, sette.	21, ventuno or	32, trentadue.	200, dugento or
8, otto.	vent' uno.	40, quaranta.	duecento.
9, nove.	22, ventidue.	50, cinquanta.	250, dugento cin-
10, dieci.	23, ventitre.	60, sessanta.	quanta.
11, undici.	24, ventiquattro.	70, settanta.	300, trecento.
12, dodici.	25, venticinque.	80, ottanta.	400, quattrocento.
13, tredici.	26, ventisei.	90, novanta.	1000, mille.
14, quattordici.	27, ventisette.	100, cento.	2000, due mila.

Uno has a feminine **una**; when used *adjectively* it has the same forms as the indefinite article; so also **ventuno**, etc.

The plural of **mille** is **mila**. *A million* is **un milione** or **milione**, of which the plural is **milioni** or **millioni**.

1. No conjunction is used between the different parts of a number: as **dugento quaranta**, *two hundred and forty*. No indefinite article is used before **cento** and **mille**: as **cento libri**, *a hundred books*.

2. **Cento, dugento**, etc., when followed by another numeral of more than two syllables may lose the final syllable –to: as **seicento cinquanta** or **seicencinquanta**, *six hundred and fifty*.

3. *Eleven hundred, twelve hundred*, etc., must be rendered **mille-cento, mille dugento**, etc.: as **mille ottocento ottantasette**, 1887.

4. *Both, all three*, etc., are **tutti** (fem. **tutte**) **e due, tutti** (fem. **tutte**) **e tre**, etc.

(*a*) If the noun modified by **ventuno, trentuno**, etc., *follows* this numeral, it is regularly in the singular; as **trentun giorno**, *thirty-one days*.   Sometimes, however, the noun *precedes* the numeral, and then it is in the plural.

> Sessantuna lira, *or* lire sessan-   *Sixty-one francs.*
> tuna.

(*b*) In dates the definite article is prefixed to the number representing the year, if that number does not follow the name of a month.   For instance, 2001 is **il 2001**.

> **Nel** mille novecento novanta-   *In* 1999.
> nove.

(*c*) *What time is it?* is **che ora e?** or **che ore sono?**   *It is six*, etc., is **sono le sei**, etc., **ore** being understood.   *One o'clock* is **il tocco**.

> Sono le due e mezzo.   *It's half past two.*
> Sono le tre e dieci.   *It's ten minutes past three.*
> Ci mancano venti minuti alle   *It's twenty minutes to four.*
> quattro.
> Sono le cinque meno un quarto. *It's a quarter to five.*

The Lute Player, Michaelangelo Caravaggio

39. The ordinal numerals are:

1st, **primo.**	12th, **duodecimo** or	20th, **ventesimo.**
2d, **secondo.**	**decimo secondo.**	21st, **ventesimo primo** or
3d, **terzo.**	13th, **tredicesimo** or	**ventunesimo.**
4th, **quarto.**	**decimo terzo.**	22d, **ventesimo secondo**
5th, **quinto.**	14th, **quattordicesimo** or	or **ventiduesimo.**
6th, **sesto.**	**decimo quarto.**	30th, **trentesimo.**
7th, **settimo.**	15th, **quindicesimo** or	100th, **centesimo.**
8th, **ottavo.**	**decimo quinto.**	101st, **centesimo primo.**
9th, **nono.**	16th, **decimo sesto.**	115th, **centoquindicesimo.**
10th, **decimo.**	17th, **decimo settimo.**	200th, **duecentesimo.**
11th, **undecimo** or	18th, **decimo ottavo.**	1000th, **millesimo.**
decimo primo.	19th, **decimo nono.**	2000th, **duemilesimo.**

All of them form their feminines and plurals like other
adjectives in –o.

> Le settantesime quinte cose.   *The 75th things.*

(*a*) Ordinal numerals are used after the words *book, chapter,*
and the names of rulers; but no article intervenes.

> Carlo **secondo.**   *Charles the Second.*
> Libro **terzo.**   *Book the Third.*
> Capitolo **quarto.**   *Chapter four.*

(*b*) For the day of the month, except the first, a cardinal number is used.

> Il dì **cinque** d' aprile *or* il   *The fifth of April.*
>   **cinque** aprile.
> Il **primo** di mággio.   *The first of May.*

(*c*) *The fourteenth century* is **il secolo decimo quarto** or **il Trecento** (*i. e.* mille trecento). **Il Duecento, il Quattrocento, il Cinquecento** are often used for the 13th, 15th, and 16th centuries,
and the later century names may be similarly abbreviated.

(*d*) *A third, a fourth, a fifth,* etc., are **un terzo, un quarto, un
quinto,** etc. *Half* is **la metà;** the adjective *half* is **mezzo.**

40. *A couple* or *a pair* is **un paio**. *A dozen* is **una dozzina**. The expressions **una decina, una ventina, una trentina**, etc., **un centinaio, un migliaio**, mean *about ten, about twenty*, etc. (see **23,** *d*). *Once, twice*, etc., are **una volta, due volte**, etc.

Un paio di scarpe.	*A pair of shoes.*
Una cinquantina di persone.	*Some fifty persons.*
L' ho visto **parecchie volte**.	*I've seen it several times.*

The Colosseum, Rome

CHAPTER 6

Demonstrative, Interrogative, Relative, and Possesive Pronouns

41. For the indefinite pronouns, see **86–91**.

DEMONSTRATIVE PRONOUNS

42. 1. The demonstratives used adjectively are **questo**,[1] *this*, and **quello** or **cotesto**, *that*. **Cotesto** (also **codesto**) is used of objects associated with the person addressed. **Questo** and **cotesto** are inflected like other adjectives; but they generally drop **o** before a vowel. **Quello** is inflected like **bello** (see **29**, *c*).

quest' uomo, *this man.*	**queste** ragazze, *these girls.*
quel bambino, *that infant.*	**quei** fanciulli, *those children.*
quell' amico, *that friend.*	**quegli** sposi, *that couple.*
quello zio, *that uncle.*	**quelle** signore, *those ladies.*

Questo and **quello** are also used substantively for *this, that, this one, that one:* as **fate questo, non fate quello**, *do this, don't do that.*

2. *This man* is translated by **questi**; *that man* by **quegli**, **quei**, or **cotesti** (rare); these words are invariable, refer only to persons, and are used only in the nominative singular. **Costui** and **colui** mean respectively the same as **questi** and

---

[1] In archaic or literary Italian **esso** is sometimes used for **questo**.

quegli, but are not defective, having a feminine singular costei, colei, and a plural (both genders alike) costoro, coloro. Costui is often used in a depreciative sense.

Questi è francese e **quegli** è tedesco.	*This man is French and that one is German.*
Chi è **costui**?	*Who is this fellow?*
Parlo di **colui**.	*I speak of that man.*

3. **Ciò**, *this*, *that*, is invariable, and represents a whole idea, not a single word:

Ciò è vero.	*That's so.*

(*a*) **Quello** and **questo**, **quegli** and **questi** mean also *the former, the latter*.

(*b*) *He who* is **colui che**, or simply **chi**. *The one who, whom, which, that which, what*, is **quello che** or **quel che**.

Chi lavora *or* **colui che** lavora.	*He who works.*
Quel che dico io.	*The one I mean.*
A **quel che** sento.	*From what I hear.*

INTERROGATIVE PRONOUNS

43. The interrogative *who, whom*, is **chi**. *What?* used substantively is **che, che cosa**, or **cosa**.[1] *What?* used adjectively is **che** or **quale**. *Which?* is **quale**.

Quale has a plural **quali**; **chi** and **che** are invariable.

How much? is **quanto** (–a); *how many?* is **quanti** (–e).

Chi vedo?	*Whom do I see?*
Di **chi** parlate?	*Of whom do you speak?*
Ditemi **chi** viene.	*Tell me who is coming.*
Che vogliono?	*What do they want?*
Che cosa dice?	*What does he say?*
Che *or* **quali** libri avete comprato?	*What books did you buy?*
Quale di questi volumi è il primo?	*Which of these volumes is the first?*
Quante volte te l'ho detto!	*How many times I have told you!*

[1] Cosa (as *cosa dice?*) is generally avoided in written Italian. Note that **chi** is used in *indirect* as well as in direct questions.

(*a*) The interrogative *whose* is **di chi**.

Di chi è questo biglietto?   *Whose card is this?*

(*b*) In exclamations *what a, what* are rendered by **che** or **quale** without any article.

Che bel paese!   *What a beautiful country!*

RELATIVE PRONOUNS

44. The principal relative pronouns are **che, cui, il quale**: they are all applied to both persons and things, and mean *who, whom, which,* or *that*. **Il quale** is inflected (**la quale, i quali, le quali**). **Che** and **cui** are invariable: in general **che** is used only as subject and direct object, **cui** only after prepositions or as indirect object. In poetry **onde** is often used to signify *of which* or *from which*.

La lingua **che** si parla.	*The language which we speak.*
L' uomo **del quale si** tratta.	*The man of whom we are speaking.*
Le persone **a cui** *or* **alle quali** parlo.	*The persons to whom I speak.*
Lo scritto **di cui** parlo.	*The work I am speaking of.*

1. As subject or direct object **che** is preferred to **il quale**, unless clearness requires the latter.

Le figlie **che** studiano.	*The daughters who are studying.*
Le figlie degli Americani, **le quali** studiano.	*The Americans' daughters, who are studying.*

2. The relative *whose* is **il cui** or **del quale**.

Una signora, **il cui** nome è Lucia.	*A lady whose name is Lucy.*
Un uomo, **le cui** figlie conosco.	*A man whose daughters I know.*
L' autore, **del cui** libro si parla.	*The author whose book we are speaking of.*
Le chiese **delle quali** si vedono le cupole.	*The churches whose domes we see.*

3. The relative cannot be omitted in Italian.

Le case **che** ho comprate.	*The houses I have bought.*

(a) *Such . . . as* is **tale . . . quale**; in poetry **tale, quale** have a plural **tai, quai** instead of **tali, quali**. *As much as* is **tanto quanto**; *as many as* is **tanti quanti**.

Quale è il padre **tale** è il figlio. *As is the father, so is the son.*

(b) *He who, him who* is **chi** or **colui che** (see **42,** b).

Chi ha la sanità è ricco. *He who has health is rich.*
Colui che lavora è contento. *He who works is satisfied.*
Amiamo **chi** ci ama. *We love him who loves us.*

(c) *Whoever* is **chiunque**; *whatever* as a pronoun is **tutto quel che** or **checchè**, as an adjective **quale che, qualunque che, qualunque, per quanto**. These words, excepting **tutto quel che**, all take the subjunctive. **Checchè** is now but little used.

Chiunque siate. *Whoever you may be.*
Checchè facciate, fatelo bene. *Whatever you do, do it well.*
Tutto quel che volete. *Whatever you wish.*
Quali che siano i vostri motivi. *Whatever your motives may be.*
Qualunque siano i suoi talenti. *Whatever his talents may be.*
In **qualunque** stato **che** io mi trovi. *In whatever condition I may find myself.*
Per quante ricchezze lui abbia. *Whatever riches he may have.*

POSSESSIVE PRONOUNS

45. The possessive pronouns and adjectives are:

	SINGULAR		PLURAL	
	MASC.	FEM.	MASC.	FEM.
my, mine:	**il mio**	**la mia**	**i miei**	**le mie**
thy, thine:	**il tuo**	**la tua**	**i tuoi**	**le tue**
his, her, hers, its:	**il suo**	**la sua**	**i suoi**	**le sue**
our, ours:	**il nostro**	**la nostra**	**i nostri**	**le nostre**
your, yours:	**il vostro**	**la vostra**	**i vostri**	**le vostre**
their, theirs:	**il loro**	**la loro**	**i loro**	**le loro**

Loro is invariable; the others agree with the object possessed:

il **mio** naso, *my nose.* i **vostri** occhi, *your eyes.*
la **sua** bocca, *his, her mouth.* le **loro** labbra, *their lips.*

When the possessive stands alone in the predicate, the article is omitted if the possessive is used adjectively. To determine whether the possessive is used adjectively, consider the sentence as the answer to a question. If the sentence answers a question beginning with *whose*, there is no article; if it answers a question beginning with *which*, the article is used.

Questo cappello è **mio**.	*This hat is* **mine**. *Whose hat? Mine.*
Questo cappello è **il mio**.	***This** hat is mine. Which hat? This one.*

(a) The article (unless it might be used in English) is omitted before the possessive:

1. When a numeral, an adjective of quantity, or a demonstrative or interrogative adjective precedes it:

Due cani suoi.	*Two dogs of his.*
BUT I due cani suoi.	*The two dogs of his* or *his two dogs.*
Molti miei amici.	*Many friends of mine.*
BUT I molti miei amici.	*The many friends of mine* or *my many friends.*
Questo tuo difetto.	*This fault of thine.*

2. When the possessive forms part of a title:

Vostra Maestà.	*Your Majesty.*
Sua Altezza.	*His Highness.*

3. When the possessive modifies a noun used in the vocative (in this case the possessive generally follows its noun): as **amico mio**, *my friend!*

4. The article is generally omitted also when the possessive precedes a noun in the *singular* expressing relationship: as **nostra madre**, *our mother;* compare **le mie figlie**, *my daughters.* But if the noun has a diminutive ending, or another adjective accompanies the noun, the article is not omitted:

Il tuo fratellino.	*Thy little brother.*
La vostra gentilissima sorella.	*Your kind sister.*

Sometimes it is omitted before a *predicate* noun that does not express relationship:

Questo signore è suo maestro.	*This gentleman is his teacher.*
Io lo credeva mio amico.	*I thought him my friend.*

5. The article is omitted also in certain standing phrases, such as:

da parte mia, *for me.*	a modo suo, *in his own way.*
per amor mio, *for my sake.*	è colpa vostra, *it's your fault.*
in casa nostra, *in our house.*	a casa sua, *to his house.*

(*b*) The possessive, when not necessary for clearness, is usually replaced by a definite article.

Come sta **la** mamma?	*How is your mother?*
Ha perduto **il** giudizio.	*He has lost his senses.*
Battono **i** piedi.	*They stamp their feet.*

(*c*) When the name of the thing possessed is direct object of a verb, the Italians often use instead of the possessive a conjunctive personal pronoun (see **47**) and a definite article.

Si strappa i capelli.	*He tears his hair* (*lit.*, he tears to himself the hairs).
Mi taglio il dito.	*I cut my finger* (I cut to myself the finger).
Il cane **gli** agguantò la gamba.	*The dog seized his leg* (seized to him the leg).

If the thing possessed be a part of the body or clothing, this construction is frequent, even when the name of the thing is not object of a verb.

Mi duole il capo.	*My head aches* (to me aches the head).

(*d*) When the possessor is not the subject of the sentence, *his, her* are, for the sake of clearness, often rendered **di lui, di lei**:

Lui non conosce il **di lei** cuore.	*He does not know her heart.*

(*e*) *A . . . of mine, of thine*, etc., is **un mio, un tuo**, etc.:

Una nostra cugína.	*A cousin of ours.*

Piazza Navona, Rome

Vittorio Emmanuel Monument, Rome

CHAPTER 7

Personal Pronouns

46. Personal pronouns are divided into two classes, conjunctive and disjunctive: the conjunctive forms are those used as direct object of a verb, and as indirect object without a preposition; the disjunctive forms are those used as subject of a verb, and as object of a preposition.

> Lui ve lo dà per me.
> He to you it gives for me.

CONJUNCTIVE FORMS

47. Conjunctive pronouns are *always unaccented*, and cannot be separated from the verb, which they sometimes follow but oftener precede, as will be explained in **48**.

They are used only as direct object of a verb or as indirect object without a preposition. The forms are:

mi, *me, to me.*	**ti**, *thee, to thee.*
ci, *us, to us.*[1]	**vi**, *you, to you.*

si (reflexive), *himself, to himself; herself, to herself; itself, to itself.*
si (reflexive), *themselves, to themselves.*

lo, *him*[1]; **gli**, *to him.*[2]	**la**, *her;* **le**, *to her.*
li, *them* (masc.); **loro**, *to them.*[2]	**le**, *them* (fem.); **loro**, *to them.*

It must be rendered by a masculine or feminine form, according to the gender of the noun it represents. *It* representing not a word, but a whole clause, is **lo**.[3]

Mi conosce.	*He knows me.*
Ti do i libri.	*I give thee the books.*
Ci vedete.	*You see us.*
Vi dico tutto.	*I tell you everything.*

[1] In old Italian and in poetry **ne** is often used for **ci**, and **il** for **lo**.

[2] In conversation **li** is often used for **gli**, and **gli** or **li** for **loro**.

[3] In certain idiomatic phrases **la** represents an indefinite object: as **pagarla cara,** *to pay dearly for it.*

Si veste.	*He dresses himself.*
Si divertono.	*They amuse themselves.*
Ecco l' oro: ve **lo** do.	*Here's the gold: I give it to you.*
Ecco la palla: **la** vedo.	*Here's the ball: I see it.*
Come poteva sapere se io veniva o no? — **Lo** ha indovinato.	*How could he tell whether I was coming or not? He guessed it.*

1. It will be seen that the third person (not reflexive) has different forms for the direct and the indirect object.

Lo trovai.	*I found him.*
Gli feci un regalo.	*I made him a present.*
La lascia.	*He leaves her.*
Le scrive.	*He writes to her.*
Li cercate.	*You seek them* (masc.).
Le salutate.	*You greet them* (fem.).
Mandiamo **loro** mille saluti.	*We send them* (masc. or fem.) *a thousand greetings.*

2. The reflexive pronouns of the first and second persons are **mi**, **ci**; **ti**, **vi**. All plural reflexive pronouns are used also as reciprocal pronouns. A verb is called *reflexive* when it has as *direct* or *indirect* object a *conjunctive* pronoun representing the same person as its subject.

Mi defendo.	*I defend myself.*
Vi lavate.	*You wash yourselves.*
Si fa onore.	*She does herself credit.*
Si odiano.	*They hate each other.*
Ci amiamo.	*We love one another.*

3. Another conjunctive pronoun is **ne**,[1] *of it, of them;* it corresponds also to *any, some* when these words mean *any, some of it, any, some of them.* It is often used pleonastically in Italian.

Ne parla.	*He speaks of it.*
Ne ho.	*I have some.*
Non **ne** abbiamo.	*We haven't any.*
Ne volete?	*Do you want any?*
Tu **ne** approfitti di questa libertà.	*You make good use of this liberty.*

---

[1] Cf. French **en**.

(*a*) **Vi**, *you*, and **ci** and **ne**, *us*, are not distinguished by form nor position from the adverbs **vi**, **ci**, meaning *there, here, to it, to them*,[1] and the adverb **ne**, *thence* (see **84**):[2]

Ci vado.	*I go there.*
Vi è stato.	*He has been there.*
Ne vengono.	*They come from there.*

The adverb **ci** or **vi** is used to express *to it, to them*, in speaking of *things*.

Ci penserò.	*I shall attend to it.*
Mi fa dei gesti, ma non **vi** rispondo.	*He makes signs to me, but I do not reply to them.*

48. The conjunctive pronouns, except **loro**, immediately precede the verb:

Mi vedete.	*You see me.*
Non **lo** capisco.	*I don't understand him.*

But when the verb is an infinitive,[3] a positive imperative,[4] a present participle, or a past participle used without an auxiliary, the pronoun follows the verb, and is written as one word with it:[5]

per veder**lo**, *to see him.*	di aver**lo** veduto, *to have seen him.*
vedete**li**, *see them.*	vedend**oci**, *seeing us.*
avend**oci** veduto, *having seen us.*	veduto**ti**, *having seen thee.*

The addition of the pronoun does not change the place of the accent.

Loro always follows the verb, but is never united to it.

Lui dà **loro** del vino.	*He gives them some wine.*
Parlate **loro**.	*Speak to them.*

---

[1] Cf. French **y**.   [2] Cf. French **en**.

[3] Not the infinitive used — with a negative — as imperative (see **72**): as **non lo fare**, *do not do it* (second pers. sing.).

[4] Not the negative imperative, nor the subjunctive used imperatively (see **77**, *a*): as **non li guardate**, *do not look at them;* **si regoli**, *let him moderate himself* (third pers. sing. pres. subj.).

[5] Students should follow strictly all of these rules; but they will find that the first is, in certain cases, not always observed by good Italian writers. In literary style a pronoun often follows a verb that begins a sentence: as **vedolo venire**, *I see him coming*

(*a*) When an infinitive depends immediately (without an intervening preposition) on another verb, a conjunctive pronoun belonging to the infinitive may go with either verb:

Posso vederti *or* **ti** posso *I can see thee.*
    vedere.

(NEVER: posso ti vedere)

A reflexive pronoun most often goes with the main verb.

Si deve correggere.   *He must correct himself.*

If both verbs have objects, the main verb regularly takes all conjunctive pronouns:

Ve lo sento dire.   *I hear you say it.*
Me lo fa capire.   *He makes me understand it.*

If, however, the main verb is impersonal, it cannot take the object of the infinitive:

Bisogna far**lo**.   *It is necessary to do it.*

If the main verb is **fare**, **lasciare**, **sentire**, **udire**, or **vedere**, it must take the pronoun:

Lo fa chiamare.   *He has him called.*

(*b*) If the main verb is **fare**, and the dependent infinitive has a direct object, the object of **fare**, if it has one, must be indirect:

Le fa avere la lettera.   *He lets her have the letter.*
Fate**li** vedere **a quel signore.**   *Let that gentleman see them.*
Dovrei far**glielo** accettare.   *I ought to make him accept it.*

This construction is generally used also with **lasciare**, *to let*, and often with **sentire** and **udire**, *to hear*, and **vedere**, *to see*. Note that the main verb takes all conjunctive pronouns.

Glielo vedo dare.   *I see it given him.*

(*c*) When a conjunctive pronoun is joined to an infinitive, that infinitive drops its final **e**; if it ends in –**rre**, it drops –**re**:

farlo (fare), *to do it.*   **condurvi** (condurre), *to conduct you* (*d*) The final vowel of **mi, ti, si** is often, and that of **lo, la** is nearly always elided before a verb beginning with a vowel:

T' amo.	*I love thee.*
L' ho visto.	*I've seen him.*

(*e*) All conjunctive pronouns except **gli** and **glie** (see **50**) double their initial consonant when added to any form of a verb that ends in an accented vowel:

Dammi (*imper.* **da'** *from* dare).	*Give me.*
Parlerolle (*antique, for* le parlerò).	*I shall speak to her.*
Dillo (*imper.* **di'** *from* dire).	*Say it.*

(*f*) Pronouns are joined to the interjection **ecco**, *see here*, just as they are joined to the imperative of a verb:

Eccomi.	*Here I am.*
Eccotelo pronto.	*Here it is ready for thee.*

49. When two conjunctive pronouns come together, the indirect object precedes the direct:

Mi vi presenta.	*He introduces you to me.*
Non vuol presentar**vimi.**	*He will not introduce me to you.*
Gli si presentò un uomo.	*A man presented himself to him.*

But see **55**, end.

Loro, however, always comes last:

Presentatela **loro.**	*Introduce her to them.*

Ne follows all forms except **loro**:

Me **ne** dà.	*He gives me some.*
Date**ne** loro.	*Give them some.*

50. Mi, ti, ci, vi, si change their **i** to **e** before **lo, la, li, le, ne** (pronoun or adverb); and if the two words follow the verb, they are joined together:[1]

Me lo dice.	*He tells me it.*
Ve ne domando.	*I ask you for some.*
Mandate**celo.**	*Send it to us.*

[1] In poetry me lo, me ne, etc., often become mel, men, etc.: as tel dico, *I tell thee so;* **sen torna**, *he returns thence.* Non lo often = nol.

Gli and **le** (*to her*) become **glie** before **lo, la, li, le, ne,** and unite with them:

Glieli mando.	*I send them to him, to her.*
Voglio dar**glielo.**	*I wish to give it to him, to her.*

DISJUNCTIVE FORMS

51. These forms are so called because they do not necessarily stand next to the verb.

Disjunctive pronouns have two cases, nominative and objective (or accusative). The objective case is used only after prepositions (for exceptions, see **51**, *a, b*).

The disjunctive forms are these:

io, *I;* **me,** *me.*	**tu,** *thou;* **te,** *thee.*
noi, *we;* **noi,** *us.*	**voi,** *you;* **voi,** *you.*

{ **egli, lui, esso,** *he;* **lui, esso,** *him.*
{ **ella, lei, essa,** *she;* **lei, essa,** *her.*
{ **essi, loro,** *they* (masc.); **loro, essi,** *them* (masc.).
{ **esse, loro,** *they* (fem.); **loro, esse,** *them* (fem.).

Lei, *you,* (polite singular); **Loro,** *you,* (polite plural).

It must be rendered by a masculine or feminine form, according to the gender of the noun it represents. *It* as subject of an impersonal verb is regularly not expressed (see, however, **51**, *h*).

La casa è grandissima, e intorno ad **essa** c' è un giardino.	*The house is very large, and around it there is a garden.*
Non è vero.	*It isn't true.*
Piove.	*It rains.*

1. The various pronouns of the third person are used as follows: In speaking of *things* the different forms of **esso** are generally employed.

---

[1] Italian formerly possessed also masc. **eglino,** fem. **elleno,** *they,* for persons; likewise pl. **egli** (or **ei**) and **elle.**

In both written and spoken Italian in speaking of *persons* use
lui, lei, loro*(plural).*

For *he who*, etc., see **42**, *b*.

Queste cose sono vere anch' **esse.**	*These things are true, too.*
Lei parla con **loro.**	*She speaks with them.*
Lei è giovane ma **lui** è vecchio.	*She is young, but he is old.*
Vennero da noi anche **loro.**	*They came to us, too.*

2. As the Italian verb denotes by its endings the person and
number of its subject, the personal pronouns of the nominative
case are generally omitted. When expressed (for clearness, emphasis, or euphony), they may precede or follow the verb; in
dependent clauses they nearly always follow. The subject of an
interrogative verb usually comes after it, as in English.

Parliamo di lui.	*We speak of him.*
Non vado.	*I don't go.*
S' **io** fossi ricco come è **lui.**	*If I were rich as he is.*
Vengono **loro?**	*Are they coming?*

3. The disjunctive reflexive pronoun of the third person is **sè,**
which is masculine and feminine, singular and plural.

Lo fecero da **sè.**	*They did it by themselves.*

In the other persons **me, noi, te, voi** are used.

(*a*) Use the objective case and not, as in English, the nominative:

(1) When a pronoun of the third person may be regarded as the
subject of an unexpressed verb:

Beato **lui!**	*Happy he!*
Tanto i genitori che **lui** sono ricchi.	*His parents as well as he are rich.*

(2) When the pronoun stands in the predicate after the verb
essere:

Credendo ch' io fossi **te.**	*Thinking I was you.*

But note carefully that *it is I*, etc., are **sono io, sei tu, è lui, è
lei, siamo noi, siete voi, sono loro.**

(*b*) (1) When the pronoun is at all emphatic, the *disjunctive* form *must* be used. In this case the conjunctive form is often inserted also.

Parlo a **voi** signore.	*I speak to **you**, sir.*
Mi piace anche a **me**.	*It pleases **me** too.*

BUT

Vi parlo.	*I **speak** to you.*
Mi piace.	*It **pleases** me.*

(2) The disjunctive form must therefore *always* be used when the verb has two direct or two indirect objects.

Vedo **lui** e **lei**.	*I see him and her.*
Lo do **a mio padre** e **a te**.	*I give it to my father and to thee.*

(*c*) In speaking of a company, a class, or a people **noi altri**, **voi altri** (which are also written as one word) are used for **noi**, **voi**.

Noi altri italiani.	*We Italians.*
Voi altri pittori.	*You painters.*

(*d*) *With me, with thee, with himself, herself, themselves* are either **con me**, etc., or **meco, teco, seco**.

(*e*) *Myself, thyself*, etc., used for emphasis with a pronoun or noun, are rendered by the adjective **stesso**.

Noi **stessi** la vedemmo.	*We saw her ourselves.*

(*f*) *One another, each other* is **l' un l' altro**.

Ci amiamo **l' un l' altro**.	*We love one another.*

(*g*) In Florence **ella** is often shortened into **la** (plural **le**), which is used of both persons and things. In poetry **egli** becomes **ei**.

La non viene.	*She doesn't come.*
Pare che **la** si possa tener in mano.	*It looks as if it might be held in the hand.*
Ei tace.	*He is silent.*

(*h*) In impersonal phrases like *it is* the subject, *it*, is occasionally expressed in Italian; it is then translated **egli**, which in the spoken language is shortened into **gli**.

Gli è che.	*It is because.*

FORMS OF ADDRESS

52. 1. The usual form of address in Italy is **Lei**. The plural of **Lei** is **Loro**, which takes the verb in the third person plural.

Lei and **Loro** are always capitalized when meaning *you*.

Lei è tedesco, signore.	*You are German, sir.*
Signorina Neri, **Lei** fu lasciata sola.	*Miss Neri, you were left alone.*
Sono lieto che **Lei** stia bene (see **51**, *g*).	*I'm glad you are well.*
E **Loro**, dove vanno?	*And you, where are you going?*
Loro erano già partiti.	*You were already gone.*
Signorine, **Loro** sono molto studiose.	*Young ladies, you are very studious.*

Like other personal pronouns, **Lei** and **Loro** are very often omitted in the nominative.

Lei è troppo gentile *or* è troppo gentile.	*You are too kind.*
Come stanno?	*How do you* (pl.) *do?*

The conjunctive forms of **Lei** are **La, Le** (or **la, le**), those of **Loro** are **Li, Le, Loro** (or **li, le, loro**); they occupy the same positions and undergo the same modifications as the corresponding pronouns of the third person (see **48, 49, 50**).

Note that regularly in the singular the same pronoun is used, whether one is addressing a man or a woman; although occasionally **lo, gli** are substituted for **la, le** in speaking to a

Paestum

male. In the *plural*, however, if the pronoun be a direct object, the sexes are regularly distinguished.

The reflexive pronoun of **Lei** and **Loro** is **si**.

Le prometto di visitarla.	*I promise (you) to visit you.*
Glielo do.	*I give it to you.*
La prego d' accomodarsi.	*I beg you to seat yourself.*
Vidi **Lei** e il babbo.	*I saw you and your father (see **51**, b, 2).*
Dico **loro**.	*I tell you (pl.).*
Le cercava.	*I was looking for you (fem. pl.).*
Non posso vederli.	*I can't see you (masc. pl.).*
Si divertono, signorini?	*Are you enjoying yourselves, young gentlemen?*

The possessive of **Lei** is **Suo** (or **suo**); that of **Loro** is **Loro** (or **loro**). See **45**.

La **Sua** gradita lettera.	*Your welcome letter.*

2. **Voi** is the form of address oftenest found in books; it is used sometimes in conversation also, but only toward inferiors or toward equals with whom one is on familiar terms.[1] It is employed for both plural and singular (like English *you*), although its verb is always plural; an adjective or participle modifying it agrees in gender and number with the person or persons it represents.

Voi qui, Pietro?	*You here, Peter?*
Voi siete alti tutti e due.	*You are tall, both of you.*

3. In speaking to an intimate friend, a near relative, a child, or an animal, the only form of address is **tu**. **Tu** is used also, like English *thou*, in poetry and poetic prose. The plural of **tu** is **voi**.

Ti chiamo Enrico.	*I call you Henry.*
Dove sei **tu**?	*Where art thou?*
Voglio veder**vi**, figliuoli miei.	*My children, I wish to see you.*

[1] Though advocated by some of the best writers and speakers of Italian, the use of **voi** instead of **Lei** and **Loro** has not become general. In Southern Italy, however, **voi** is the form popularly used.

CHAPTER 8

Auxiliary Verbs

AUXILIARIES OF VOICE AND TENSE
(essere, avere)

53. The irregular verbs **essere**, *to be*, and **avere**, *to have*, are the ones most used as auxiliaries in Italian. They are conjugated as follows:

(*a*) INFINITIVES: **essere**, *to be;* **essere stato**, *to have been.*

PARTICIPLES: **essendo**, *being;* **essendo stato**, *having been;* **stato**, *been.*

INDICATIVE

PRESENT *I am, etc.*	PAST DESCRIPTIVE *I was, etc.*	PAST ABSOLUTE *I was, etc.*	FUTURE *I shall be, etc.*
sono	era	fui	sarò
sei	eri	fosti	sarai
è	era	fu	sarà
siamo	eravamo	fummo	saremo
siete	eravate	foste	sarete
sono	erano	furono	saranno

PRESENT PERFECT *I have been, etc.*	PAST PERFECT *I had been, etc.*	SECOND PAST PERFECT *I had been, etc.*	FUTURE PERFECT *I shall have been, etc.*
sono stato (stata) etc.	era stato (stata) etc.	fui stato (stata) etc.	sarò stato (stata) etc.
siamo stati (state) etc.	eravamo stati (state) etc.	fummo stati (state) etc.	saremo stati (state) etc.

IMPERATIVE	SUBJUNCTIVE		PAST FUTURE
Be, etc.	PRESENT *I be, etc.*	PAST *I were, etc.*	*I should be, etc.*
	sia	fossi	sarei
sii or sia	sia	fossi	saresti
	sia	fosse	sarebbe
siamo	siamo	fossimo	saremmo
siate	siate	foste	sareste
	siano or sieno	fossero	sarebbero

SUBJUNCTIVE		PAST FUTURE
PRESENT PERFECT *I have been, etc.*	PAST PERFECT *I had been, etc.*	PERFECT *I should have been, etc.*
sia stato (stata) etc.	fossi stato (stata) etc.	sarei stato (stata) etc.

(*b*) INFINITIVES: avere, *to have;* avere avuto, *to have had.*
PARTICIPLES: avendo, *having;* avendo avuto, *having had;* avuto, *had.*

INDICATIVE

PRESENT *I have, etc.*	PAST DESCRIPTIVE *I had, etc.*	PAST ABSOLUTE *I had, etc.*	FUTURE *I shall have, etc.*
ho	aveva	ebbi	avrò
hai	avevi	avesti	avrai
ha	aveva	ebbe	avrà
abbiamo	avevamo	avemmo	avremo
avete	avevate	aveste	avrete
hanno	avevano	ebbero	avranno

PRESENT PERFECT *I have had, etc.*	PAST PERFECT *I had had, etc.*	SECOND PAST PERFECT *I had had, etc.*	FUTURE PERFECT *I shall have had, etc.*
ho avuto etc.	aveva avuto etc.	ebbi avuto etc.	avrò avuto etc.

IMPERATIVE	SUBJUNCTIVE		PAST FUTURE
Have, etc.	PRESENT *I have, etc.*	PAST *I had, etc.*	*I should have, etc.*
	abbia	avessi	avrei
abbi	abbi or abbia	avessi	avresti

Park d'Alassio Fountain, Riviera

Trevi Fountain, Rome

abbiamo	abbia	avesse	avrebbe
abbiate	abbiamo	avessimo	avremmo
	abbiate	aveste	avreste
	abbiano	avessero	avrebbero

PRESENT PERFECT	PAST PERFECT	PAST FUTURE PERFECT
I have had, etc.	*I had had, etc.*	*I should have had, etc.*
abbia avuto etc.	avessi avuto etc.	avrei avuto etc.

54. 1. The auxiliary of the passive is **essere**, *to be*.

L' esercito **fu** sconfitto.   *The army was defeated.*

2. The future (*shall, will*) and the past future or conditional (*should, would*) are formed in Italian without any auxiliary.

Io **andrò** ed lui **verrà**.   *I shall go, and he will come.*
Vorrei vederlo.   *I should like to see him.*

3. The auxiliary of the perfect, past perfect, second past perfect, and future perfect tenses is **avere**, *to have*, if the verb be active and transitive.

If the verb be passive, reflexive, or reciprocal, the auxiliary is always **essere**. For the definition of a reflexive verb, see **47**, 2, on p. 39.

If the verb be intransitive, the auxiliary is generally **essere**, but sometimes **avere**.[1]

Ho parlato.	*I have spoken.*
Avevano fatto queste cose.	*They had done these things.*
Mi **sono** fatto male.	*I have hurt myself.*
Le donne si **erano** sbagliate.	*The women had made a mistake.*
Sarò venuto.	*I shall have come.*
È nevicato.	*It has snowed.*
Aveva viaggiato.	*He had traveled.*

[1] The use of **avere** with intransitive verbs must be learned by practice.

(*a*) A past participle used with the auxiliary **essere** must agree with its *subject* in gender and number.

La ragazza è tornat**a**.	*The girl has returned.*
Le donne si sono disputat**e**.	*The women have argued.*

But when the verb has a reflexive pronoun as *indirect* object, and some other word as *direct* object, the past participle may agree with the subject, or with the direct object, or remain invariable.

La sorella si è fatta male.	*Our sister has hurt herself.*
Ci siamo fatti onore.	*We have done ourselves credit.*
Ci siamo data (*or* dato) parola d' onore.	*We have pledged our word of honor.*

(*b*) A past participle used with **avere** may or may not agree with its *direct object*, according to the choice of the writer. It usually does not agree when the object follows; and it nearly always does agree when the object is a personal pronoun preceding the verb.

La birra che aveva bevut**o** (*or* bevut**a**).	*The beer he had drunk.*
Ho vedut**o** molte cose.	*I have seen many things.*
Li ho trovati.	*I have found them.*

(*c*) *To be*, expressing a state or condition, is often rendered by **stare** (**92**, 4), instead of **essere**. **Stare per** or **essere per** (followed by the infinitive) means *to be on the point of.*

Sto bene.	*I'm well.*
Come sta?	*How are you?*
Stava per uscire.	*I was just going out.*

(*d*) English *am* (or *was*)+the present participle, when expressing duration, is rendered either by the simple present (or past descriptive) or by the same tense of **stare**[1]+the present participle; when denoting futurity, it is translated by the future (or past future), sometimes by the present (or past descriptive).

Camminava.	*He was walking.*
State lavorando.	*You are working.*
Leggevano *or* stavano leggendo.	*They were reading.*

[1] **Andare** (**92**, 1) and **venire** (**92**, 166) are sometimes used instead of **stare**.

Medito *or* sto meditando.	*I am meditating.*
Dice che verrà (*or* viene).	*He says he is coming.*
Disse che verrebbe.	*He said he was coming.*

(*e*) A verb with the auxiliary *used to* (or *would=used to*) is translated either by the simple past descriptive, or by the infinitive with **solere**, *to be accustomed* (**92**, 14).

| Vi **andava** (*or* **soleva andare**) ogni sera. | *He used to go* (or *would go*) *there every evening.* |

(*f*) **Venire**, *to come* (**92**, 166), and **rimanere**, *to remain* (**92**, 16), are sometimes used as auxiliaries in the simple tenses of the passive, instead of **essere**. **Andare**, *to go* (**92**, 1), is similarly used, but always implying duty or obligation.

I ladri **vennero** arrestati.	*The thieves were arrested.*
Rimase sorpresa.	*She was surprised.*
Il fucile non **va** toccato.	*The gun mustn't be touched.*

(*g*) The English auxiliary *do* is not expressed in Italian.

| Non viene. | *He does not come.* |

(*h*) *To have a thing done* is **far fare una cosa** (**92**, 2).

| Il re lo **fece** ammazzare. | *The king had him killed.* |

55. The third person of the passive is very often replaced by the reflexive construction with **si**:

Si racconta.	*It is related.*
Questo libro **si** legge.	*This book is read.*
La spada che mi **si** diede.	*The sword that was given me.*
Quelle cose **si** facevano.	*Those things were done.*

Many writers always make the verb agree with its subject in number; but in popular speech the verb is nearly always in the singular when its subject follows (as if **si** were the subject of the verb, and the original subject were the object):

| Si **vedono** (*or* **vede**) moltissime cose. | *Many things are seen.* |

| Non si **può** (*or* **possono**) leggere questi libri. | *These books can't be read.* |

Si belonging to a dependent infinitive regularly goes with the main verb (see **48**, *a*).

The construction with **si** is generally used also to render the English indefinite *they* followed by a verb: as **si dice**, *they say*. In this sense it is employed with neuter as well as with transitive verbs: as **si va spesso**, *people often go*. See also **63**, *a*. In this construction an object pronoun may precede **si**: as **lo si fa**, *it is done*.

56. Following are synopses of the compound tenses of transitive, neuter, reflexive, and passive verbs. In the paradigms given henceforth these forms will be omitted.

(*a*) Following is a synopsis of the compound tenses of **trovare**, *to find*, and **venire**, *to come:*

avere trovato, *to have found.*	essere venuto, *to have come.*
avendo trovato, *having found.*	essendo venuto, *having come.*
ho trovato, *I have found.*	sono venuto, *I have come.*
aveva trovato, *I had found.*	era venuto, *I had come.*
ebbi trovato, *I had found.*	fui venuto, *I had come.*
avrò trovato, *I shall have found.*	sarò venuto, *I shall have come.*
avrei trovato, *I should have found.*	sarei venuto, *I should have come.*
abbia trovato, *I have found.*	sia venuto, *I have come.*
avessi trovato, *I had found.*	fossi venuto, *I had come.*

(*b*) Following is a synopsis of the compound tenses of **alzarsi**, (*to raise one's self*), *to get up*, and **andarsene**,[1] *to go away*.

INFINITIVE: PAST	essersi alzato	essersene andato
PARTICIPLE: PAST	essendosi alzato	essendosene andato
INDICATIVE: PRES. PERF.	mi sono alzato	me ne sono andato
PAST PERFECT	mi era alzato	me ne era andato
SECOND PAST PERFECT	mi fui alzato	me ne fui andato

---

[1] **Andarsene** is composed of the verb **andare**, *to go*, the reflexive **si**, and the adverb **ne**, *thence* (see **47**, *a*).

FUTURE PERFECT	mi sarò alzato	me ne sarò andato
PAST FUTURE: PERFECT	mi sarei alzato	me ne sarei andato
SUBJUNCTIVE: PRES. PERF.	mi sia alzato	me ne sia andato
PAST PERFECT	mi fossi alzato	me ne fossi andato

(*c*) Following is a synopsis of the entire passive of **amare**, *to love:*

INFINITIVE: PRESENT	essere amato, *to be loved.*
PAST	essere stato amato, *to have been loved.*
PARTICIPLE: PRESENT	essendo amato, *being loved.*
PAST	essendo stato amato, *having been loved.*
INDICATIVE: PRESENT	sono amato, *I am loved.*
PRESENT PERFECT	sono stato amato, *I have been loved.*
PAST DESCRIPTIVE	era amato, *I was loved.*
PAST PERFECT	era stato amato, *I had been loved.*
PAST ABSOLUTE	fui amato, *I was loved.*
SECOND PAST PERFECT	fui stato amato, *I had been loved.*
FUTURE	sarò amato, *I shall be loved.*
FUTURE PERFECT	sarò stato amato, *I shall have been loved.*
PAST FUTURE	sarei amato, *I should be loved.*
PERFECT	sarei stato amato, *I should have been loved.*
IMPERATIVE	sii amato, *be loved.*
SUBJUNCTIVE: PRESENT	sia amato, *I be loved.*
PRESENT PERFECT	sia stato amato, *I have been loved.*
PAST	fossi amato, *I were loved.*
PAST PERFECT	fossi stato amato, *I had been loved.*

MODAL AUXILIARIES

57. *May, might, can, could* are generally rendered by the proper tense of **potere**[1]; *must, ought, shall* = *must, should* = *ought,* by **dovere**[1]; *will* and *would* expressing volition, by **volere**.[1]

Può essere vero.	*It may be true.*
Non **poteva** parlare.	*He couldn't speak.*
Deve pagarlo.	*He must pay him, he shall pay him.*
Dovrebbe farlo.	*He ought to do it, he should do it.*
Voglio sapere.	*I will know.*
Non **vorrei** andare.	*I wouldn't go.*

[1] See **92**, 21, 8, 19. The auxiliary of these verbs is regularly **avere**; but some writers use with them the auxiliary that belongs to the dependent infinitive: as **hanno potuto venire** or **sono potuti venire**, *they have been able to come.*

Note that *ought* must be expressed by the *past future* (or *conditional*) of **dovere**.

Dovremmo parlare.	*We ought to speak.*
Avrei dovuto farlo.	*I ought to have done it.*

No preposition intervenes between these verbs and the dependent infinitive.

Hanno potuto dormire.	*They have been able to sleep.*
Potremo partire.	*We shall be able to start.*
Dovemmo venire.	*We had to come.*
Dovrete trovarla.	*You will have to find her.*
Vorrà tornare.	*He will want to return.*
Vorrei sapere.	*I should like to know.*

These verbs are not defective, like the English modal auxiliaries; hence in Italian the tense is expressed by the auxiliary itself, and not by the dependent infinitive. To find the proper form of **potere**, **dovere**, or **volere**, replace *may*, etc., by the correct tense of *to be able; must*, etc., by *to be obliged; will*, etc., by *to want* or *to like:* as *I could have said it*=*I should have* (**avrei**) *been able* (**potuto**) *to say it* (**dirlo**)=**avrei potuto dirlo**.

Avrebbe dovuto tacere.	*He ought to have kept still.*
Avremmo voluto restare.	*We would have stayed.*

(*a*) *Must* is also expressed by the impersonal verb **bisognare**, *to be necessary*, followed by the infinitive or by **che**, *that*, with the subjunctive. *To have to* is **avere da**.

Bisogna farlo.	*It must be done.*
Bisogna che andiamo.	*We must go.*
Ho da scrivere una lettera.	*I have to write a letter.*

(*b*) *To be able* meaning *to know how* is **sapere** (see **92**, 6). *Not to be able to help* doing a thing is **non poter a meno di non** (with infinitive) or **non poter fare a meno di** (with infinitive).

Non **seppe** farlo.	*He couldn't do it.*
Sa leggere e scrivere.	*He can read and write.*
Non **potè a meno di non** ridere.	*He couldn't help laughing.*

CHAPTER 9

Regular and Irregular Verbs

58. Italian verbs are divided into four conjugations, according as the infinitive ending is –**are**, accented –**ere**, unaccented –**ere** (or –**rre**), or –**ire**. Regular verbs of the second and third conjugations are, however, inflected just alike.

(*a*) The final **e** of the infinitive may be dropped before any word except one beginning with **s** impure.[1]

THE REGULAR VERB

59. Parlare, *to speak*, will serve as a model for the first conjugation. All compound tenses are omitted (see **56**):

INFINITIVE AND PARTICIPLES

parlare	parlando	parlato

INDICATIVE

PRESENT	PAST DESCRIPTIVE	PAST ABSOLUTE	FUTURE
parlo	parlava	parlai	parlerò
parli	parlavi	parlasti	parlerai
parla	parlava	parlò	parlerà
parliamo	parlavamo	parlammo	parleremo
parlate	parlavate	parlaste	parlerete
parlano	parlavano	parlarono	parleranno

IMPERATIVE	SUBJUNCTIVE		PAST FUTURE
	PRESENT	PAST	
	parli	parlassi	parlerei
parla	parli	parlassi	parleresti
	parli	parlasse	parlerebbe
parliamo	parliamo	parlassimo	parleremmo
parlate	parliate	parlaste	parlereste
	parlino	parlassero	parlerebbero

[1] Cf. **10,** *b;* **14,** *b.* Italians find it hard to pronounce three consecutive consonants of which the middle one is **s.**

(*a*) Verbs whose infinitives end in –care or –gare insert **h** after the **c** or **g** in all forms where those letters precede **e** or **i**:

Paghi (pagare).	*Let him pay.*
Cercherò (cercare).	*I shall search.*

Verbs in –ciare and –giare drop the **i** before **e** or **i**:

Mangi (mangiare).	*Thou eatest.*
Comincerà[1] (cominciare).	*He will begin.*

But all other verbs in –iare drop the **i** only before another **i**:

Picchi (picchiare).	*Let him strike.*
Pigli (pigliare).	*Thou takest.*

BUT

Picchierà, piglierei.   *He will strike, I should take.*

Equestrian statue of Gattamelta, Padua

---

[1] Some writers retain the i before e: as **comincierà.**

60. Verbs of the second and third conjugations[1] are conjugated like **credere**, *to believe:*

INFINITIVE AND PARTICIPLES

credere	credendo	creduto

INDICATIVE

PRESENT	PAST DESCRIPTIVE	PAST ABSOLUTE	FUTURE
credo	credeva	credei (credetti)	crederò
credi	credevi	credesti	crederai
crede	credeva	credè (credette)	crederà
crediamo	credevamo	credemmo	crederemo
credete	credevate	credeste	crederete
credono	credevano	crederono (credettero)	crederanno

IMPERATIVE	SUBJUNCTIVE		PAST FUTURE
	PRESENT	PAST	
	creda	credessi	crederei
credi	creda	credessi	crederesti
	creda	credesse	crederebbe
crediamo	crediamo	credessimo	crederemmo
credete	crediate	credeste	credereste
	credano	credessero	crederebbero

The following verbs and their compounds do not have in the past absolute the forms in parentheses:

battere	mescere	stridere
competere	mietere	tessere
convergere	pascere	tondere
divergere	prudere	
lucere	ripetere	

Verbs in –**cere** and –**gere** insert after the **c** or **g** an **i** before the **u** of the past participle, but not before the **o** or **a** of the singular or third person plural of the present indicative or subjunctive:

mescere; mesco, mesci, mesce, mesciamo, mescete, mescono; mesca, etc., **mescano; mesciuto.**

---

[1] Many grammars and dictionaries class these two together as the "second conjugation."

Gondola tour, Venice

61. Most verbs of the fourth conjugation[1] are conjugated like **finire,** *to finish:*

INFINITIVE AND PARTICIPLES

finire   finendo   finito

INDICATIVE

PRESENT	PAST DESCRIPTIVE	PAST ABSOLUTE	FUTURE
finisco	finiva	finii	finirò
finisci	finivi	finisti	finirai
finisce	finiva	finì	finirà
finiamo	finivamo	finimmo	finiremo
finite	finivate	finiste	finirete
finiscono	finivano	finirono	finiranno

IMPERATIVE	SUBJUNCTIVE		PAST FUTURE
	PRESENT	PAST	
	finisca	finissi	finirei
finisci	finisca	finissi	finiresti
	finisca	finisse	finirebbe
finiamo	finiamo	finissimo	finiremmo
finite	finiate	finiste	finireste
	finiscano	finissero	finirebbero

Though conjugated like **finire** in all other parts, **dormire, fuggire,**[2] **pentire, sentire, servire, vestire** are always, **aborrire, bollire,** and verbs in –**vertire** are generally, and **assorbire, inghiottire, mentire, nutrire, tossire** are often, in the present indicative, imperative, and subjunctive, conjugated

---

[1] Many grammars and dictionaries call this the "third conjugation."
[2] **Fuggire** inserts no extra i (see last sentence of **60**).

after the model below. **Partire** and **sortire** are, when transitive, conjugated like **finire**, when intransitive, like **sentire**.[1]

INDICATIVE	IMPERATIVE	SUBJUNCTIVE
sento		senta
senti	senti	senta
sente		senta
sentiamo	sentiamo	sentiamo
sentite	sentite	sentiate
sentono		sentano

62. The present participle of all verbs is invariable.

Stavamo parlando.   *We were speaking.*

63. In all conjugations a form of the first person singular
of the past descriptive ending in –o instead of –a is nearly
always used in conversation, and occurs often in the works
of modern authors:

Leggevo.   *I was reading.*

(*a*) In popular speech the first person plural of all tenses is
generally replaced by the third person singular preceded by **si**:

Noi altri **si crede.**   *We believe.*
Noi **si era** venuti.   *We had come.*
Ci **si decise.**   *We decided (ourselves).*

(*b*) Final **o** of the third person plural is frequently omitted:

Parlan di lui.   *They speak of him.*

Forms in **–anno** sometimes drop **–no**:

Diran tutto.   *They will tell everything.*

(*c*) The past descriptive endings **–avamo, –avate, –evamo,
–evate, –ivamo, –ivate** are often pronounced **–avamo, –avate**, etc.

(*d*) Occasionally, especially in poetry, –at– is omitted from the
ending of the past participle of the first conjugation: **destato =
desto.**

___
[1] Compounds are conjugated like their simple verbs.

THE IRREGULAR VERB

64. Certain parts of Italian irregular verbs are always regular: the example given below will show which they are. **Essere** (see **53,** *a*) is an exception to all rules.

65. Many irregular verbs that belong or once belonged to the third conjugation have the infinitive contracted (**fare** for **facere, dire** for **dicere, condurre** for **conducere**): in this case the future and past future are formed from this contracted infinitive (**farò, direi, condurrebbe**), while the present participle, the past descriptive and past subjunctive, and certain persons of the present and past absolute are formed from the uncontracted stem (**facendo, diceva, conduciamo**).

66. Porre (for **ponere**), *to put,* a verb of the third conjugation, will serve to show which are the regular and which the irregular parts of irregular verbs: the forms printed in boldface are regular in all verbs except **dare, dire, essere, fare, stare;** those in Roman type may be irregular.

INFINITIVE AND PARTICIPLES

porre　　　　　**ponendo**　　　　posto

INDICATIVE

PRESENT	PAST DESCRIPTIVE	PAST ABSOLUTE	FUTURE
pongo	**poneva**	posi	porrò
poni	**ponevi**	ponesti[2]	porrai
pone	**poneva**	pose	porrà
poniamo	**ponevamo**	ponemmo[2]	porremo
ponete[1]	**ponevate**	poneste[2]	porrete
pongono	**ponevano**	posero	porranno

[1] See **66, 4.**　　　　[2] See **66, 3.**

Il Duomo, Florence

Santa Maria del Fiore Cathedral, Florence

Imperative	Subjunctive		Past Future
	PRESENT	PAST	
	ponga	ponessi[1]	porrei
poni	ponga	ponessi	porresti
	ponga	ponesse	porrebbe
poniamo	poniamo	ponessimo	porremmo
ponete	poniate	poneste	porreste
	pongano	ponessero	porrebbero

It will be seen that the present participle, the past descriptive and past subjunctive, and certain persons of the present and past absolute are always regular.

1. **Dare** and **stare** have in the future and past future **darò, darei; starò, starei.** Otherwise the only irregularity in the future and past future is that they are contracted in many verbs even when the infinitive is uncontracted: as **vedere**, *to see*, **vedrò; venire**, *to come*, **verrei.**

2. From the first person singular of the past absolute the other irregular persons can be constructed, the third person singular by changing the ending –i to –e, the third person plural by adding –ro to the third person singular.[2]

3. The *regular* persons of the past absolute and the whole past subjunctive are slightly irregular in **dare** and **stare**, which substitute **e** for **a** in those forms (**desti, demmo, deste, dessi; stesti, stemmo, steste, stessi**).

4. **Dire** (for **dicere**) and **fare** (for **facere**) have **dite** and **fate** in the second person plural of the present indicative.

(*a*) Verbs whose stem ends in –l, –n, or –r often drop final **e** or **i** in the singular of the present indicative and imperative:

Non **vuol** andare.	*He will not go.*
Vien qui.	*Come here.*

See also **63**, *a, b, c.*

---

[1] See **66**, 3.

[2] This rule applies only to an *irregular* past absolute.

(b) The three forms of the imperative are exactly like the corresponding persons of the present indicative, except in **avere, sapere,** and **volere,** where they follow the subjunctive:

abbi	abbiamo	abbiate
sappi	sappiamo	sappiate
vogli	vogliamo	vogliate

and in **andare, dare, dire, fare,** and **stare,** which have in the singular **va', da', di', fa', sta'.**

(c) The third person plural of the present indicative can always be constructed from the first person singular, from which can be formed also the whole present subjunctive except the first and second persons plural: these can be made from the first person plural of the present indicative.

EXCEPTIONS to this rule are **andare, avere, dare, fare, sapere,** and **stare,** which have in the third person plural of the present indicative **vanno, hanno, danno, fanno, sanno, stanno;** while **avere, dare, sapere,** and **stare** have in the present subjunctive **abbia, dia, sappia, stia.**

67. With the aid of the above notes any verb except **essere** can be constructed from the infinitive, the participles (the present participle often being necessary to show the uncontracted form of the infinitive), the present indicative, and the first person singular of the past absolute and future. A list of irregular verbs begins on page 86.

(a) In general, compound verbs not differing in conjugation from their simple verbs will be omitted from this list. All compounds of **dare** and **fare** are accented on the same syllable as the simple verbs:

Fa.　　*He does.*　　　　　　**Disfà.**　　*He undoes.*

The compounds of **stare** demand special mention: **ristare, soprastare, sottostare, sovrastare** are conjugated like **stare (ristà, soprastetti, sottostiano); distare** has no present participle, is regular in the present of all moods (**disto,** etc.), but otherwise is conjugated like **stare** (distetti, etc.); constare, contrastare, instare, ostare, prestare, restare, sostare are regular throughout (**consta, contrastano, instai, ostarono, presterò, resti, sostassi**).

68. In old Italian and in poetry both regular and irregular verbs differ in many ways from the normal types: some of the commonest variations are given below.

(*a*) In the first and third persons singular and the third person plural of the past descriptive **v** is often dropped, but never in the first conjugation: **voleva=volea** (also **volia**); **finivano=finiano**. Some of these forms are not uncommon in modern prose.

(*b*) The past future endings **–ei, –ebbe, –ebbero** are generally replaced in poetry by **–ia, –ia, –iano**: **crederei=crederia**.

(*c*) The future endings **–ò, –anno** are sometimes replaced by **–aggio** or **–abbo, –aggiono** or **–abbono**: **amerò=ameraggio; ameranno=amerabbono**.

(*d*) In the third person plural of the past absolute **–no** or **–ono** is often dropped: **amarono=amaro** or **amar** (also **amorno, amonno**). In the third person singular we find **amao, credeo, sentio**.

(*e*) Final **–ero** is often replaced by **–ono**: **avrebbero=avrebbono**.

(*f*) In the first person plural final **o** is often dropped, and then the **m** sometimes becomes **n**: **andiamo=andiam** or **andian**.

(*g*) In the first person plural of the present indicative of the second and third conjugations **–iamo** may be replaced by **–emo**.

(*h*) Final **–iano**, wherever it occurs (also **–eano** in the imperfect), may be replaced by **–ieno** or **–ieno**: **avevano=avieno**.

(*i*) At the end of a word we often find **e** for **i**, sometimes **i** for **e**: **pensi=pense; ascoltate=ascoltati**.

(*j*) **E** is sometimes added to a word ending in an accented vowel: **amò=amoe**.

CHAPTER 10

Moods and Tenses

INFINITIVE AND PARTICIPLE

69. The English gerund in *–ing* used as subject, predicate nominative, or direct object of a verb must be rendered in Italian by the *infinitive*, nearly always preceded by the definite article.

Mi piace **il viaggiare**.	*I like traveling.*
Rifarsela cogli animali è da sciocchi.	*Taking vengeance on animals is silly.*
La nostra prima cura fu **il cercare** una pensione.	*Our first care was hunting up a boarding house.*
Odio **lo studiare**.	*I hate studying.*

70. The English gerund preceded by a preposition is translated as follows:

1. If the preposition is a necessary part of the thought, it is expressed in Italian, and the English gerund is rendered by the infinitive with the definite article. This article is, however, omitted (unless it would be used in English) after the following prepositions:

di, *of.*	**invece di,** *instead of*	**senza,** *without.*
dopo di, *after.*	**prima di,** *before.*	

Parlai **contra il trarre** utile di quella disgrazia.	*I spoke **against** utilizing that misfortune.*
Il vizio **di fumare**.	*The habit **of** smoking.*
Ho l' abitudine **di coricarmi** tardi.	*I am in the habit **of** going to bed late.*
Invece di dirmi tutto.	***Instead of** telling me everything.*
Prima di morire.	***Before** dying.*
Parliamo **senza riflettere**.	*We speak **without** thinking.*

2. If in English the omission of the preposition, although it made the construction awkward, would not essentially change the meaning, the phrase is rendered in Italian by the present participle without any preposition.

Studiando si impara.	(*Through*) *studying we learn.*
Dovrei corrispondere alla sua cortesia **ascoltandola**.	*I ought to acknowledge her courtesy* (*by*) *listening to her.*
Partendo incontrò un amico.	(*On*) *going away he met a friend.*
Copiando non fa errori.	(*In*) *copying he makes no mistakes.*

3. *To amuse one's self by* . . . and *to weary one's self by* . . . are **divertirsi a** . . . and **affannarsi a** . . . with the infinitive:

Si diverte a tirar sassi.	*He amuses himself throwing stones.*

Some other verbs often take this construction.

71. Following are some other rules for the use of the infinitive and participles:

(*a*) When any verb is used as an auxiliary, the mood and tense are expressed in that verb, and not in the dependent infinitive (see **57**).

Avrei potuto farlo.	*I could have done it.*

(*b*) After **fare**, *to make* or *to have* (=*to cause*), **sentire** and **udire**, *to hear*, and **vedere**, *to see*, the Italian present infinitive is used to render an English past participle. After **lasciare**, *to let*, and often after the preposition **da** an Italian active infinitive is used to translate a passive one in English.

Si fa **capire**.	*He makes himself understood.*
Farò **fare** un paio di scarpe.	*I shall have a pair of shoes made.*
L' ho sentito **dire**.	*I have heard it said.*
Lo vide **ammazzare**.	*He saw him killed.*
Si lascia **ingannare**.	*He lets himself be deceived.*
Non c' è niente da **fare**.	*There is nothing to be done.*

(*c*) The Italian past participle is inflected like any other adjective. The present participle (which was originally an ablative gerund) is invariable.

When in English the present participle is used adjectively, without any verbal force whatsoever, it is translated, not by the form we have called the participle, but by a verbal adjective, which can be formed from almost any Italian verb by changing the infinitive ending into –**ante** for the first conjugation, and into –**ente** for the others. This adjective may be used substantively. It was originally a present participle, and some Italian writers have used it as such.

Questi vasi sono rotti.	*These vases are broken.*
La donna sta cucendo.	*The woman is sewing.*
Stavano parlando.	*They were speaking.*
Un animale **parlante**.	*A speaking animal.*
Acqua **bollente**.	*Boiling water.*
Due **amanti**.	*Two lovers.*

(*d*) A whole conditional clause (or protasis) is often replaced in Italian by a present participle, or by an infinitive with **a**.

Andandovi lo vedrebbe.	*If he went there, he would see it.*
A bucarsi esce il sangue.	*If you prick yourself, blood comes.*

(*e*) Writers sometimes use, instead of a clause in indirect discourse, an infinitive followed by the word that would have been subject of the clause.

Disse **essere questo** l' uomo che cercavamo.	*He said this was the man we were looking for.*

72. In negative commands the infinitive is always used instead of the second person *singular* of the imperative.

Trovalo.	*Find it.*
Non lo **trovare**.	*Do not find it.*

But the negative of **trovatelo** is **non lo trovate**.

PAST, PRESENT, AND FUTURE

73. When an action is represented as having taken place and still continuing, the English uses the present perfect or past perfect tense, the Italian the present or the past descriptive.

Studio l' italiano da otto mesi.	*I have studied Italian for eight months.*

74. In subordinate clauses referring to the future and introduced by a conjunction of time, where the present is often used in English, the future tense must be employed in Italian.

Quando vi **andrò**, glielo dirò.   *When I go there, I'll tell him.*

(*a*) The future is often used, without any idea of future time, to express probability.

Sarà uscito.   *He has probably gone out.*
Avrà molto denaro.   *He probably has a great deal of money.*

75. The difference between the past descriptive (or imperfect) and the past absolute (or preterit) is this: the latter is used of an event that occurred at a definite date in the past, the former is used in a description or in speaking of an accessory circumstance or an habitual action in past time — the preterit is a narrative, the imperfect a descriptive tense.

The second past perfect (or preterit perfect) is used — instead of the past perfect (or pluperfect) — only after conjunctions meaning *as soon as* (**appena che, subito che, tosto che**), and sometimes after **quando**, *when*, or **dopo che**, *after*, when immediate sequence is denoted.[1]

Entrò mentre **dormivamo**.   *He came in while we slept.*
Facevo così ogni mattina.   *I did so every morning.*
Lo **fece** l' anno scorso.   *He did it last year.*
Tosto che l' **ebbe visto**, uscì.   *As soon as he had seen it, he went.*

(*a*) In conversation the present perfect is often used instead of the past absolute, when the event is not remote. This use is, however, far more restricted than it is in French.

Vi **sono andato** ieri.   *I went there yesterday.*

---

[1] It is used also in phrases like: **in cinque minuti ebbe finita la lettera**, *in five minutes he had the letter finished.*

PAST, PRESENT, OR CONDITIONAL

76. The past future (or conditional), like the English *should* and *would*, has two uses: in *indirect discourse* after a principal verb in a past tense it expresses the tense which in direct discourse would be future[1]; in the *conclusion* of a conditional sentence it is used when the conditional clause is (or, if expressed, would be) in the past subjunctive (see **77**).

Disse che lo **farebbe**.	*He said he would do it.*
Se fosse vero lo **crederei**.	*If it were true, I should believe it.*
Questa casa mi **converrebbe**.	*This house would suit me.*

SUBJUNCTIVE

77. When a condition is contrary to *present* fact, or consists of a more or less unlikely supposition referring to *future* time,[2] the conditional clause has the past (or imperfect) subjunctive, the conclusional clause has the past future (or conditional).

If the unreal condition refers to *past* time, the conditional clause has the past perfect subjunctive, the conclusional clause has the past future perfect.[3]

Otherwise both condition and conclusion are in the indicative.

Se l' **avessi** te lo **darei**.	*If I had it, I should give it thee.*
Se **fosse tornato** l' **avrei veduto**.	*If he had returned, I should have seen him.*
Se **venisse** noi ce ne **andremmo**.	*If he came, we should go.*
Se vi **andassi morrei**.	*If I should go there, I should die.*
Se non è vero è ben trovato.	*If it isn't true, it's a good invention.*
Se lo **fece sarà punito**.	*If he did it, he will be punished.*

---

[1] The perfect of the future or the conditional is sometimes used where the simple tense would be expected: **disse che non l' avrebbe fatto più,** *he said he would do it no more.*

[2] Rendered in English by the past, or by the auxiliary *should.*

[3] The imperfect indicative is occasionally used to replace the past or past perfect subjunctive of the condition (or protasis) and the past future or past future perfect of the conclusion (or apodosis): as **se veniva, mi diceva tutto,** *if he had come, he would have told me everything.*

(*a*) The missing persons of the imperative are supplied from the present subjunctive. The past subjunctive is used to express a wish that is not likely to be realized.

Si **accomodi**.	*Be seated* (sing.).
Stiano zitti.	*Be quiet* (plur.).
Sia pure.	*Be it so.*
Vengano subito.	*Let them come at once.*
Fosse pure!	*Would it were so!*

(*b*) When a relative clause restricts its antecedent to one of all its possible conditions or actions, the verb of that relative clause is in the subjunctive, — the present subjunctive if the verb on which it depends be present or future, the past if it be past or past future.

Non c' è animale piu bellino d' un gatto giovane che **faccia** il chiasso.	*There is no animal prettier than a kitten that is at play.*
Vorrei vedere un bel quadro che non **fosse** antico.	*I should like to see a fine picture that is not old.*

(*c*) The verb of a subordinate clause depending on an impersonal verb, on a superlative, or on one of the words *first, last,* and *only,* is in the subjunctive. This rule does not apply to reflexive verbs, nor to affirmative phrases meaning *it is true* or *it is because.*

Bisognò ch' io vi **andassi**.	*I had to go there.*
È giusto che **siano puniti**.	*It's right they should be punished.*
Il più bello ch' io **conosca**.	*The finest that I know.*
Si vede che non è così.	*You see it isn't so.*
È vero che ci **sono stato**.	*It's true that I've been there.*

(*d*) The subjunctive is used after all conjunctions meaning *although, as if, unless, provided that, in order that, in such a way that* (denoting purpose), *before, until* (referring to future), *whenever, wherever, without.*

Benchè **stia** nascosto, lo troverò, dovunque **sia**.	*Although he be hidden, I shall find him, wherever he is.*
Partirò a meno che egli non **venga**.	*I shall go unless he comes.*

Lo fece perchè io **venissi**.	*He did it that I might come.*
La divise in modo che le due parti **fossero** uguali.	*He divided it in such a way that the two parts should be equal.*
Aspetta finchè io **torni**.	*Wait until I return.*
Parti senza che ti **veda**.	*Go without his seeing you.*

(*e*) The subjunctive is used after the indefinite words and phrases **quale che, qualunque, chiunque, checchè, per quanto**.

Chiunque **venga**.	*Whoever comes.*
Qualunque disgrazia che **succeda**.	*Whatever misfortune happens.*
Per quante volte ci **vada**.	*However many times I go there.*
Per quanto ricco egli **sia**.	*However rich he may be.*

(*f*) The verb of an indirect question is nearly always in the subjunctive when it depends on a main verb in a past tense.[1]

Domandano se il re è morto.	*They ask whether the king is dead.*
Domandò se il padre **fosse** uscito.	*He asked whether his father was out.*

(*g*) In a clause dependent on a verb of saying the subjunctive is used if the main verb is negative, or interrogative, or in a past tense.[1]

It is generally not used, however, after an affirmative verb in a past tense when the author himself wishes to imply that the indirect statement is true.

Dice che la cosa è chiarissima.	*He says the thing is perfectly clear.*
Non dico che questo **sia** vero.	*I don't say this is true.*
Dissero che lo zio **fosse** ammalato.	*They said their uncle was ill.*
Gli dissi che mi **chiamava** Enrico.	*I told him my name was Henry.*

(*h*) The subjunctive is used after verbs expressing causation, concession, desire, emotion, prevention, and uncertainty: i.e., after verbs of bringing about; granting, permitting; commanding, hoping, requesting, wishing; fearing, regretting, rejoicing; forbidding, hindering; being ignorant, denying, disbelieving, doubting, expect-

---

[1] The term *past tense* includes the past future.

ing, pretending, supposing, suspecting, thinking.   But **sperare**, *to hope*, very often does not take the subjunctive.

Non so chi **siano**.	*I don't know who they are.*
Vorrei che non **fosse accaduto**.	*I wish it had not happened.*
Supponiamo che **sia provato**.	*Let us suppose that it is proved.*
Spero che **verrà**.	*I hope he will come.*

(*i*) **Se**, *if*, is occasionally omitted before a past subjunctive; in this case the subject, if expressed, must follow the verb.

Sarei felíce **venisse egli**.	*I should be happy, should he come.*

Vigo di Fassa Church

CHAPTER 11

Conjunctions, Prepositions, and Adverbs

CONJUNCTIONS

78. The principal conjunctions are:

after, dopo che.
also, anche, pure.
although, benchè, sebbene, non ostante che.
and, e.
as, come, quanto (after tanto).
as (*=since*), siccome, poichè.
as fast as, via via che.
as if, come se, quasi.
as long as, finchè.
as well as, come anco.
because, perchè.
before, prima che, avanti che.
both . . . and, e . . . e.
but, ma.
either . . . or, o . . . o.
even if, anche se, ancorchè.
except that, se non che.
for, chè.
granting that, dato che.
however (*=nevertheless*), però, pure.
however (before an adj.), qualunque, per quanto.
if, se (occasionally quando, ove).
in case, caso.
in order that, perchè, acciochè, affinchè.
much less, non che.
neither . . . nor, nè . . . nè.
nevertheless, tuttavia, nondimeno, però.

nor, nè, nemmeno, neppure.
nor . . . either, nemmeno, neppure.
nor even, neanche, neppure.
not to say . . . but even, non che . . . ma.
or, o, ovvero, ossia.
or else, ossia.
provided that, purchè.
rather, anzi.
since (temporal), dacchè.
since (causal), poichè, siccome.
so, dunque, adunque.
so that (result), di modo che, sicchè.
so that (*=in order that*), perchè.
than, che.
that, che.
that (*=in order that*), perchè.
then, dunque.
therefore, dunque, però, perciò, adunque (at the beginning of a clause).
too, pure, anche.
unless, a meno che non, eccetto che non, senza che.
until, finchè non.
when, quando.
whence, donde.
where, dove, ove, là dove.
wherever, dovunque.
whether, se.
while, mentre, mentre che.

The final vowel of **anche, che, dove, neppure,** and **ove** is generally elided before **e** or **i.**

(*a*) Of the above conjunctions the following require the subjunctive:

acciochè	come se	prima che
affinchè	dato che	purchè
a meno che non	dovunque	qualunque
ancorchè	eccetto che non	quasi
avanti che	non ostante che	sebbene
benchè	perchè meaning *in order that*	senza che
caso	per quanto	

For the use of **che,** *that,* with the subjunctive, see **77,** *c, g, h.* **Come** is occasionally used for **come se,** and then it takes the subjunctive. **Finchè** when referring to the future sometimes has the sense of **finchè non,** and then it generally takes the subjunctive. **Se** is followed by the subjunctive when it introduces an indirect question or statement dependent on a verb in a past tense, or a condition contrary to fact. **Quando** and **ove,** meaning *if,* frequently take the subjunctive when **se** would not. — For examples, see **77,** *c, d, f, g, h.*

(*b*) **Che** cannot be omitted in Italian as *that* is in English:[1]

Disse **che** fosse vero.   *He said it was true.*

Se can be omitted before an imperfect subjunctive (see **77,** *i*).

(*c*) **E** and **o** are often written **ed** and **od** before a vowel.

Mio padre **ed** io.   *My father and I.*

(*d*) Between a verb of motion and an infinitive *and* is rendered by the preposition **a.**

Andrò **a** cercarlo.   *I'll go and look for it.*

---

[1] It is omitted, however, in the following peculiarly Italian construction: il **ragazzo pareva fosse felice,** *the boy seemed to be happy;* that is, between a verb of seeming and the subjunctive dependent on it, when in English the construction would be a verb of seeming with a dependent infinitive. It is occasionally omitted also after verbs of wishing, hoping, and fearing: as **spero mi scriva presto,** *I hope you will write to me soon.*

(*e*) When **anche**, *also* or *too*, relates to a personal pronoun, the disjunctive form of that pronoun must follow **anche**, even if some form of the same pronoun has already been expressed.

Andremo anche **noi**.	*We shall go too.*
Parte anche **lui**.	*He goes away too.*
Trovai anche **lui**.	*I found him too.*
Vennero anch' **essi**.	*They came too.*
Lo *or* me lo diede anche **a me**.	*He gave it to me too.*
Ti piace anche **a te**.	*You like it too.*

PREPOSITIONS

79. The principal prepositions are:

about (=*approximately*), **circa**.
about (=*around*), **intorno a, attorno a**.
above, **sopra**.
according to, **secondo**.
after, **dopo, dopo di**.
against, **contra, contro**.
along, **lungo**.
among, **fra, tra**.
around, **intorno a, attorno a**.
as far as, **fino a, sino a**.
as for, **per, quanto a, in quanto a**.
as to, **rispetto a**.
at, **a**.
because of, **per motivo di**.
before (time), **prima di, innanzi**.
before (place), **davanti a, innanzi**.
behind, **dietro**.
below, **sotto**.
beside (place), **accanto a**.
besides, beside (=*in addition to*), **oltre**.
between, **fra, tra**.
beyond, **oltre, al di là di**.
by, **da, accanto a** (=*beside*).
by means of, **per mezzo di**.
during, **durante**.
except, **tranne, eccetto, fuori di**.
from, **da, fin da**.

in, **in**.
in front of, **davanti a, innanzi**.
inside of, **dentro di**.
instead of, **invece di**.
in the midst of, **in mezzo a**.
into, **in**.
near, **vicino a**.
of, **di**.
on, **su** (before a vowel, **sur**), **sopra**.
on this side of, **al di qua di**.
on to, **su** (before vowels, **sur**), **sopra**.
opposite, **dirimpetto a**.
out of, **da, di, fuori di**.
outside of, **fuori di**
over, **sopra**.
round and round, **torno torno a**.
since, **da**.
to, **a**.
toward, **verso**.
through, **per**.
under, **sotto**.
upon, **su** (before vowels, **sur**), **sopra**.
up to, **fino a, sino a**.
with, **con**.
within, **fra, tra**.
within (=*inside of*), **dentro di**.
without, **senza**.
without (=*outside of*), **fuori di**.

Rialto Bridge, Venice

Il Battistero with Duomo, Pisa

When governing a personal pronoun **contra**, **dietro**, **dopo**, **senza**, **sopra**, **sotto**, and often **fra** and **verso** take **di** after them:

    sénza di me, *without me.*   **fra di** loro, *among themselves.*

After **con**, **in**, **per**, a word beginning with **s** impure generally prefixes **i**:[1]

    la strada, *the street.*   in istrada, *in the street.*

(*a*) *To* before the name of a country, after a verb of motion, is **in**.

    Andiamo **in** Francia.   *Let us go to France.*

(*b*) *To* before an infinitive is rendered in Italian as follows:

1. After the verbs

bastare, *suffice*	**fare**, *make*	**sentire**, *hear, feel*
bisognare, *need*	**lasciare**, *let*	**solere**, *be accustomed*
convenire, *suit*	**parere**, *seem*	**udire**, *hear*
desiderare, *desire*	**potere**, *can, be able*	**vedere**, *see*
dovere, *must, ought*	**sapere**, *know*	**volere**, *wish*

to before a following infinitive is omitted. It is omitted also in exclamations and indirect questions consisting only of an interrogative and an infinitive.

    Dovrei capire.   *I ought to understand.*
    Bisogna pensarci.   *It is necessary to look out for it.*
    Potremo venire.   *We shall be able to come.*
    Non sa che fare nè dove avvol-   *He doesn't know what to do nor*
       gersi.   *where to turn.*

2. After verbs of accustoming, attaining, beginning, compelling, continuing, hastening, helping, inviting, learning, preparing, teaching, and after verbs of motion, *to* before a following infinitive is **a**.

    Andranno **a** vederla.   *They will go to see her.*
    Si affrettò **a** rispondere.   *He hastened to reply.*

3. After all other verbs it is **di**; but *to* denoting purpose or result is **per**, and *to* indicating duty or necessity is **da**.

    Gli dissi **di** scrivere.   *I told him to write.*
    Mi è grato **di** dirlo.   *I am happy to say so.*

[1] Cf. **58**, *a*.

Legge **per** divertirsi.   *He reads to amuse himself.*
È troppo basso **per** arrivarci.   *He's too short to reach it.*
Ho qualchecosa **da** fare.   *I have something to do.*

(c) *By* denoting the agent is **da.**

Fu fatto **da** lui.   *It was done by him.*

(d) *In* is **in**; but when expressing future time it is **fra.**

Fra tre giorni sarà finito.   *In three days it will be finished.*

(e) *For* is **per**: as l' **ha fatto per me**, *he has done it for me.* But, in the sense of *since*, in speaking of past time, *for* is **da.** *For* meaning *during* is omitted or translated **durante.** Sentences like *it is right for him to do it* must be translated by **che** with the subjunctive: **è giusto che lo faccia.**

Dimora **da** molti anni a Firenze.   *He has lived for many years at Florence* (see **73**).
Resterò cinque settimane.   *I shall stay for five weeks.*
Piovve **durante** un mese.   *It rained for a month.*
Bisogna **ch'** io vada.   *It is necessary for me to go.*

(f) *From* is **da**; but before adverbs and sometimes after verbs of departing it is **di.** In speaking of time it is generally **fin da.**

Arriva **da** Parigi.   *He arrives from Paris.*
È lontano **di** qua.   *It is far from here.*
Esco **di** casa.   *I go out of the house.*
Fin **dal** principio.   *From the beginning.*

(g) **Da** has, in addition to the meanings *by, from, since,* another sense hard to render in English: it may be translated *as, characteristic of, destined for, such as to,* or *suited to,* according to the context. **Da** means also *at the house of* or *to the house of.* **Da** corresponds to English *on, at,* or *to* before the word *side,* **parte,** used in its literal sense.

Prometto **da** uomo d' onore.   *I promise as a man of honor.*
Il Salvini **da** Otello.   *Salvini as Othello.*
Sareste tanto buono **da** venire?   *Would you be so good as to come?*
Questo è **da** sciocchi.   *This is acting like a fool.*
Il bambino ha un giudizio **da** grande.   *The child has the judgment of a grown person.*

La sala **da** pranzo.	*The dining-room.*
Una tazza **da** caffè.	*A coffee-cup.*
L' ho veduto **dal** Signor Neri.	*I saw him at Mr. Neri's.*
Viene **da** me.	*He comes to my house.*
Da questa parte.	*On this side.*

(*h*) **A** is often used before a noun — not indicating material (which is expressed by **di**) nor purpose (expressed by **da**) — that describes another noun, when in English these two substantives would form a compound word.

Una macchina **a** vapore.	*A steam-engine.*
Una sedia **a** dondolo.	*A rocking-chair.*
Uno sgabello **a** tre piedi.	*A three-legged stool.*

(*i*) **Essere per** or **stare per** means *to be about to.*

Stava **per** parlare.	*He was on the point of speaking.*

(*j*) In some idiomatic phrases **di** is used in Italian when another preposition would be employed in English.

Di giorno, **di** notte.	*By day, by night.*
Essere contento **di** una cosa.	*To be satisfied with a thing.*
Vivo **di** pane.	*I live on bread.*
Che faceva **delle** forbici?	*What did he do with the scissors?*

ADVERBS

80. 1. Adverbs, unless they begin the clause, are generally placed immediately after the verb; **non**, however, always precedes the verb. When a compound tense is

Old Fortifications, Umbria, Assisi

used, the adverb nearly always follows the past participle, but **già, mai, più,** and **sempre** usually precede it. See also **84.**

Non precedes a conjunctive and follows a disjunctive pronoun.

Non ci vado **mai.**	*I never go there.*
Ho parlato **spesso.**	*I have often spoken.*
Non ha **sempre** parlato così.	*He hasn't always talked so.*
Io **non** lo vedo.	*I don't see him.*

2. Adverbs are compared like adjectives (see **31**); but *better, worse, more, less* are respectively **meglio, peggio, più, meno.**

81. *Yes* is **sì** or **già**: **sì** when it expresses real affirmation, **già** when it denotes passive assent. *No* is **no.** *Not* is **non.** *Or not* at the end of a clause is **o no:**

Le piace? — **Sì.**	*Do you like it? — Yes.*
Che tempaccio! — **Già.**	*What nasty weather! — Yes.*
Sta bene? — **No.**	*Is he well? — No.*
Non sta bene.	*He isn't well.*
Sia vero **o no.**	*Whether it be true or not.*

(a) *What?* meaning *what do you say?* is **come? Che** and the interjection **o** are often used to introduce questions.

O perchè non rispondete? — **Come?** — **Che** siete sordo, signore?	*Why don't you answer? — What? — Are you deaf, sir?*

(b) *Very* is **molto** (see, however, **35**, *a*). Instead of using a word or suffix for *very*, the Italians often repeat the emphasized adjective or adverb.

E **molto** bello *or* è **bellissimo.**	*It is very beautiful.*
I suoi genitori erano **poveri poveri.**	*His parents were very poor.*

82. *Only* may be translated by the adverb **solo, soltanto,** or **solamente;** or by the adjective **solo.** When it modifies anything but a verb, it is often rendered by **non . . . che**, with the whole verb intervening, and with the word modified by *only* immediately after **che**.

Non ne ho comprato **che** due.   *I have bought only two of them.*

83. *Never* is **non . . . mai**, with the inflected part of the verb intervening. *Just*, as an adverb of time, is **or ora**. *Early* is **presto, per tempo**, or **di buon' ora**. *This morning* is **stamane**; *last night* is **stanotte**. *The day after to-morrow* and *the day before yesterday* are respectively **doman l' altro** and **ier l' altro**. *A week, a fortnight from to-day* are **oggi a otto, a quindici**. *Ago* is translated by **fa**, which follows the substantive of time; if this substantive is plural, *ago* may be rendered also by **sono** (**erano** or **saranno** if the date from which time is counted be past or future).

Non ti ha **mai** veduto.	*He has never seen thee.*
Son arrivati **or ora**.	*They have just arrived.*
Tre anni **fa**.	*Three years ago.*
Quattro giorni **sono**.	*Four days ago.*
Lunedì **erano** due settimane.	*Two weeks ago Monday.*
Domani **saranno** cinque mesi.	*Five months ago to-morrow.*

84. *Here* and *there*, when they denote a place already mentioned, and no particular stress is laid upon them, are **ci** and **vi**, which are often used in Italian when they would be superfluous in English; *there is, there are*, etc., are **c' è** or **vi è, ci sono** or **vi sono**, etc. (sometimes **vi ha**). **Ci, vi**, and also **ne**, *thence*, occupy the same positions with regard to the verb, and undergo the same changes, as the pronouns **ci, vi, ne** (**48, 50**); they precede conjunctive pronouns beginning with **l** or **n**, and follow all others: **ce lo manda, ti ci mando**.

When emphasized, *here* is **qui** or **qua**, *there* indicating a place near the person addressed is **costì** or **costà**, and *there* denoting a point remote from both speaker and hearer is **lì** or **là**.

Carlo **vi** è tornato.	*Charles has gone back there.*
Alla scuola non **ci** vado.	*I don't go to school.*
Voi rimarrete **costà**, lui resterà **laggiù**, ed io non partirò di **qui**.	*You will remain where you are, he will stay down there, and I shall not move from here.*

(a) *Here I am, here it is*, etc., are **eccomi, eccolo**, etc.

85. Most adverbs of manner are formed by adding –**mente** to the feminine singular of the corresponding adjective. Adjectives in –**le** and –**re** drop their final **e** in forming the adverb. See **35**, *a*.

franco, *frank.*	**francamente**, *frankly.*
felice, *happy.*	**felicemente**, *happily.*
piacevole, *pleasant.*	**piacevolmente**, *pleasantly.*

(a) *So* meaning *it* is translated **lo**:

Lo faccio.	*I do so.*
Lo crede.	*He thinks so.*
Lo dicono.	*They say so.*

CHAPTER 12

Indefinite Pronouns

86. *One, people, we, you, they,* used in an indefinite sense, are rendered in Italian by the reflexive construction with **si** (see **55**).

Si canta bene in Italia.	*They sing well in Italy.*
Si fa così.	*You do this way.*
Se ne parla.	*People speak of it.*
Si fanno spesso queste cose.	*One often does these things.*

87. *All* as a substantive is **tutto** (**tutti**, etc.):

Tacevano tutti.	*All were silent.*

Castle of Cornedo

The adjective *all, the whole* is **tutto** followed by the definite article.

Tutta la terra.	*The whole earth.*
Tutto il giorno.	*All day.*
Tutte le romane son belle.	*All Roman ladies are beautiful.*

88. *Any*, when it really adds nothing to the sense, is omitted:

Non ha libri.	*He hasn't (any) books.*
Volete vino?	*Do you want (any) wine?*

When, however, this redundant *any* might be replaced by *any of the*, it is translated by the partitive construction (see **12**, *a*):

Volete **del** vino?	*Do you want any (of the) wine?*

Any used substantively in the sense of *any of it, any of them* is **ne** (see **47**, 3):

Non **ne** ho.	*I haven't any.*
Non **ne** ha più.	*He hasn't any more.*
Ne avete?	*Have you any?*

Any used adjectively and meaning *any whatsoever* is **qualunque**:

Lo fa meglio di **qualunque** altra persona.	*He does it better than any other person.*

89. *Some*, when it adds nothing to the sense, is omitted or rendered by the partitive construction:

Volete burro *or* volete **del** burro?	*Will you have some butter?*

Some meaning *some of it, some of them* is **ne**:

Ne ha.	*He has some.*

Otherwise *some* is **alcuno** or **qualche**. **Qualche** is always singular (even when the meaning is plural), and is never used substantively.

Alcune persone *or* **qualche** persona.	*Some persons.*
Alcuni lo dicono.	*Some say so.*

90. *Some . . . others, the one . . . the other, one . . . another* are translated by **chi . . . chi, altri . . . altri, l' uno . . . l'altro,** or **alcuni . . . alcuni.**

Alcuni used in this way is always plural. A verb whose subject is **chi** or **altri** (used in this sense) is always singular; **altri** is not used after prepositions. But **l' uno** and **l' altro** can be used in any case or number.

Tutti, **chi** più tosto, e **chi** meno, morivano.	*All died, some sooner, some later.*
Altri cade, **altri** fugge.	*Some fall, others flee.*
Gli **uni** son buoni, gli **altri** cattivi.	*Some are good, others bad.*

91. Following is a list of some other indefinite pronouns and adjectives:

anybody, **qualcuno, qualcheduno, chicchessía,** pronouns.

any more, **più, ne . . . più,** pron.

anything, **qualchecosa,** pron.

anything else, **altro,** pron.

both, **tutti e due, l' uno e l' altro, ambedue,** pron. or adj.

certain, **certo,** adj.

each, **ogni, ciascuno, ognuno,** adj.

either, **l' uno o l' altro,** pron. or adj.

every, **ogni, ciascuno, ognuno, ciascheduno,** adj.

everybody, **tutti** (pl.), **ciascheduno, ciascuno, ognuno,** pron.

everything, **tutto,** pron.

few, a few, **pochi** (pl.), pron. or adj.

however much (*or many*), **per quanto** (–ti), adj.

little, **poco,** pron. or adj.

less, **meno,** pron. or adj.[1]

many, **molti,** pron. or adj.[2]

more, **più,** pron. or adj.

much, **molto,** pron. or adj.

neither, **non . . . l' uno nè l' altro, nè l' uno nè l' altro,** pron. or adj.

no, **non . . . nessuno, non . . . alcuno,** adj.

nobody, **non . . . nessuno,** pron.

---

[1] *Less=smaller* is **più piccolo.**

[2] *A great many* is **moltissimi.**

no more, **non ne . . . più**, pron.,
  non . . . più, adj.

none, **non ne . . .**, pron.

nothing, **non . . . niente, non . . .**
  nulla, pron.

nothing else, **non . . . più niente,**
  non . . . più nulla, pron.

others, **altrui** (see **91**, *d*), pron.

several, **parecchi** (fem. **parecchie**),
  pron. or adj.

somebody, **qualcheduno, qualcuno,**
  pron.

something, **qualchecosa, qualcosa,**
  pron.

something else, **altro**, pron.

such, **tale**, adj.

such a, **un tale**, adj. (but also pron.
  in Ital., meaning *so-and-so*).

whatever, **qualunque** (invariable),
  adj.

(*a*) The verb used with **nessuno, alcuno, niente, nulla** (meaning *no, nobody, nothing*) must be preceded by **non**, *not*, unless this pronoun or adjective precedes the verb.

Non ho visto **nessuno**.	*I have seen nobody.*
Nessun popolo lo possiede.	*No people possesses it.*

(*b*) *Nothing*, followed by an adjective, is **niente di**.

Non avete **niente di** buono.	*You have nothing good.*

(*c*) **Ciascuno, ciascheduno, ognuno, nessuno,** and **alcuno** when used adjectively are inflected like **uno** (see **14, 15**).

(*d*) **Altrui**, *another, others, our neighbor*, is invariable, and is not used as subject of a verb:

Con **altrui**.	*With other people.*
Chi ama **altrui** ama sè stesso.	*He who loves his neighbor loves himself.*

The prepositions **di** and **a** are sometimes omitted before **it**:

La mostro **altrui**.	*I point her out to others.*
La voglia **altrui**.	*The will of another.*

CHAPTER 13

List of Irregular Verbs

92. This list contains no compound verbs except those which differ in conjugation from their simple verbs and those for which no simple verb exists in Italian. With every verb its irregular forms are given: in the same line with the infinitive are the present participle (if it be needed to show the original form of the infinitive), the first person singular of the past absolute indicative, the past participle, and the first person singular of the future indicative (if the future be contracted); immediately below are the present indicative, the imperative, and the present subjunctive, if these parts be peculiar. For **dare** and **stare** the whole past absolute and the first person singular of the past subjunctive are given also. **Essere** is irregular throughout. *All tenses not mentioned are regular.* For peculiar *endings*, see **63, 68**. Note the following rules:

(*a*) If the *present participle* is given, the following forms, unless expressly mentioned, are to be constructed from its stem: all *past absolute forms with accented endings*, and the whole *past descriptive* and *past subjunctive*. E.g., **fare**, pres. part. **facendo**: hence past abs. 2d sing. and 1st and 2d pl., **facesti, facemmo, faceste**; past descr., **faceva**, etc.; past subj., **facessi**, etc.

If the present participle is not given, these forms, unless they be mentioned, are to be constructed from the stem of the infinitive. E.g., **venire**: past abs., **venisti, venimmo, veniste**; past descr., **veniva**; past subj., **venissi**.

---

[1] Reference to these tables is facilitated by an Alphabetical List of Irregular and Defective Verbs (see page 100). Students are advised not to learn forms in parentheses nor any verbs or forms marked *rare* or *poetical*.

(*b*) A past absolute whose 1st pers. sing. ends in **–ai, –ei, –ii,** or **–etti** (except **detti** and **stetti**) is regular throughout. In any *other* past absolute the third person singular can be formed from the first person by changing final **i** to **e**, and the third person plural by adding **–ro** to the third person singular. E.g., **fare**, p. abs. feci: 3d sing., fece; 3d pl., fecero.

(*c*) If the future is not given, it is to be constructed from the infinitive. The past future always has the same stem as the future. See **65**, p. 57.

(*d*) The imperative, when not given, is like the corresponding forms of the present indicative. See **66**, *b*.

The Three Graces, Botticelli

Mantua, Lombardy

FIRST CONJUGATION

1. **Andare,** *go,* andai, andato; andrò (anderò).

PRES. IND.		IMPER.	PRES. SUBJ.	
vado or vo	andiamo	va'	vada	andiamo
vai	andate	andiamo	vada	andiate
va	vanno	andate	vada	vadano

2. **Fare,** *do,* facendo, feci,[1] fatto; farò. **Fare** (*formerly also* **facere**) *was originally a verb of the third conjugation (see* **92,** *a).*

PRES. IND.		IMPER.	PRES. SUBJ.	
faccio or fo	facciamo	fa'	faccia	facciamo
fai[2]	fate	facciamo	faccia	facciate
fa[2]	fanno	fate	faccia	facciano

3. **Dare,** *give,* diedi *or* detti, dato; darò. *Past subj.* dessi.

PRES. IND.	PAST. ABS.	IMPER.	PRES. SUBJ.
do	diedi or detti		dia
dai	desti	da'	dia
dà	diede or dette[3]		dia
diamo	demmo	diamo	diamo
date	deste	date	diate
danno	diedero or dettero[3]		diano or dieno

[1] In poetry we sometimes find a past abs. fei, festi, fe or feo, femmo, feste, ferono or fero or fenno; and past descr. fea, etc.

[2] Also faci face.

[3] Also diè, sing.; dier or diero or dierono, pl.

4. **Stare** (**67**, *a*), *stand*, stetti, stato; starò. *Past subj.* stessi.

PRES. IND.	PAST. ABS.	IMPER.	PRES. SUBJ.
sto	stetti		stia
stai	stesti	sta'	stia
sta	stette		stia
stiamo	stemmo	stiamo	stiamo
state	steste	state	stiate
stanno	stettero		stiano or stieno

SECOND CONJUGATION

5. **Avere**, *have*, ebbi, avuto; avrò. See **53**, *b*.[1]

6. **Sapere**, *know*, seppi, saputo; saprò.

PRES. IND.		IMPER.	PRES. SUBJ.	
so	sappiamo	sappi	sappia	sappiamo
sai	sapete	sappiamo	sappia	sappiate
sa	sanno	sappiate	sappia	sappiano

7. **Cadere**, *fall*, caddi, caduto; cadrò.

PRES. IND.		PRES. SUBJ.	
cado (caggio)	cadiamo (caggiámo)	cada (caggia)	cadiamo (caggiamo)
cadi	cadete	cada (caggia)	cadiate (caggiate)
cade	cadono (caggiono)	cada (caggia)	cadano (caggiano)

8. **Dovere**, *owe*, dovei (dovetti), dovuto; dovrò. *Imperative lacking.*

PRES. IND.	PRES. SUBJ.
devo (debbo or deggio)	debba (deva or deggia)
devi (debbi)	debba (deva or deggia)
deve (debbe)	debba (deva or deggia)
dobbiamo (deggiamo)	dobbiamo
dovete	dobbiate
devono (debbono or deggiono)[2]	debbano (devano or deggiano)

9. **Sedere**, *sit*, sedei *or* sedetti, seduto.

PRES. IND.		PRES. SUBJ.	
siedo or seggo	sediamo (seggiamo)	sieda or segga	sediamo (seggiamo)
siedi	sedete	sieda or segga	sediate
siede	siedono or seggono	sieda or segga	siedano or seggano

[1] In poetry we find: aggio, abbo, or aio for ho; ave for ha; aggia or aia for abbia; ei for ebbi; a future arò, etc., or averò, etc., and similar forms in the past future.

[2] Also deo, dei, dee, dovemo, dovete, deono or denno.

10. **Vedere,** *see,* vidi, veduto *or* visto; vedrò. **Provvedere** *has a future* provvederò; **prevedere** *has* prevederò *or* prevedrò. *All other compounds are like* vedere.

PRES. IND.	PRES. SUBJ.
vedo (veggo or **veggio)**	veda (vegga or veggia)
vedi	veda (vegga or veggia)
vede	veda (vegga or veggia)
vediamo (veggiamo)	vediamo (veggiamo)
vedete	vediate (veggiate)
vedono (veggono or **veggiono)**	vedano (veggano or veggiano)

11. **Giacere,** *lie,* giacqui, giaciuto.

PRES. IND.		PRES. SUBJ.	
giaccio	giacciamo	giaccia	giacciamo
giaci	giacete	giaccia	giacciate
giace	giacciono	giaccia	giacciano

12. **Piacere,** *please: like* giacere (11).

13. **Tacere,** *be silent: like* giacere (11).

14. **Solere,** *be wont,* solito. *No past. abs., fut., past fut., nor imperative.*

PRES. IND.		PRES. SUBJ.	
soglio	**sogliamo**	soglia	sogliamo
suoli	**solete**	soglia	sogliate
suole	**sogliono**	soglia	sogliano

15. **Dolere,** *grieve,* dolsi, doluto; dorrò.

PRES. IND.		PRES. SUBJ.	
dolgo (doglio)	dogliamo [1]	dolga (doglia)	dogliamo [1]
duoli	dolete	dolga (doglia)	dogliate
duole	dolgono (dogliono)	dolga (doglia)	dolgano (dogliano)

16. **Rimanere,** *remain,* rimasi, rimasto *or* rimaso; rimarrò.

PRES. IND.		PRES. SUBJ.	
rimango	**rimaniamo** [2]	rimanga	rimaniamo [2]
rimani	**rimanete**	rimanga	rimaniate
rimane	**rimangono**	rimanga	rimangano

[1] Also **dolghiamo:** a popular form.
[2] Also **rimanghiamo:** a popular form.

17. Tenere, *hold*, tenni, tenuto; terrò.

PRES. IND.		PRES. SUBJ.	
tengo	teniamo[1]	tenga	teniamo[1]
tieni	tenete	tenga	teniate
tiene	tengono	tenga	tengano

18. Valere, *be worth*, valsi, valuto *or* valso; varrò.

PRES. IND.		PRES. SUBJ.	
valgo (vaglio)	vagliamo	valga (vaglia)	vagliamo[1]
vali	valete	valga (vaglia)	vagliate
vale	valgono (vagliono)	valga (vaglia)	valgano (vagliano)

19. Volere, *wish*, volli,[2] volúto; vorrò.

PRES. IND.		IMPER.	PRES. SUBJ.	
voglio (vo')	vogliamo	vogli	voglia	vogliamo
vuoi[3]	volete	vogliamo	voglia	vogliate
vuole	vogliono	vogliate	voglia	vogliano

20. Parere, *seem*, parvi, paruto *or* parso; parrò.

PRES. IND.		PRES. SUBJ.	
paio	paiamo *or* pariamo	paia	paiamo *or* pariamo
pari	parete	paia	paiate
pare	paiono	paia	paiano

21. Potere, *be able*, potei, potuto; potrò.[4] *No imperative.*

PRES. IND.		PRES. SUBJ.	
posso	possiamo	possa	possiamo
puoi	potete	possa	possiate
può[5]	possono[5]	possa	possano

22. Persuadere, *persuade*, persuasi, persuaso. *Pres.* persuado, etc.

23. Calere, *matter*, calse, caluto. *Impersonal. No fut., past fut., nor imperative. Not modern.*

PRES. IND.	PRES. SUBJ.
cale	caglia

---

[1] Also tenghiamo; valghiamo: popular forms.
[2] Also volsi.   [3] Also vuogli or vuoli.
[4] In poetry we find a fut. porò and a past fut. poria.
[5] Also puote; ponno.

THIRD CONJUGATION

(*e*) All irregular verbs of the third conjugation are accented, in the singular and third person plural of the present indicative and subjunctive, on the same syllable as in the infinitive.

(*f*) Verbs in –**cere** and –**gere** insert no **i** between the **c** or **g** and the **o** or **a** of the present indicative and subjunctive endings, except in the first person plural of both moods and the second person plural of the subjunctive. Cf. **60**, last paragraph.

(*g*) See chapter on Pronunciation, **4**, **s**, **d**.

Present Regular

24. **Accendere**, *light*, accesi, acceso.
25. **Affliggere**, *afflict*, afflissi, afflitto.
26. **Algere**, *be cold*, alsi. *Defective. Rare.*
27. **Alludere**, *allude*, allusi (alludei), alluso.
28. **Ardere**, *burn*, arsi, arso.
29. **Arrogere**, *add*, arrosi, arroso *or* arroto. *Defective. Rare.*
30. **Assidere**, *besiege*, assisi, assiso. *Rare.*
31. **Assolvere**, *absolve*, assolvetti *or* assolvei *or* assolsi, assolto *or* assoluto. *So* risolvere (*determine*). *For* **solvere, dissolvere,** *and* **risolvere** (*dissolve*), see 107.
32. **Assorbere**, *absorb*, assorsi (*not in use*), assorto. *Rare.*
33. **Avellere**, *uproot*, avulse, avulso. *Defective. Rare.*
34. **Chiudere**, *shut*, chiusi, chiuso. *So all verbs in* –chiudere *or* –cludere. *See, however,* **4**, **s**, **d**.
35. **Colere**, *revere*, colto *or* culto. *Defective. Rare.*
36. **Connettere**, *connect*, connessi (connettei), connesso (connettuto). *Rare.*
37. **Conoscere**, *know*, conobbi, conosciuto.
38. **Conquidere**, *conquer*, conquisi, conquiso. *Rare.*
39. **Consumere**, *consume*, consunsi, consunto. *Rare.* **Presumere** *has also* presumei.
40. **Contundere**, *bruise*, contusi, contuso.
41. **Correre**, *run*, corsi, corso.
42. **Crescere**, *grow*, crebbi, cresciuto.
43. **Cuocere**, *cook*, cocendo, cossi, cotto. *Pres.* cuocio *or* cuoco, *etc.*[1]

---

[1] In the 1st and 2d persons plural of the pres. ind., subj., and imperative, uo is generally replaced by o: cociamo, etc. The uo occurs in those parts of the verb where the accent falls on that syllable.

44. **Decidere,** *decide,* decisi, deciso.
45. **Difendere,** *defend,* difesi (difendei), difeso.
46. **Dirigere,** *direct,* diressi, diretto.
47. **Discutere,** *discuss,* discussi (discutei), discusso.
48. **Distinguere,** *distinguish,* distinsi, distinto.
49. **Dividere,** *divide,* divisi, diviso.
50. **Elidere,** *elide,* elisi (elidei), eliso.
51. **Eludere,** *elude,* elusi (eludei *or* eludetti), eluso.
52. **Ergere,** *erect,* ersi, erto. *Rare.*
53. **Esigere,** *exact,* esigei (esigetti), esatto.
54. **Esistere,** *exist,* esistei (esistetti), esistito.
55. **Espellere,** *expel,* espulsi, espulso. *Rare.*
56. **Esplodere,** *explode,* esplosi, esploso.
57. **Esprimere,** *express,* espressi, espresso. *So all other verbs in* –primere. **Premere** *and its compounds with* e *are regular.*
58. **Fendere,** *split,* fendei (fendetti *or* fessi), fenduto *or* fesso.
59. **Figgere (figere),** *fix,* fissi, fitto.
60. **Fingere,** *feign,* finsi, finto.
61. **Fondere,** *melt,* fusi (fondei), fuso (fonduto).
62. **Frangere,** *break,* fransi, franto.
63. **Friggere,** *fry,* frissi, fritto.
64. **Genuflettere,** *kneel,* genuflessi, genuflesso. *Rare.*
65. **Intridere,** *dilute,* intrisi, intriso.
66. **Intrudere,** *intrude,* intrusi, intruso.
67. **Invadere,** *invade,* invasi, invaso.
68. **Ledere,** *offend,* lesi (*not in use*), leso. *Rare.*
69. **Leggere,** *read,* lessi, letto.
70. **Licere** *or* **lecere,** *be lawful,* lecito *or* licito. *Impersonal. Defective. Poetical.*
71. **Ludere,** *play,* lusi, luso. *Rare.*
72. **Mergere,** *plunge,* mersi, merso. *Rare.*
73. **Mettere,** *put,* messi *or* misi, messo.
74. **Molcere,** *soothe,* mulse. *Defective. Rare.*
75. **Mordere,** *bite,* morsi, morso.
76. **Muovere,** *move,* movendo, mossi, mosso.[1]
77. **Nascere,** *be born,* nacqui, nato.
78. **Nascondere,** *hide,* nascosi, nascosto.
79. **Negligere** (*see* **5**, gli), *neglect,* neglessi, negletto.
80. **Offendere,** *offend,* offesi, offeso.
81. **Ostendere,** *show. Defective. Rare.*
82. **Percipere,** *perceive,* percetto. *Defective. Rare.*
83. **Perdere,** *lose,* perdei *or* perdetti *or* persi, perduto *or* perso.
84. **Piovere,** *rain,* piovve (piovè), piovuto. *Impersonal.*

[1] See page 92, footnote.

85. **Porgere**, *present*, porsi, porto.
86. **Prediligere**, *prefer*, predilessi, prediletto.
87. **Prendere**, *take*, presi, preso.
88. **Proteggere**, *protect*, protessi, protetto.
89. **Radere**, *shave*, rasi (radei), raso.
90. **Redimere**, *redeem*, redensi (redimei), redento.
91. **Reggere**, *support*, ressi, retto.
92. **Rendere**, *render*, resi (rendei *or* rendetti), reso (**renduto**).
93. **Ridere**, *laugh*, risi, riso.
94. **Riflettere**, *reflect*, riflettei *or* riflessi, riflettuto *or* riflesso. **Riflettere**, *reflect light, is generally irregular;* riflettere, *meditate, is usually regular.*
95. **Rifulgere**, *shine*, rifulsi. *Past part. lacking. Poetical.*
96. **Rilucere**, *shine*, rilussi *or* rilucei. *Past part. lacking.*
97. **Rispondere**, *answer*, risposi, risposto.
98. **Rodere**, *gnaw*, rosi, roso.
99. **Rompere**, *break*, ruppi, rotto.
100. **Scendere**, *descend*, scesi, sceso.
101. **Scindere**, *sever*, scindei *or* scissi, scisso.
102. **Sciolvere**, *breakfast*, sciolsi *or* sciolvetti, sciolto. *Rare.*
103. **Scorgere**, *perceive*, scorsi, scorto.
104. **Scrivere**, *write*, scrissi, scritto.
105. **Scuotere**, *shake*, scotendo, scossi, scosso.[1]
106. **Soffolcere**, *support*, soffolse, soffolto. *Defective. Rare.*
107. **Solvere**, *undo*, solvei (solvetti), soluto. *Poetical. So* dissolvere; *for* assolvere *and* risolvere (*determine*), see 31.
108. **Sorgere**, *rise*, sorsi, sorto.
109. **Sospendere**, *suspend*, sospesi, sospeso. *So* appendere, impendere. **Pendere** *is reg.;* dipendere *either reg. or irreg.*
110. **Spandere**, *spill*, spandei *or* spandetti, spanto.
111. **Spargere**, *scatter*, sparsi, sparso *or* sparto.
112. **Spendere**, *spend*, spesi, speso.
113. **Spergere**, *disperse*, spersi, sperso. *Rare.*
114. **Sporgere**, *project*, sporsi, sporto.
115. **Struggere**, *melt*, strussi, strutto.
116. **Succedere**, *happen*, successi *or* succedei, successo *or* succeduto. *So* **concedere**, *which has also* concedetti; **cedere** *and its other compounds are generally regular.*
117. **Suggere**, *suck*, suggei *or* sussi. *Past part. lacking. Rare.*
118. **Tendere** (*transitive*), *extend*, tesi, teso. *The intrans. verb is reg. but has no past participle.*
119. **Tergere**, *wipe*, tersi *or* tergei, terso. *Rare.*
120. **Torcere**, *twist*, torsi, torto.

[1] See page 92, footnote.

121. **Uccidere,** *kill,* uccisi, ucciso.
122. **Vincere,** *conquer,* vinsi, vinto.
123. **Vivere,** *live,* vissi, vissuto *or* vivuto; viverò *or* vivrò.
124. **Volgere,** *turn,* volsi, volto.
125. **Volvere,** *turn,* volsi, volto. *Rare.* **Devolvere** *has a past part.* devoluto.

Present Irregular

126. **Essere,** *be,* fui, stato; sarò. See **53,** *a.*[1]
127. **Bere** *or* **bevere,** *drink,* bevendo, bevvi (bevetti *or* bevei), bevuto (beuto); berò *or* beverò.

PRES. IND.		PRES. SUBJ.	
bevo or beo	beviamo or beiamo	beva or bea	beviamo or beiamo
bevi or bei	bevete or beete	beva or bea	beviate or beiate
beve or bee	bevono or beono	beva or bea	bevano or beano

128. **Chiedere,** *ask,* chiesi (chiesi *or* chiedei), chiesto.

PRES. IND.	PRES. SUBJ.
chiedo (chieggo)[2]	chieda (chiegga)[2]
chiedi	chieda (chiegga)
chiede	chieda (chiegga)
chiediamo	chiediamo
chiedete	chiediate
chiedono (chieggono)[2]	chiedano (chieggano)[2]

129. **Condurre,** *conduct,* conducendo, condussi, condotto; condurrò.

PRES. IND.		PRES. SUBJ.	
conduco	conduciamo	conduca	conduciamo
conduci	conducete	conduca	conduciate
conduce	conducono	conduca	conducano

130. **Nuocere,** *harm,* nocendo, nocqui, nociuto.

PRES. IND.		PRES. SUBJ.	
nuoco or noccio	nociamo	nuoca or noccia	nociamo
nuoci	nocete	nuoca or noccia	nociate
nuoce	nuocono or nocciono	nuoca or noccia	nuocano or nocciano

[1] In the past descriptive **eramo** is often used for **eravamo.** We find in poetry: **sete** for **siete; enno** or **en** for **sono** (third pl.); **sie** for **sia; eramo, erate** for **eravamo, eravate; u** for **o** in the past absolute and past subjunctive; **foro** for **furono; fia, fiano** or **fieno** for **sarà, saranno; fora, forano** for **sarei, sarebbe, sarebbero; sendo** for **essendo; suto, essuto,** or **issuto** for **stato.**

[2] Also **chieggio, chieggiono, chieggia, chieggiano.**

131. **Porre,** *put,* ponendo, posi, posto; porrò.

PRES. IND.		PRES. SUBJ.	
pongo	poniamo (ponghiamo)	ponga	poniamo (ponghiamo)
poni	ponete	ponga	poniate
pone	pongono	ponga	pongano

132. **Trarre (traere),** *drag,* traendo, trassi, tratto; trarrò.

PRES. IND.		PRES. SUBJ.	
traggo	traiamo or traggiamo[1]	tragga	traiamo or traggiamo[1]
trai (traggi)	traete	tragga	traiate
trae (tragge)	traggono	tragga	traggano

133. **Vellere (verre),** *tear up,* velsi, velto; vellerò (verrò *or* velgerò).
     Vellere, *which is rare, has not all the forms given here; but its compound,* **svellere,** *has them all.*

PRES. IND.		PRES. SUBJ.	
vello or velgo	velliamo (velgiamo)	vella or velga	velliamo (velgiamo)
velli (velgi)	vellete	vella or velga	velliate (velgiate)
velle (velge)	vellono or velgono	vella or velga	vellano or velgano

134. **Cogliere (corre),** *gather,* colsi, colto; coglierò *or* corrò.

PRES. IND.		PRES. SUBJ.	
colgo (coglio)	cogliamo (colghiamo)	colga (coglia)	cogliamo (colghiamo)
cogli	cogliete	colga (coglia)	cogliate
coglie	colgono (cogliono)	colga (coglia)	colgano (cogliano)

135. **Scegliere (scerre),** *choose:* like cogliere (134).
136. **Sciogliere (sciorre),** *untie:* like cogliere (134).
137. **Togliere (torre),** *take:* like cogliere (134).
138. **Giungere (giugnere),** *to arrive,* giunsi, giunto; giungerò (giugnerò).

PRES. IND.	PRES. SUBJ.
giungo (giugno)	giunga (giugna)
giungi (giugni)	giunga (giugna)
giunge (giugne)	giunga (giugna)
giungiamo (giugniamo)	giungiamo (giugniamo)
giungete (giugnete)	giungiate (giugniate)
giungono (giugnono)	giungano (giugnano)

139. **Cingere (cignere),** *gird:* like giungere (138).
140. **Mugnere (mungere),** *milk:* like giungere (138).

---

[1] Also **tragghiamo.**

141. **Piangere (piagnere)**, *weep: like* giungere (138).
142. **Pingere (pignere)**, *paint: like* giungere (138).
143. **Pungere (pugnere)**, *prick: like* giungere (138).
144. **Spegnere (spengere)**, *extinguish: like* giungere (138), *except that the forms with* **gn** *are far commoner than those with* **ng**.
145. **Spingere (spignere)**, *push: like* giungere (138).
146. **Stringere (strignere)**, *bind: like* giungere (138), *except that the past part. is* stretto *or* strinto. **Costringere**, *compel, has for past part. only* costretto.
147. **Tingere (tignere)**, *dye: like* giungere (138).
148. **Ungere (ugnere)**, *anoint: like* giungere (138).

FOURTH CONJUGATION

Present Regular

149. **Aprire**, *open,* aprii *or* apersi, aperto. *Pres.* apro, *etc.*
150. **Coprire (cuoprire)**, *cover,* coprii *or* copersi, coperto. *Pres.* copro (cuopro), *etc.*
151. **Offrire (offerire)**, *offer,* offrii (offerii) *or* offersi, offerto. *Pres.* offro (offerisco), *etc.*
152. **Soffrire**, *suffer: like* offrire (151).
153. **Convertire**, *convert,* convertii *or* conversi, convertito *or* converso. *Pres.* converto *or* convertisco, *etc. All other verbs in* –vertire *are reg.*
154. **Costruire (construire)**, *construct,* co(n)strussi *or* co(n)struii, co(n)struito *or* co(n)strutto. *Pres.* co(n)struisco, *etc.*
155. **Digerire**, *digest,* digerii, digerito (digesto). *Pres.* digerisco, *etc.*
156. **Esaurire**, *exhaust,* esaurii, esaurito *or* esausto. *Pres.* esaurisco, *etc.*
157. **Seppellire** *or* **sepellire**, *bury,* sep(p)ellii, seppellito *or* sepolto. *Pres.* sep(p)ellisco, *etc.*

Present Irregular

158. **Cucire**, *sew,* cucii, cucito. *Pres.* cucio *or* cucisco. *This verb inserts* i *before* o *and* a, *but not before* e *and* i.
159. **Sdrucire** *or* **sdruscire**, *rip: like* cucire (158).
160. **Empire** *or* **empiere**, *fill,* empiendo, empii, empito. *All but the present from the stem of* empire. *So* **compire** *or* **compiere**, *which has also a past part.* compiuto.

PRES. IND.		PRES. SUBJ.	
empio (empisco)	empiamo	empia	empiamo
empi (empisci)	empite	empia	empiate
empie (empisce)	empiono (empiscono)	empia	empiano

161. **Morire,** *die,* morii, morto; morrò *or* morirò.

<table>
<tr><td colspan="2">PRES. IND.</td><td colspan="2">PRES. SUBJ.</td></tr>
<tr><td>muoio (muoro)</td><td>moriamo or muoia-
mo</td><td>muoia (muora)</td><td>moriamo or muoi-
amo</td></tr>
<tr><td>muori or muoi</td><td>morite</td><td>muoia (muora)</td><td>muoiate</td></tr>
<tr><td>muore</td><td>muoiono (muoro-
no)</td><td>muoia (muora)</td><td>muoiano (muora-
no)[1]</td></tr>
</table>

162. **Seguire,** *follow,* seguii, seguito. *Pres.* seguo, *etc. The verb is generally regular; but the* **e** *may be changed to* **ie** *in all forms where it is accented.* **Proseguire** *has* –seguo *or* –seguisco.

163. **Sparire,** *disappear,* sparii *or* sparvi, sparito. *Pres. (regular)* sparisco, *etc.* **Apparire** *has* apparvi *or* –si *or* –ii, apparito *or* apparso; **comparire** *has* comparvi *or* –si *or* –ii, comparso; *otherwise they are like* sparire, *but they have in the present the additional forms:* –paio, –pare, –paiono; –paia, –paiano.

164. **Dire,** *say,* dicendo, dissi, detto; dirò. Dire (*formerly* dicere) *belongs really to the third conjugation:* dicesti, –eva, –essi.

<table>
<tr><td colspan="2">PRES. IND.</td><td>IMPER.</td><td colspan="2">PRES. SUBJ.</td></tr>
<tr><td>dico</td><td>diciamo</td><td>di'</td><td>dica</td><td>diciamo</td></tr>
<tr><td>dici</td><td>dite</td><td>diciamo</td><td>dica</td><td>diciate</td></tr>
<tr><td>dice</td><td>dicono</td><td>dite</td><td>dica</td><td>dicano</td></tr>
</table>

165. **Salire,** *ascend,* salii *or* salsi, salito.

<table>
<tr><td colspan="2">PRES. IND.</td><td colspan="2">PRES. SUBJ.</td></tr>
<tr><td>salgo (salisco)</td><td>saliamo or sagliamo[2]</td><td>salga (salisca)</td><td>saliamo or sagliamo[2]</td></tr>
<tr><td>sali (salisci)</td><td>salite</td><td>salga (salisca)</td><td>sagliate</td></tr>
<tr><td>sale (salisce)</td><td>salgono (saliscono)</td><td>salga (salisca)</td><td>salgano (saliscano)</td></tr>
</table>

166. **Venire,** *come,* venni, venuto; verrò.

<table>
<tr><td colspan="2">PRES. IND.</td><td colspan="2">PRES. SUBJ.</td></tr>
<tr><td>vengo (vegno)</td><td>veniamo[2]</td><td>venga (vegna)</td><td>veniamo[2]</td></tr>
<tr><td>vieni</td><td>venite</td><td>venga (vegna)</td><td>veniate</td></tr>
<tr><td>viene</td><td>vengono (vegnono)</td><td>venga (vegna)</td><td>vengano (vegnano)</td></tr>
</table>

167. **Udire,** *hear,* udii, udito; udirò (udrò).

<table>
<tr><td colspan="2">PRES. IND.</td><td colspan="2">PRES. SUBJ.</td></tr>
<tr><td>odo</td><td>udiamo</td><td>oda</td><td>udiamo</td></tr>
<tr><td>odi</td><td>udite</td><td>oda</td><td>udiate</td></tr>
<tr><td>ode</td><td>odono</td><td>oda</td><td>odano</td></tr>
</table>

[1] In all forms where **uo** occurs, it may be replaced by **o**.
[2] Also **salghiamo; venghiamo:** popular forms.

168. Uscire (escire), *go out,* uscii, uscito.

PRES. IND.		PRES. SUBJ.	
esco	usciamo	esca	usciamo
esci	uscite	esca	usciate
esce	escono	esca	escano

169. Orire, *be born,* orto. *Defective. Rare.*

Portrait of Dante, National Museum, Capella

CHAPTER 14

Alphabetical List of Irregular and Defective Verbs

93. Every irregular verb in this list is followed by a number referring to the table of Irregular Verbs arranged according to Conjugation. Obsolete defective verbs that present no irregularity have not been mentioned.

(a) Compound verbs have, in general, been excluded from this list, unless they differ in conjugation from the simple verbs from which they come (see **67,** a). The commonest prefixes are: **a–** (corresponding in meaning to the preposition **a**); **as–** (=Latin abs–); **co–, com–, con–, cor–** (=prep. **con**); **contra–** (=prep. **contra**); **de–, di–** (=Lat. de–); **dis–** (=Lat. dis–); **e–, es–** (=Lat. ex); **i–, im–, in–, ir–** (=prep. **in**); **o–** (=Lat. ob); **per–** (=prep. **per**); **pre–** (=Lat. prae–); **pro–** (=Lat. pro–); **r–, re–, ri–** (=Lat. re–); **s–** (=Lat. ex– or dis–); **so–, sos–, su–** (=Lat. sub); **sopra–, sopr–, sor–** (=prep. **sopra**); **sott–, sotto–** (=prep. **sotto**); **stra–** (=Lat. extra); **tra–** (=prep. tra). After several of these prefixes the initial consonant of the simple verb is generally found doubled: **a+cadere** =accadere. **S–** is sometimes combined with **con–,** **r–** with **a–** or **in–**: **scoscendere, raccogliere, rincorrere.**

Accadere, *see* cadere, 7.
Accendere, 24.
Accludere, *see* chiudere, 34.
Accorgere, *see* scorgere, 103.
Acquisire *has only* acquisito.
Addurre, *see* condurre, 129.

Affliggere, 25.
Algere, 26.
Alludere, 27.
Ancidere, *see* uccidere, 121.
Andare, 1.
Annettere, *see* connettere, 36.

Anteporre, *see* porre, 131.
Antivedere, *p. p. only* antiveduto, *otherwise like* vedere, 10.
Apparire, *see* sparire, 163.
Appartenere, *see* tenere, 17.
Appendere, *see* sospendere, 109.
Aprire, 149.
Ardere, 28.
Arrogere, 29.
Ascendere, *see* scendere, 100.
Asciolvere, *see* sciolvere, 102.
Ascondere, *see* nascondere, 78.
Aspergere, *see* spergere, 113.
Assalire, *see* salire, 165.
Assidere, 30.
Assistere, *see* esistere, 54.
Assolvere, 31.
Assorbere, 32.
Assumere, *see* consumere, 39.
Avellere, 33.
Avere, 5.
Bere, 127.
Bevere, *see* bere, 127.
Cadere, 7.
Calere, 23.
Cedere, *generally reg., sometimes has p. abs.* cessi, *p. p.* cesso.
Chiedere, 128.
Chiudere, 34.
Cignere, *see* cingere, 139.
Cingere, 139.
Circoncidere, *see* decidere, 44.
Cogliere, 134.
Coincidere, *reg. verb, has no p. p.*
Colere, 35.
Colludere, *see* ludere, 71.
Comparire, *see* sparire, 163.
Competere, *reg. verb, has no p. p.*
Compiere, *see* empire, 160.
Compire, *see* empire, 160.
Comprimere, *see* esprimere, 57.
Concedere, *see* succedere, 116.
Concludere, *see* chiudere, 34.
Concutere, *see* discutere, 47.

Condurre, 129.
Connettere, 36.
Conoscere, 37.
Conquidere, 38.
Consistere, *see* esistere, 54.
Constare *is reg.*
Construire, *see* costruire, 154.
Consumere, 39.
Contendere, *see* tendere, 118.
Contrastare *is reg.*
Controvertere, *see* vertere.
Contundere, 40.
Convergere, *reg. verb, has no p. p.*
Convertire, 153.
Coprire, 150.
Corre, *see* cogliere, 134.
Correre, 41.
Corrispondere, *see* rispondere, 97.
Cospargere, *see* spargere, 111.
Cospergere, *see* spergere, 113.
Costruire, 154.
Crescere, 42.
Cucire, 158.
Cuocere, 43.
Cuoprire, *see* coprire, 150.
Dare, 3.
Decidere, 44.
Dedurre, *see* condurre, 129.
Delinquere, *reg. verb, has no p. p., and its p. abs.,* delinquetti, *is rare.*
Deprimere, *see* esprimere, 57.
Desistere, *see* esistere, 54.
Devolvere, *see* volvere, 125.
Difendere, 45.
Digerire, 155.
Dipendere, *see* sospendere, 109.
Dire, 164.
Dirigere, 46.
Dirimere, *reg. verb, has no p. p.*
Discendere, *see* scendere, 100.
Discutere, 47.
Dispergere, *see* spergere, 113.
Dissolvere, *see* solvere, 107.
Dissuadere, *see* persuadere, 22.

Distare, *reg. in pres. of all moods, no pres. p., otherwise like* stare, 4.

Distinguere, 48.

Distruggere, *see* struggere, 115.

Divedere *has nothing but infin.*

Divergere, *reg. verb, has no p. p.*

Dividere, 49.

Dolere, 15.

Dovere, 8.

Eleggere, *see* leggere, 69.

Elidere, 50.

Eludere, 51.

Empiere, *see* empire, 160.

Empire, 160.

Ergere, 52.

Erigere, *see* dirigere, 46.

Esaurire, 156.

Escire, *see* uscire, 168.

Escludere, *see* chiudere, 34.

Esigere, 53.

Esimere, *reg. verb, has no p. p.*

Esistere, 54.

Espellere, 55.

Esplodere, 56.

Esprimere, 57.

Essere, 126.

Estinguere, *see* distinguere, 48.

Evadere, *see* invadere, 67.

Fare, 2.

Fendere, 58.

Fervere, *reg. verb, has no p. p., and is rare except in the third pers. of the pres. ind. and past descr.*

Figere, *see* figgere, 59.

Figgere, 59.

Fingere, 60.

Fondere, 61.

Frangere, 62.

Friggere, 63.

Genuflettere, 64.

Giacere, 11.

Gire, *defect.: pres.* giamo, gite; *past descr.* giva *or* gia, *etc.; imper.* giamo, gite; *pres. subj.* giamo, giate; *no pres. p.; rest reg.*

Giugnere, *see* giungere, 138.

Giungere, 138.

Illudere, *see* ludere, 71.

Impellere, *see* espellere, 55.

Impendere, *see* sospendere, 109.

Imprimere, *see* esprimere, 57.

Incidere, *see* decidere, 44.

Includere, *see* chiudere, 34.

Incutere, *see* discutere, 47.

Indurre, *see* condurre, 129.

Insistere, *see* esistere, 54.

Instare *is reg.*

Instruire, *see* construire, 154.

Intendere, *see* tendere, 118.

Intercedere, *see* succedere, 116.

Intridere, 65.

Introdurre, *see* condurre, 129.

Intrudere, 66.

Invadere, 67.

Invalere, *p. p. only* invalso, *otherwise like* valere, 18.

Ire, *defect.: pres.* ite; *p. des.* iva, *etc.; p. abs.* isti, iste, iro; *fut.* iremo, irete, iranno; *imper.* ite; *past subj.* isse, iste, issero; *p. p.* ito.

Istruire, *see* costruire, 154.

Lecere, *see* licere, 70.

Ledere, 68.

Leggere, 69.

Licere, 70.

Lucere, *reg. verb, has no p. p.*

Ludere, 71.

Mantenere, *see* tenere, 17.

Mergere, 72.

Mettere, 73.

Molcere, 74.

Mordere, 75.

Morire, 161.

Mugnere, 140.

Mungere, *see* mugnere, 140.

Muovere, 76.

Nascere, 77.

Nascondere, 78.
Negligere, 79.
Nuocere, 130.
Offendere, 80.
Offerire, *see* offrire, 151.
Offrire, 151.
Opprimere, *see* esprimere, 57.
Orire, 169.
Ostare *is reg.*
Ostendere, 81.
Parere, 20.
Percipere, 82.
Percuotere, *see* scuotere, 105.
Perdere, 83.
Permanere, *see* rimanere, 16.
Persistere, *see* esistere, 54.
Persuadere, 22.
Piacere, 12.
Piagnere, *see* piangere, 141.
Piangere, 141.
Pignere, *see* pingere, 142.
Pingere, 142.
Piovere, 84.
Porgere, 85.
Porre, 131.
Posporre, *see* porre, 131.
Possedere, *see* sedere, 9.
Potere, 21.
Precidere, *see* decidere, 44.
Precludere, *see* chiudere, 34.
Prediligere, 86.
Premere *is reg.*
Prendere, 87.
Prestare *is reg.*
Presumere, *see* consumere, 39.
Prevedere, *see* vedere, 10.
Produrre, *see* condurre, 129.
Proteggere, 88.
Provvedere, *fut. and past fut. un-contracted, otherwise like* vedere, 10.
Prudere, *reg. verb, has no p. p., and is used only in the third pers.*
Pugnere, *see* pungere, 143.

Pungere, 143.
Raccogliere, *see* cogliere, 134.
Radere, 89.
Raggiungere, *see* giungere, 138.
Recidere, *see* decidere, 44.
Redimere, 90.
Reggere, 91.
Rendere, 92.
Repellere, *see* espellere, 55.
Reprimere, *see* esprimere, 57.
Resistere, *see* esistere, 54.
Restare *is reg.*
Ridere, 93.
Ridurre, *see* condurre, 129.
Riflettere, 94.
Rifulgere, 95.
Rilucere, 96.
Rimanere, 16.
Risolvere (*dissolve*), *see* solvere, 107.
Risolvere (*determine*), *see* assolvere, 31.
Rispondere, 97.
Ristare, *see* stare, 4.
Risumere, *see* consúmere, 39.
Rodere, 98.
Rompere, 99.
Salire, 165.
Sapere, 6.
Scegliere, 135.
Scendere, 100.
Scerre, *see* scegliere, 135.
Scindere, 101.
Sciogliere, 136.
Sciolvere, 102.
Sciorre, *see* sciogliere, 136.
Scommettere, *see* mettere, 73.
Scoprire, *see* coprire, 150.
Scorgere, 103.
Scrivere, 104.
Scuotere, 105.
Sdrucire, 159.
Sdruscire, *see* sdrucire, 159.
Sedere, 9.

Sedurre, *see* condurre, 129.
Seguire, 162.
Sepellire, *see* seppellire, 157.
Seppellire, 157.
Sofferire, *see* soffrire, 152.
Soffolcere, 106.
Soffrire, 152.
Solere, 14.
Solvere, 107.
Sopprimere, *see* esprimere, 57.
Soprastare, *see* stare, 4.
Sorgere, 108.
Sospendere, 109.
Sostare *is reg.*
Sottostare, *see* stare, 4.
Sovrastare *see* stare, 4.
Spandere, 110.
Spargere, 111.
Sparire, 163.
Spegnere, 144.
Spendere, 112.
Spengere, *see* spegnere, 144.
Spergere, 113.
Spignere, *see* spingere, 145.
Spingere, 145.
Sporgere, 114.
Stare, 4.
Stridere, *reg. verb, has no p. p.*
Strignere, *see* stringere, 146.
Stringere, 146.
Struggere, 115.
Subire *is reg.*: *pres.* subisco.
Succedere, 116.
Suggere, 117.
Sussistere, *see* esistere, 54.

Svellere, *see* vellere, 133.
Tacere, 13.
Tendere (*trans.*), 118.
Tendere (*intrans.*), *reg. verb, has no p. p.*
Tenere, 17.
Tergere, 119.
Tignere, *see* tingere, 147.
Tingere, 147.
Togliere, 137.
Torcere, 120.
Torre, *see* togliere, 137.
Tradurre, *see* condurre, 129.
Traere, *see* trarre, 132.
Transigere, *see* esigere, 53.
Trarre, 132.
Uccidere, 121.
Udire, 167.
Ugnere, *see* ungere, 148.
Ungere, 148.
Uscire, 168.
Valere, 18.
Vedere, 10.
Vellere, 133.
Venire, 166.
Verre, *see* vellere, 133.
Vertere, *reg. verb, is used only in the pres. and past descr.*
Vilipendere, *see* sospendere, 109.
Vincere, 122.
Vivere, 123.
Volere, 19.
Volgere, 124.
Volvere, 125.

CHAPTER 15

Lessons and Exercises

LESSON 1. PRONUNCIATION

Study sections **1, 2, 3.**

NOTE. — In this and in all other lessons the assignment of a section number means that the *whole* section, including all subdivisions, is to be studied, unless special directions to the contrary are given.

EXERCISE 1

1. *State the quality of the* e (*close or open*) *in each of these words, and pronounce each word:* te, tre, nè, sè, potè, è, diedi, fieno, Siena, desti, debito, Alfredo, presto, merito, Valerio.

2. *State the quality of the* o *in each of these words, and pronounce each word:* fo, no, canterò, però, muore, suona, noi, ricoveri, Roma, bove, opera, Modena.

3. *Pronounce:* abitudine, alfabeto, Alfieri, altrui, America, Amleto, andatevene, animato, augurerai, balenio, benedirono, benevolo, bibliofilo, cavaliere, colui, conservatorio, contadino, Costantinopoli, costui, credulo, cui, demolirete, Demostene, Domenico, dove, ei, Emanuele, eroe, esprimereste, Faraone, formidabile, fui, Galileo, Goldoni, idea, impermalito, impero, insubordinato, io, linea, Lombardia, lui, lunedi, maestro, miei, mio, Napoli, naufrago, neutro, nobiltà, nuora, ode, oibò, onorevole, ortografia, Orvieto, ovest, Panamà, Paolo, patata, paura, perdè, perpendicolo, personalità, poi, povero, responsabilità, restituiti, rimanevate, Rimini, Romolo, Rovere, Serao, Severino, suoi, Taormina, umile, uno, vendè, voi, volontà, vuoto.

LESSON 2. PRONUNCIATION (continued)

Study 4 [*omitting* (*a*), (*b*), (*c*), (*d*) *under* s], 5, 6, 7. *Read* (*a*), (*b*), (*c*) *under* s *in* 4, *and* 8.

EXERCISE 2

1. *Pronounce:* cane, panca, tasca, come, Pascoli, cura, alcuni, scudo, classe, Tecla, credo, sacro, ascrivere, che, chetare, oche, panche, maschera, chi, chino, bachi, parchi, boschi, chiudo, richiamo, manchiamo, schiavo, Ischia, Peschiera, cena, celare, voce, vivace, Nocera, elce, incendio, ci, civile, Cimabue, dieci, taci, Lucia, Medici, porci, Pulci, Vinci, ciarla, diciannove, oncia, marcia, cielo, specie, ciò, bacio, commercio, Pincio, ciurma, fanciullo, accendere, uccello, accidente, piccino, faccia, boccia, taccio, piccione, Duccio, acciuffo, ricciuto, scena, nasce, discepolo, scibile, lasci, disciplinai, sciame, poscia, lasciò, mesciuto.

2. *Pronounce:* gala, targa, sgarbato, pago, valgo, sgombro, gusto, augurare, guardia, Guido, sangue, gloria, anglomania, magro, sgridare, ghetto, pagherò, alghe, sghembo, ghirlanda, ghinea, Ghiberti, sughi, Inghilterra, ghianda, ghiotto, paghiamo, Alighieri, ringhiera, gelare, genere, Genova, agevole, Eugenio, stringendo, Angelico, sgelare, giro, agitato, antologia, Perugino, piangi, cangia, Borgia, giorno, giovedì, Giovanni, adagio, mangio, giù, giusto, Giulio, digiúno, ingiuria, friggere, piagge, oggi, fuggire, piaggia, foggiare, leggiero, maggiore, solfeggio, Reggio, aggiunta, raggiustare, magli, begli, tigli, moglina, medaglia, pigliare, Cagliari, moglie, cogliendo, taglio, luglio, pagliucola, figliuolo, gli, pugnare, Campagna, Bologna, spugne, mugnere, compagnia, Mascagni, stagno, sogno, Foligno, ognuno, piagnucolare.

3. *Pronounce the words in* (*a*) *under* s *on p.* 3; *then pronounce these words, in which the* s *has the sound of English* z: basilico, brindisi, caso, causa, confusione, deserto, desinare, elemosina, enfasi.

4. *Pronounce these words, in which the* z (*or* zz) *is pronounced like* ts: grazie, ozio, Venezia, Abruzzi, altezza, Arezzo, mazzo, pozzo, alzo, calzoni, anzi, denunzia, Firenze, Monza, senza, forza, marzo, zampa, zio, zolfo; *then pronounce the words in* (*a*) *under* z *on p.* 4.

5. *Pronounce:* debbo, gabbare, Lecco, pacco, addio, freddo, affare, goffo, bello, Donatello, commedia, somma, fanno, Ravenna, appena, troppo, arrivo, terra, essa, Messina, metto, otto, avvenire.

LESSON 3. ARTICLES

Study **9, 10, 11, 12, 14, 15.**

EXERCISE 3

1. *State the gender and number of each of these combinations, as indicated by the form of the definite article:* gli abiti, il balcone, i bambini, la barba, le immagini, gl' impeti, le scarpe, lo scherzo, gli zecchini; cogli affari, del campo, sulla faccia, ai ladri, dallo scoglio, negli stati, delle unioni.

2. *Place the proper form of the definite article before each of these nouns [those in* (a) *are masculine singular, those in* (b) *masculine plural, those in* (c) *feminine singular, those in* (d) *feminine plural]:*
(a) albero, dente, fatto, impero, sguardo, spedale, uccello, zingaro.
(b) alberi, denti, fatti, imperi, sguardi, spedali, uccelli, zingari.
(c) aria, campana, evoluzione, mente, ombra, scena, zampa.
(d) arie, campane, evoluzioni, menti, ombre, scene, zampe.

3. *Translate into Italian the prepositions and articles in these combinations [the nouns in* (a) *are masculine singular, those in* (b) *masculine plural, those in* (c) *feminine singular, those in* (d) *feminine plural]:* (a) *of the* anno, *by the* effetto, *to the* gatto, *in the* gesto, *with the* idolo, *on the* leone, *with the* quadro, *in the* scudo, *to the* spirito, *by the* umore, *of the* zappatore. (b) *of the* anni, *by the* effetti, *to the* gatti, *in the* gesti, *with the* idoli, *on the* leoni, *with the* quadri, *in the* scudi, *to the* spiriti, *by the* umori, *of the* zappatori. (c) *of the* acqua, *by the* estate, *to the* notte, *in the* opera, *with the* scala, *on the* tavola. (d) *of the* acque, *by the* estati, *to the* notti, *in the* opere, *with the* scale, *on the* tavole.

4. *Place the proper form of the indefinite article before each of these nouns [those in* (a) *are masculine, those in* (b) *are feminine]:*
(a) idilio, nome, oceano, specchio, strido, teatro, uovo, zoccolo.
(b) età, maestra, onda, spina, uva, valle.

LESSON 4. NOUNS

Study **17–25** *inclusive* [*omitting* (*a*), (*b*) *under* **22**, *and* (*a*), (*b*), (*c*). (*d*) *under* **23**].

EXERCISE 4

1. *State the gender and number of each of these combinations:* gli animali, nei caffè, la canzone, colla fede, del fucile, gl' ingegni, i lupi, dagli onori, le parole, il poeta, sulle questioni, lo scherzo, allo schioppo.

2. *Give the plural of each of these nouns* [*those in* (*a*) *are masculine, those in* (*b*) *are feminine*]: (*a*) brindisi, cane, castello, despota, dolore, libro, lume, maestro, padrone, pericolo, podestà, problema, uomo. (*b*) bellezza, bontà, capitale, fonte, luna, moglie, origine, polvere, serie, sintesi, terra, vittoria.

3. *Give the plural of each of these combinations:* l' acqua, l' artista (*masculine*), l' anno, l' azione (*feminine*), la barbarie, la bestia, il bue, il cavallo, la chiave, il cuore, la dama, il dono, l' errore (*m.*), l' estasi (*f.*), l' età, la fanciulla, la felicità, la festa, il frate, la gente, il giurì, la gravità, l' idea, l' inchiostro, l' istante (*m.*), il lavoro, la lira, la mano, il mare, la metropoli, il ministro, la morale, della nazione, all' oggetto, nell' opinione (*f.*), della padrona, dal palazzo, sulla pelle, col prete, dal profeta, della ragazza, al re, dal santo, sullo scaffale, della sete, nel sistema, nello stato, sulla superficie, dell' umore (*m.*), nella valle, sul vapore, della verità, colla virtù.

LESSON 5. *ESSERE*

Study **53** (*a*) [*omitting the compound tenses*].

EXERCISE 5

1. *Identify* (*that is, state the person, number, and tense of*) *and translate these forms:* erano, sarete, fummo, siamo, essendo, sarebbe, saremo, fu, sei, sareste, era, stato, sarà, siete, saremmo, eravate, saranno, sono, foste, sarebbero, furono.

2. *Translate into Italian:* we[1] are, he will be, they were (*past descriptive*), they were (*past absolute*), I should be, she is, we were (*desc.*), they would be, I was (*abs.*), we shall be, we should be, being, it was (*abs.*), they will be, thou art, you are,[2] thou wast (*desc.*), you were (*desc.*), thou wast (*abs.*), you were (*abs.*), you will be, you would be, to be, been, let us be, be.[3]

[1] English subject pronouns are to be omitted in translation, until other directions are given.

[2] English verbs which have 'you' as subject are to be translated by second person plural forms, until other directions are given.

[3] English imperatives without an expressed subject are to be translated by second person plural forms, until other directions are given.

VOCABULARY

giornale, m., *newspaper.*
Giovanni, *John.*
libro, *book.*
padre, m., *father.*
ragazzo, *boy.*
signore, m., *gentleman.*
uomo, *man.*

casa, *house, home.*
città, *city.*
donna, *woman.*
Firenze, f., *Florence.*
madre, f., *mother.*
Maria, *Mary.*
Napoli, f., *Naples.*
porta, *door.*

ragazza, *girl.*
Roma, *Rome.*
scrivania, *desk.*
signora, *lady.*
tavola, *table.*

a, *to, at, in.*[1]
domani, *tomorrow.*
dove, *where.*
già, *already.*
ieri, *yesterday.*
là, *there.*
oggi, *today.*
ora, *now.*
quando, *when.*
qui, *here.*

[1] English 'in' is ordinarily to be translated by *in*, but before the name of a city it is to be translated by *a*.

3. *Study these sentences:*[1] 1. Il signore è il padre di Giovanni. 2. Dove siete ora? Sono qui. 3. Quando sarà coi signori? 4. I libri

[1] The student should enable himself to translate the sentences, to read them aloud in Italian accurately and intelligently, and to translate them without reference to the book.

Casa de Fauna, Pompei

Radda Square

dei ragazzi erano sulla tavola. 5. Domani saremo nella città. 6. Sarà qui oggi? 7. La donna è già alla porta della casa. 8. Ora è qui: domani dove sarà? 9. Il giornale è là, sulla scrivania. 10. Ieri le signore erano a Napoli, oggi sono a Roma, domani saranno a Firenze.

4. *Translate into Italian:* 1. The lady is Mary's mother. 2. The girls will be here tomorrow. 3. The newspapers were[1] on the tables. 4. Where are the boy's books? Are they on the desk? 5. I shall be there with the men. 6. Were[1] you already at the door? 7. Would he be in the house now? 8. John's father is in the city. 9. When will you be in Naples? 10. Today they are here, tomorrow they'll be there.

[1] Use the past descriptive.

LESSON 6. ADJECTIVES

Study **26–34** *inclusive. Learn the first twelve cardinal numerals, as given in* **38**.

EXERCISE 6

1. *Give the feminine singular and the masculine and feminine plural of each of these adjectives:* cattivo, fedele, forte, rosso, semplice, vero.

2. *Insert the proper form of* bello *in each of these phrases:* il — albero, il — cappello, il — fanciullo, il — ingegno, il — stato; i — alberi, i — cappelli, i — fanciulli, i — ingegni, i — stati.

3. *Place the proper form of* Santo *before each of these names:* Agostino, Carlo, Elmo, Giovanni, Lorenzo.

4. *Insert the proper form of* grande *in each of these phrases:* un — cappello, un — errore, un — fuoco, un — ingegno, un — stato.

5. *Insert the proper form of* buono *in each of these phrases:* un — amico, un — cuore, un — fanciullo, un — ingegno, un — schioppo.

VOCABULARY

centro, *centre.*
fiore, m., *flower.*
fratello, *brother.*
giardino, *garden.*
tempo, *time, weather.*

chiesa, *church.*
lezione, f., *lesson.*
sorella, *sister.*
stanza, *room.*
via, *street.*

alto, *high, tall.*
bello, *beautiful, pretty, handsome, fine.*
facile, *easy.*
felice, *happy.*

francese, *French.*
gentile, *gentle, polite, kind.*
giovane, *young.*
grande, *great, large, big.*
interessante, *interesting.*
italiano, *Italian.*
molto, *much;* as adverb, *much, very.*
piccolo, *little, small.*
povero, *poor.*
rosso, *red.*
rotondo, *round.*

ci, *here, there.*[1]
dopo, *after, afterward.*
forse, *perhaps.*
non,[2] *not.*

[1] *Ci* is used when the 'here' or 'there' is quite unemphatic, *qui* and *là* when the 'here' or 'there' bears some emphasis. *Ci* is called a conjunctive adverb, and its position is governed by special rules. Until other directions are given, it should be placed directly before the verb.

[2] Placed before the verb.

6. *Study these sentences:*[1] 1. Ci sono dei bei fiori nel piccolo giardino. 2. Per i poveri non è facile essere felici. 3. La tavola rotonda era nel centro della stanza. 4. C' è qualche giornale francese sulla scrivania. 5. Le vie di Napoli sono molto interessanti. 6. Oggi siete più felice che ieri. 7. Le tre signore francesi erano molto gentili. 8. La chiesa è più alta della casa. 9. Il ragazzo più giovane è il fratello di Maria. 10. Domani forse il tempo sarà migliore.

[1] See the statement on p.163.

7. *Translate into Italian:*[1] 1. The big red book is for John's brother. 2. He is the happiest of the boys. 3. The lesson for tomorrow will

[1] See the statement on p.179.

be very easy. 4. The Italian newspaper was[1] on the round table. 5. The largest house is as high as the church. 6. Mary's four sisters will not be here after tomorrow. 7. The boys were[1] more polite when they were younger. 8. Yesterday the weather was fine. 9. The prettiest flowers are in the garden. 10. There are some interesting streets in the centre of the city.[2]

[1] Use the past descriptive.

[2] Write this sentence in two ways, first using the partitive construction, then using *qualche*.

LESSON 7. *AVERE*

Study **53** (*b*) [*omitting the compound tenses*].

EXERCISE 7

1. *Identify and translate:* aveste, hanno, avreste, avremo, ebbi, avevi, avendo, avrà, avuto, avrebbero, avevano, avrete, abbiamo, ebbero, hai, avranno.

2. *Translate into Italian:* they will have, she had (*past abs.*), we should have, I had (*past desc.*), having, we have, thou wilt have, they have, let us have, you will have, we had (*abs.*), I should have.

3. *Translate:* furono, ha, foste, avevate, sarà, avete, essendo, ebbe, siate, avremmo, sarei, avemmo, sareste, aveva.

4. *Translate into Italian:* I am, I have, you are, you have, he is, he has, we were (*desc.*), we had (*desc.*), they were (*desc.*), they had (*desc.*), I was (*abs.*), I had (*abs.*), you were (*abs.*), you had (*abs.*), he was (*abs.*), he had (*abs.*), we shall be, we shall have, they would be, they would have.

VOCABULARY

albero, *tree.*
anno, *year.*
giorno, *day.*
inverno, *winter.*
mese, m., *month.*

pranzo, *dinner.*
quadro, *picture.*
salotto, *parlor.*
sole, m., *sun, sunlight.*
teatro, *theatre.*

matita, *pencil.*
pazienza, *patience.*
penna, *pen.*
rosa, *rose.*
settimana, *week.*
storia, *history.*

caldo, *hot, warm.*
freddo, *cold.*
importante, *important.*
nuovo, *new.*
pieno, *full.*

scuro, *dark.*
stretto, *narrow.*
vero, *true.*

benchè, *although.*[1]
e, *and.*
ma, *but.*
o, *or.*
poi, *then.*
presto, *soon, early.*
sempre, *always.*
soltanto, *only.*

[1] The verb of the clause introduced by *benchè* is always in the subjunctive.

5. *Study these sentences:* 1. Avranno soltanto tre o quattro giorni a Firenze. 2. La chiesa più interessante era in una via stretta e scura. 3. Il giovane aveva sempre qualche libro italiano sulla scrivania. 4. Benchè le stanze non siano grandi, sono calde e piene di sole. 5. Abbiamo per domani delle lezioni molto facili. 6. Non ho una penna, ma Giovanni ha delle matite. 7. Dopo pranzo le signore sarebbero nel salotto. 8. Poi avrà delle tavole nuove. 9. Il libro è una storia importante dei teatri di Napoli. 10. Oggi avrò dei giornali francesi e italiani.

6. *Translate into Italian:* 1. The trees are much higher than the houses. 2. A year has twelve months, a month has four weeks, and a week has seven days. 3. They have a large house with a beautiful garden. 4. Have patience, they will be here soon. 5. Although the room is small, it will not be cold in the winter. 6. The most beautiful flowers were large red roses. 7. He had ten books on the desk, and seven or eight on the round table. 8. Have you a pen or a good pencil? 9. It is a pretty theatre, it's true, but it isn't very large. 10. The churches of the city were very beautiful; they had many interesting pictures.

LESSON 8. DEMONSTRATIVES AND INTERROGATIVES

Study **42, 43.**

EXERCISE 8

1. *Place the proper form of* quello *before each of these nouns:* albero, cappello, fanciullo, ingegno, stato, uccello; alberi, cappelli, fanciulli, ingegni, stati, uccelli.

2. *Translate into Italian:* who is it? whom have you there? of whom are-you-speaking (*parlate*)? what is it? what have you? of what are you speaking? what book is that? which book is that? whose book is that? what a beautiful book!

VOCABULARY

biglietto, *ticket.*
cappello, *hat.*
denaro, *money.*
fanciullo, *child.*
lavoro, *work.*
numero, *number.*
occhiali, m. pl., *glasses.*
studente, m., *student.*

foglia, *leaf.*
gita, *trip, excursion.*
mano, f., *hand.*
mattina, *morning.*
Milano, f.,[1] *Milan.*
poesia, *poem, poetry.*
Venezia, *Venice.*

certo, *certain.*
corto, *short.*
difficile, *difficult.*
fortunato, *fortunate.*
necessario, *necessary.*
ogni,[2] *every.*
possibile, *possible.*
pronto, *ready.*
verde, *green.*

come, *as, like.*
finalmente, *finally, at last.*
lunedì, *Monday.*
se, *if.*[3]
sì, *yes.*
troppo, *too, too much.*

[1] Names of cities are regarded as feminine, whatever the ending.

[2] Invariable.

[3] The verb of the clause introduced by *se* is present *indicative* if the tense is present, past *subjunctive* if the tense is past.

3. *Study these sentences:* 1. Queste foglie sono più belle di quei fiori. 2. Ho dei giornali e dei libri: questi sono per le signore, quelli per i signori. 3. Ciò è possibile, ma non è certo. 4. Chi ha un padre come quello è molto fortunato. 5. Chi è? È quello studente francese. 6. Che cosa avete in quella mano? Dei biglietti per una gita a Venezia. 7. Quale è il numero della casa di quel signore? 8. Quale lezione era la più difficile? 9. Quanti quadri in quel salotto! 10. Di chi è quel cappello verde?

4. *Translate into Italian:* 1. What handsome children! Who are they? 2. Those poems are shorter than this one. 3. How much money would he have then? 4. At last he has what is necessary for the work. 5. These boys are here every morning. 6. Are you ready? Have you those tickets? 7. Which churches are more interesting, those of Venice or those of Milan? 8. That red is pretty. Yes, if it isn't too dark for the room. 9. How many will be here Monday? More than ten or twelve? 10. Whose glasses are these? Are they John's?

LESSON 9. THE FIRST CONJUGATION

Study **58, 59** [*omitting* (*a*), (*b*)], **62, 63** [*omitting* (*a*)–(*d*)], *the first sentence of* **75**, *and the first sentence of* **77** (*a*).

EXERCISE 9

1. *Identify and translate:* parlò, parlerete, parli, parlaste, parlate, parliamo, parlerei, parlerai, parlino, parlerà, parlai, parlavano.

2. *Translate into Italian:* I spoke, she would speak, we were speaking, I shall speak, they spoke, speak, let us speak, let him speak, speaking, they speak, we should speak, he spoke.

VOCABULARY

baule, m., *trunk.*
esame, m., *examination.*
forestiere, m., *foreigner.*
guanto, *glove.*
momento, *moment.*
palazzo, *palace.*
pane, m., *bread.*

paniere, m., *basket.*
poeta, m., *poet.*

chiave, f., *key.*
galleria, *gallery.*
stazione, f., *station.*
università, *university.*

amare, *to love.*
aspettare, *to wait, wait for.*
cantare, *to sing.*
comprare, *to buy.*
costare, *to cost.*
desiderare, *to desire.*
entrare, *to enter, go in, come in.*

guardare, *to look, look at, watch.*
lavorare, *to work.*
passare, *to pass.*
telefonare, *to telephone.*
tornare, *to come back, return.*
trovare, *to find.*
visitare, *to visit.*

3. *Translate:* compriamo, costerebbe, entrava, tornerà, desiderate, trovaste, entreranno, amerebbero, torni, trovato, trovati, comprammo, guarda, guardai, amarono, trovando, telefonò, lavorereste, aspettano, cantino.

4. *Translate into Italian:* it will cost, I waited, buying, they would watch, she came in, they returned, I should telephone, he loved, sing, we found, let him work.

5. *Study these sentences:* 1. Comprerò un baule, se non costa troppo. 2. Quando ci entrammo, guardavano quel bel quadro degli alberi. 3. Quanto costano questi guanti? 4. Se non lavorasse, non passerebbe gli esami. 5. Parlava delle poesie di quel poeta francese. 6. Lunedì visitammo l'università di Napoli. 7. Che cosa cantavano quei ragazzi nella via? 8. Aspetti un momento: non sono pronto. 9. Non entrò nel palazzo, benchè avesse le chiavi. 10. Chi più ha, più desidera.

6. *Translate into Italian:* 1. Look at[1] that girl with the basket full of roses. 2. They were waiting for that foreigner. 3. You will find some[2] interesting pictures in that gallery. 4. Did you telephone to that French gentleman? 5. With whom did you come back from the station? 6. I went in, although he was working. 7. Let's wait for[1] John: he will be here soon. 8. Let him buy the bread, and then come back. 9. Where did she find those keys? 10. If I find the money, I'll telephone.

[1] Do not use a preposition after an Italian verb which may be in itself equivalent to an English verb and preposition.

[2] Use *qualche*.

LESSON 10. RELATIVES AND POSSESSIVES

Study **44** [*omitting* (*a*), (*b*), (*c*)], **45** [*omitting* (*a*)–(*e*)], **59** (*a*). *Read* **44** (*a*), (*b*), (*c*), **63** (*a*), (*b*), (*c*).

EXERCISE 10

1. *Insert the proper relative pronoun in each of these phrases:* il ragazzo — è qui, i libri — trovai, i ragazzi con — tornai, il libro di — parlo, i libri — sono sulla tavola, il ragazzo — cercavamo.

2. *Translate into Italian:* my garden, his house, our books, your pencils, their garden, my house, her books, our pencils, your garden, their house, my books, his pencils, our garden, your house, their books.

VOCABULARY

cugino, *cousin.*
mercato, *market.*
ombrello, *umbrella.*
pittore, m., *painter.*
romanzo, *novel.*

finestra, *window.*
fotografia, *photograph.*
mela, *apple.*
pera, *pear.*
testa, *head.*

giallo, *yellow.*
moderno, *modern.*
tutto, *all.*
ultimo, *last, latest.*

arrivare, *to arrive.*
bisognare,[1] *to be necessary.*
cercare, *to seek, search, look for, try.*
cominciare, *to begin.*
mangiare, *to eat.*
menare, *to lead, take.*
pagare, *to pay.*
portare, *to carry, bring.*
studiare, *to study.*

bene, *well.*
ecco, *here is, here are, there is, there are.*[2]
perchè, *why, because.*
stamane, *this morning.*
subito, *at once.*

[1] Impersonal.

[2] When 'there is,' 'there are,' are quite unemphatic (as in 'There are some pretty flowers in the garden'), or when the 'is' or 'are' is emphatic (as in 'There are men who don't believe it'), they are to be translated by *c' è* or *ci sono.* When the 'there' is emphatic (as in 'There is John') they are to be translated by *ecco.* 'Here is,' 'here are,' are always to be translated by *ecco.* *C' è* and *ci sono* correspond to the French *il y a; ecco* to the French *voici* and *voilà.*

3. *Give all the forms of* pagare *in which an* h *is inserted.*

4. *Translate into Italian:* I search, we search, let him search, I shall search; I pay, we pay, let him pay, I shall pay; I begin, we begin, let him begin, I shall begin; I eat, we eat, let him eat, I shall eat; I study, we study, let him study, I shall study.

5. *Study these sentences:* 1. È un uomo che trova subito quel che cerca. 2. C' erano all' ultima finestra due signori, uno dei quali era quel forestiere con cui parlai ieri. 3. Il palazzo che visitammo stamane è uno dei più interessanti della città. 4. La loro sorella portava sulla testa un gran paniere giallo pieno di mele e di pere. 5. Mangeremo quel che troveremo, e pagheremo bene. 6. Il quadro che guardavano nel salotto è di uno dei nostri migliori pittori italiani moderni. 7. Ecco quel signore. Perchè desidera parlare ai vostri fratelli? 8. Che bei fiori! Sono tutti del vostro giardino? 9. La via più stretta è quella che mena dalla chiesa di San Giovanni al mercato. 10. Bisognava aspettare Maria, che cercava l' ombrello.

6. *Translate into Italian:* 1. Who is the tall gentleman who arrived this morning? 2. Which of the lessons that you studied yesterday is the easiest? 3. This novel is more interesting than the one that he brought from the city. 4. My glasses are larger and rounder than his. 5. What are you looking for? Those tickets that I bought this morning. 6. Here is the umbrella I found at the door the day that you were here. Is it yours? 7. Whose is that poem of which they were speaking? 8. There are the men they were waiting for: why don't they begin? 9. Which of those three trunks is yours? This one, the largest. 10. Here is what he brought, — what is it? It's the latest photograph of my cousin.

LESSON 11. THE SECOND AND THIRD CONJUGATIONS

Study **60.**

EXERCISE 11

1. *Identify and translate:* credè, crederete, creda, crederò, credeste, credete, credetti, crediamo, crederei, credettero, crederai, credei, crederà, credevano, crederemo.

2. *Translate into Italian:* I believed, she would believe, we were believing, believe, they believed, let us believe, let him believe, believing, they believe, we should believe, he believed, you believe.

VOCABULARY

bottone, m., *button.*
caffè, m., *coffee.*
ferro, *iron.*
lume, m., *light.*
onore, m., *honor.*
servitore, m., *servant.*

battaglia, *battle.*
cosa, *thing.*
frase, f., *sentence.*
preghiera, *prayer, entreaty.*
salute, f., *health.*
torre, f., *tower.*
villa, *villa.*
vista, *sight, view.*
vita, *life.*
volta, *time.*[1]

godere, *to enjoy.*
temere, *to fear, be afraid.*

battere, *to beat, strike.*
cedere, *to yield.*
combattere, *to fight.*
credere, *to believe, think.*
perdere, *to lose.*
premere, *to press.*
ricevere, *to receive, get.*
ripetere, *to repeat.*

ancora, *yet, still, again, even.*
che, conjunction, *that.*
fuorchè, *except.*
meglio, *better.*
mentre, *while.*

[1] 'Time' is ordinarily to be translated by *tempo;* but when it has the sense of 'occasion' (as in 'three or four times') it is to be translated by *volta.*

3. *Translate:* battiamo, temeva, perderà, godete, ricevei, cedettero, combattè, premendo, ripeta, cederebbe, riceveste, goderanno, perderebbero, temano, perduto, perduti, tememmo, combatte, perderono, ricevono.

4. *Translate into Italian:* he will lose, I enjoyed, fearing, they would beat, she received, let them yield, they fought, repeat, they are pressing.

5. *Study these sentences:* 1. Oggi è felice: riceverà il denaro per quel quadro della signora coi guanti. 2. Benchè combattessero bene, perdettero la battaglia, e molti perdettero la vita. 3. Avremo quel che bisogna, non temete. 4. Non ho ricevuto ancora le mie fotografie.

5. Ripetevano ancora quel che avevano già ripetuto molte volte. 6. Non ho studiato la lezione: ieri perdei i miei libri. 7. Se non tornasse, perderebbe ogni cosa. 8. Credeva che fosse meglio essere temuto che amato. 9. Tutto è perduto fuorchè l' onore. 10. Bisogna battere il ferro mentre è caldo.

6. *Translate into Italian:* 1. She pressed a button, and the servant came in with the coffee. 2. The students had to (*a*) repeat the sentence three or four times. 3. The trees were losing the last red and yellow leaves. 4. If I receive the money, I'll telephone at once to my father. 5. Finally she came back and repeated that *ária* from the *Trovatóre* (*m.*). 6. Although she is still young, she does not enjoy good health. 7. That room has only one small window, but it gets light from the parlor. 8. From their villa they enjoy a beautiful view of the towers of the city. 9. If he doesn't yield to their entreaties, he won't yield to mine. 10. They think that he is[1] even poorer than his cousin.

[1] Use the subjunctive.

LESSON 12. CONJUNCTIVE PRONOUNS

Study **46, 47** [*omitting* 3 *and* (*a*)], **48** [*omitting* (*a*), (*b*), (*d*), (*e*), *and* (*f*), *but including* (*c*)].

EXERCISE 12

1. *Translate into Italian:* he finds me, he finds thee, he finds him, he finds her, he finds it (*m.*), he finds it (*f.*), he finds us, he finds you, he finds them (*m.*), he finds them (*f.*); I find myself, thou findest thyself, he finds himself, she finds herself, we find ourselves, you find yourself, you find yourselves, they (*m.*) find themselves, they (*f.*) find themselves; we find each other, you find each other, they find each other; to find him, finding him, let us find him, find him, do not find him, finding himself.

2. *Translate into Italian:* he speaks to me, he speaks to thee, he speaks to him, he speaks to her, he speaks to us, he speaks to you, he speaks to them (*m.*), he speaks to them (*f.*); I speak to myself, thou speakest to thyself, he speaks to himself, she speaks to herself, we speak to ourselves, you speak to yourself, you speak to yourselves, they (*m.*) speak to themselves, they (*f.*) speak to themselves; we speak to each other, you speak to each other, they speak to each other; to speak to him, speaking to him, let us speak to him, let's not speak to him, speak to him, speaking to himself.

3. *Translate:* lo trovai, le parlano, mi parlerebbe, ripetetelo, vi aspettavano, li compraste?, cediamo loro, la guardavano?, gli telefonerò, si trovò, lo perdemmo, cercatela, le riceverono, lo perdette, trovarvi, ci visiteranno, ci visiteremo, temendoli, non le parlate, ci ceda, vi telefonò, studiamolo, si cercano, compratolo, li portate.

4. *Study these sentences:* 1. Se non mi trovate qui, aspettatemi coi biglietti alla porta della stazione. 2. Che cosa cerca? Le chiavi di quel baule. Le trovò ieri, poi le perdette ancora. 3. Si ripetevano le frasi della lezione. 4. Che ragazzo! Comprare cinque mele, e mangiarle subito! 5. Quanto gli costerebbe un cappello come quello? 6. Parlava come se ci fosse stato. 7. Quando riceverò il denaro, vi pagherò. 8. Di che cosa le parlava nel salotto? 9. Dove ci mena? Alla chiesa di cui vi parlò quel pittore. 10. Ecco quell' ombrello: temeva che lo avesse perduto.

5. *Translate into Italian:* 1. When he came back from the market, he brought me some[1] apples. 2. When will she begin to (*a*) sing to them? 3. If you study the lesson, you will find it easy. 4. If he had them, he would bring them to my father. 5. When they came in, he was beginning to (*a*) eat it. 6. Here are the books I lost yesterday. Who found them? 7. We were here this morning, but she did not receive us. 8. I waited for them three days in Naples. 9. Now that you have it again, don't lose it. 10. Whose photograph is this? It's of my cousin. I received it yesterday.

---

[1] Use the partitive construction.

Piero di Lorenzo de Medici, Domenico Ghirlandaio

Duomo Cathedral, Milan

LESSON 13. CONJUNCTIVE PRONOUNS (continued)

Study **46–50** *inclusive.*

EXERCISE 13

1. *Translate each of these phrases in two ways:* glielo porto, gliela porto, glieli porto, gliele porto, gliene parlo, portateglielo, parlategliene.

2. *Translate into Italian:* he leads him to me, he leads him to thee, he leads him to him, he leads him to her, he leads him to us, he leads him to you, he leads him to them; he leads her to me, he leads her to thee, he leads her to him, he leads her to her, he leads her to us, he leads her to you, he leads her to them; he leads them (*m.*) to me, he leads them to thee, he leads them to him, he leads them to her, he leads them to us, he leads them to you, he leads them to them; he leads them (*f.*) to me, he leads them to thee, he leads them to him, he leads them to her, he leads them to us, he leads them to you, he leads them to them.

3. *Translate into Italian:* he speaks of it to me, he speaks of it to thee, he speaks of it to him, he speaks of it to her, he speaks of it to us, he speaks of it to you, he speaks of it to them.

4. *Translate into Italian:* I repeat it to myself, thou repeatest it to thyself, he repeats it to himself, she repeats it to herself, we repeat it to ourselves, you repeat it to yourself, you repeat it to yourselves, they repeat it to themselves; we repeat it to each other, you repeat it to each other, they repeat it to each other.

VOCABULARY

automobile, m., *automobile.*
complimento, *compliment.*
ritardo, *delay;* **in ritardo,** *late.*
treno, *train.*

cortesia, *courtesy.*
lira, *lira,* coin

notte, f., *night.*
occasione, f., *occasion.*
ora, *hour.*

altro, *other.*
stesso, *same.*
venti, *twenty.*

chiamare, *to call;* come si chiama?
   what is the name of?
domandare, *to ask.*[1]
incontrare, *to meet.*
insegnare, *to teach.*
lasciare, *to leave, let.*[2]
mandare, *to send.*

mostrare, *to show.*
presentare, *to present.*
prestare, *to lend.*
raccontare, *to narrate, tell, tell about.*[1]
ringraziare, *to thank.*
spiegare, *to explain.*

[1] The personal object of *domandare* or *raccontare* is indirect: *gli domandai,* 'I asked him'; *le raccontai,* 'I told her.'

[2] *Lasciare* is to be used in translating 'let' only when the idea is one of permission rather than one of command. For example, if 'let him speak' really means 'I command that he speak,' it is to be translated *parli;* if it really means 'allow him to speak,' it is to be translated *lasciatelo parlare.*

5. *Translate:* vi aspetto, ne cercava, ce lo cantarono, ne parlaste, non ne avrebbe, eccoli, portandoglielo, ripeteteglielo, gliene parlerò, bisogna portarglielo, eccola, ce li cedette, portiamogliene, me le mandò?, glielo prestai, ve lo spiegheranno, mandatemeli, glielo prestino, mi si presenta, gli si presentano, se lo presentano, lo mostrai loro, ve ne mandarono?, me lo spieghi, glielo presterete?

6. *Study these sentences:* 1. Quell' ombrello era il suo, e stamane glielo mandai. 2. Se non credesse quel che gli raccontammo, non glielo ripeterebbe. 3. Cominciava a domandargli perchè ne avesse parlato agli altri. 4. Ve lo spiegherà quando gli si presenterà una buona occasione. 5. Lo ringraziai della cortesia, e gli raccontai tutto. 6. Ogni volta che s' incontrano, si ripetono gli stessi complimenti. 7. Come si chiama quel giovane che v' insegna il francese? 8. Il treno era in ritardo, e l' aspettarono un' ora e più. 9. Ora lasciateli studiare; parleremo dopo. 10. Ho a pagare subito, e non ho una lira: Giovanni ha ricevuto oggi venti lire, non è vero?[1] Me ne presterebbe dieci?

[1] *non è vero?* 'hasn't he?'

7. *Translate into Italian:* 1. He is in the garden. Call him — they are looking for him. 2. He presented himself to me yesterday. I believe him even younger than the others. 3. Where are my pencils? didn't I leave them on the desk? 4. If he loses it, it will cost him **10,000** *lire.* 5. It is necessary to[1] watch them day and night. 6. He has a French automobile, and he'll show it to us Monday. 7. Whose tickets are those? Are they your cousin's? Why don't you send them to him? 8. If I didn't believe what she told me, I wouldn't repeat it to you. 9. If he receives that money, he will pay me at once. 10. If she finds this lesson too difficult, he will explain it to her tomorrow.

[1] No preposition is used between *bisognare* and a dependent infinitive.

LESSON 14. THE FOURTH CONJUGATION

Study **61.**

EXERCISE 14

1. *Identify and translate:* finì, finirete, finiscono, finirò, finiste, finivano, finii, finiranno, finirei, finisci, finirono, finirai, finite, finiremo, finisca, finivo.

2. *Translate into Italian:* I finished, she would finish, we were finishing, he is finishing, finish, they finished, let us finish, finishing, they finish, we should finish, he finished, you finish, let him finish.

VOCABULARY

autunno, *autumn.*
colore, m., *color.*
pericolo, *danger.*
spedale, m., *hospital.*
vento, *wind.*
vestito, *dress.*

cura, *care.*
stoffa, *stuff, goods.*

cattivo, *bad.*
chiaro, *clear, bright.*
tanto, *so much.*[1]

applaudire, *to applaud.*
avvertire, *to warn.*
capire, *to understand.*
divertire, *to amuse.*
dormire, *to sleep.*
ferire, *to wound.*
fuggire, *to flee.*
garantire, *to guarantee.*
partire, *to depart, leave.*[2]
preferire, *to prefer.*
restituire, *to give back.*
sentire, *to feel, hear.*
servire, *to serve.*

[1] 'So much' is to be translated by *tanto;* not by the separate words for 'so' and 'much.'

[2] When 'leave' is transitive, it is to be translated by *lasciare;* when intransitive, by *partire.*

almeno, *at least.*   senza, *without.*
invece, *instead.*   stanotte, *last night.*
nondimeno, *nevertheless.*   stasera, *this evening.*
prima di, *before.*   subito che, *as soon as.*[1]

[1] 'As soon as' is to be translated by *subito che;* not by the separate words for 'as' and 'soon.'

3. *Give the present indicative of each of these verbs:* capire, divertire, dormire, fuggire, garantire, preferire.

4. *Translate:* dormiamo, capirebbe, serviva, avvertirà, applaudite, garantiscano, diverte, fuggirono, ferisce, servendo, preferimmo, fuggii, avvertito, ferite, preferirebbero, divertono, sentiste, serviranno, senta, capiscono.

5. *Translate into Italian:* he will amuse, I was sleeping, fleeing, they prefer, we understood, she served, they will applaud, you fled, I should guarantee, sleep.

6. *Study these sentences:* 1. Subito che me ne parlò, capii che l' aveva perduto. 2. Se ci serve bene, le pagheremo venti lire la settimana. 3. Glielo restituiranno subito che torna. 4. L' avvertii che c' era pericolo, ma partì nondimeno. 5. Se si divertono ora invece di lavorare, domani avranno a lavorare invece di divertirsi. 6. Aveva cantato molto bene, e tutti l' applaudivano. 7. Che vento stanotte! Lo sentiste? Sì, non dormii un' ora in tutta la notte. 8. Il ferito fu portato allo spedale. 9. Partirono senza ringraziarci, benchè avessimo cercato tanto di divertirli. 10. Il mese cominciò con una settimana di bel tempo — giorni chiari e caldi — ma finì con dieci giorni freddi e scuri.

7. *Translate into Italian:* 1. If he doesn't guarantee it for a year at least, we won't buy it. 2. Although he heard them speak, he fled like the wind. 3. I explained it to him with much care, but he doesn't understand it yet. 4. If he is still sleeping, he won't finish that lesson. 5. The trees are losing the last leaves: the autumn is ending, and the winter is beginning. 6. Did you hear what he told them? 7. This room is warm, but in the parlor we felt the cold. 8. We shall leave this evening if the weather isn't too bad. 9. What goods and what color does she prefer for the dress? 10. When will you finish that work? I shall not have the time to (*di*) finish it before Monday.

LESSON 15. DISJUNCTIVE PRONOUNS

Study **51.**

EXERCISE 15

1. *Translate into Italian, expressing the subject pronouns* (*use* lui, lei, *and* loro *for the third person*): I am, thou hast, he speaks, she fears, we finish, you feel, they are, I had, thou didst enter, he yielded, she understood, we slept, you were, they had, I shall pay, thou wilt receive, he will guarantee, she will depart, we shall be, you will have, they will enter.

VOCABULARY

avvocato, *lawyer.*
bicchiere, m., *glass.*
facchino, *porter.*
latte, m., *milk.*
mezzogiorno, *noon.*

aria, *air.*
lettera, *letter.*
libertà, *liberty, freedom.*
moglie, f., *wife.*
seggiola, *chair.*
valigia, *valise, bag.*

aiutare, *to help.*
restare, *to stay.*

accanto a, *beside.*
contro, contro di,[1] *against.*
davanti a, *in front of.*
dietro, dietro a,[1] *behind.*
secondo, *according to.*

avanti, *forward; come in.*[2]
così, *so.*
eh, *eh.*
mai, *ever, never;* **non . . . mai,**[3] *never.*
nemmeno, non . . . nemmeno,[3] *not even.*
perfettamente, *perfectly.*
prima, *first.*

[1] The compound form is used before a disjunctive pronoun, the simple form in other cases.

[2] As an exclamation.

[3] When *mai* (meaning 'never') or *nemmeno* follows the verb, *non* is placed before the verb.

2. *Study these sentences:* 1. Portate a questo signore un caffè, e a me un bicchiere di latte. 2. Se loro ce l' hanno raccontato a noi, perchè non glielo racconteremmo noi a lui? 3. Felici voi, che godete quell' aria e quella libertà, mentre io resto qui in città a lavorare come un facchino! 4. Chi è? Sono io. Chi, io? Io, Giovanni. Siete voi, eh? avanti. 5. Se non glielo spiega bene, gli è che non lo capisce bene nemmeno lui. 6. A quel teatro me non mi ci troverete mai più. 7. Porta sempre con sè una valigia tutta piena di libri, ma poi non ne guarda nemmeno uno. 8. Lui le parlava contro di me — e io avevo lavorato tanto per lui! 9. Quando entrai, lei era qui; accanto a lei, Giovanni, che le parlava di sè stesso, come sempre; e davanti a lui, in questa seggiola, la piccola sorella di lei, che guardava ora l' uno ora l' altra. 10. Quando lo perdei, loro mi aiutarono a cercarlo.

3. *Translate into Italian:* 1. They spoke of it to us, to you, and to him. 2. If it's he, call him, and show him that letter. 3. I myself telephoned to you, and asked you if he would arrive there before noon. 4. *I* think that you will receive it tomorrow. 5. If *you* were here with them, they would be perfectly happy. 6. If he stays, they will leave. 7. He was speaking to us, but we thought that he was speaking to them. 8. He and his cousin left before us, but we arrived there an hour before them. 9. According to him, she was staying at home because the weather was so bad. 10. The lawyer's wife came in first; then, behind her, the two girls; behind them, three porters with the trunks; and finally the lawyer himself.

LESSON 16. COMPOUND TENSES

Study the compound tenses in **53** (*a*) *and* **53** (*b*), **54** [*omitting* (*c*)–(*h*)] **55, 56,** *and the second sentence in* **75.**

EXERCISE 16

1. *Identify and translate:* ho trovato, aveva trovato, ebbe trovato, avremo trovato, avreste trovato; sono trovato, era trovato, fu trovato, saremo trovati, sarebbero trovati; sono stato trovato, era stato trovato, saremo stati trovati, sareste stato trovato; sono tornato, era tornato, fu tornato, saremo tornati, sareste tornati; mi sono divertito, si era divertito, ci saremo divertiti, si sarebbero divertiti.

2. *Translate each of these phrases in six ways (as true reflexive, masculine and feminine; as substitute for the passive, masculine, feminine, and neuter; and as indefinite)*: si presenta, si trova, si servì, si perderà.

3. *Translate each of these phrases in three ways: (as true reflexive, as reciprocal, and as substitute for the passive)*: si capiscono, si chiamano, si trovarono.

4. *Translate:* l' hanno avuto, c' era stato, l' avrò cominciato, mi avrebbe telefonato, siete ferito, vi siete ferito, vi furono trovati, gli saranno restituiti, gli si restituiranno, saremmo presentati loro, gli è spiegato, gli si spiega, gli è stato spiegato, gli si è spiegato, ci siamo spiegati, ce lo siamo spiegati, si erano incontrati, siamo arrivati, vi fu mostrato, gli si presenterà, le era stato raccontato, le si era raccontato, si è presentata, si sono presentate, li avrebbe aspettati, ci ha capito, ci avevano ringraziati, si era perduto, erano fuggiti, si è ferito, vi sono arrivati, ci erano stati mandati, ci si erano mandati, vi aveva aiutato, essendo temuto, ci si spiega, glielo avevano raccontato, vi avremmo ringraziato.

5. *Translate into Italian:* we have found you, we have been there, they had had it, he will have eaten it, we should have sent it to you, he had[1] arrived, they are received,[2] they would have presented themselves to us, you would have found each other, they had[1] come in, he had left them, they would have[1] fled, it has been told to me.[2]

[1] Translate by the proper form of *essere*.
[2] Translate this phrase in two ways.

6. *Study these sentences:* 1. Sono certo che se ci fosse stato cogli altri, ce ne avrebbe parlato. 2. Perchè non ha cominciato a cercare quel che perdette? 3. Quando loro saranno tornati, noi saremo già partiti. 4. Non li avrà finiti prima di domani. 5. Non ha mai visitato quel giardino? Gliene abbiamo parlato tante volte. 6. Le seggiole che mi si mostravano erano molto belle, e le avrei comprate se avessi avuto il denaro. 7. Mi si era raccontato che lui ci fosse stato, ma non l' avevo creduto. 8. Se hanno ricevuto la sua lettera, saranno già partiti per la città. 9. Lui aveva temuto che cedessero alle nostre preghiere. 10. Si mangia a mezzogiorno, e un' ora dopo si torna al lavoro.

7. *Translate into Italian:* 1. If he had had any, he would have sent us some. 2. Being called, I entered, and found myself where I had been the day before. 3. That bag that he had lost has been given back to him. 4. Let him explain to her why they hadn't telephoned to her. 5. I would have sent it to you if I had found it. 6. As soon as he had called them, he came back into the house. 7. When I arrived, they had[1] already left. 8. If they had begun them, they would have finished two or three of them. 9. He told me that he had[1] arrived there before the others. 10. I should have preferred a room with at least two windows.

[1] Translate by the proper form of *essere.*

LESSON 17. REVIEW

EXERCISE 17

1. *Pronounce Exercise* **A** *on p.* 158.

2. *Give the plural of each of these combinations:* all' avvocato gentile, che bel salotto!, col loro fratello, dalla sua bella mano, dell' uomo felice, il gran baule, il mio cugino, il poeta francese, il suo bell' ombrello, la città moderna, la giovane moglie, l' altra finestra, lo stesso ragazzo, nell' università nuova, quale stanza?, quel buon padre, quello studente italiano, quel piccolo caffè, quel servitore fedele, questa lezione difficile, sulla torre alta.

3. *Translate:* se lui ci aiutasse, erano stati amati, aspettandole, l' avevamo, ne avrai, li hanno battuti, si capisce, lo cedemmo loro, lo comprano, si erano divertiti, ci entrarono, se loro non ci fossero, s' incontrarono, glielo mandai, lui lo mangerà, ve ne avevo parlato, chi li perdette?, che cosa preferirebbe lei?, se lo premesse, ci sarei restato, le telefonavo, lasciatolo, benchè ci capisca, ve lo restituirà, non l' hánno ricevuta, ripeteteglielo, vi sareste, glielo restituii, non gli cedano, siete chiamato, se lo spiegheranno, sono stati ricevuti, gli si è restituito, le sarà spiegato, si è perduto, ve lo manderanno, glieli avrebbero mostrati, se vi avessero sentito, la servano, benchè lo temano, lui li avvertì, non gliene parlate, ce lo spiegarono, gli si erano presentati.

4. *Translate into Italian:* there they are, we shall be there, if they should buy it, they would carry it to him, he will applaud them, *I* feared it, are they fighting there?, they are not fleeing, we should have gone in, they would have had it, did he have any?, although they had lost it, will they pay me?, I should prefer it, what has he received?, wait for us.

5. *Study these proverbs:* [1] 1. A ogni uccello suo nido è bello. 2. Buona compagnia, mezza la via. 3. Chi cerca, trova. 4. Chi dorme non piglia pesci. 5. Chi ha fiorini trova cugini. 6. Chi non lavora non mangia. 7. Chi s' aiuta, il ciel l' aiuta. 8. Chi tardi arriva, male alloggia. 9. Gli assenti han sempre torto. 10. Il buon vino non ha bisogno di frasca. 11. Il passo più duro è quello dell' uscio. 12. La fame non ha legge. 13. La fine corona l' opera. 14. La notte porta consiglio. 15. L' aurora indora. 16. L' età porta senno. 17. Meglio tardi che mai. 18. Non v' è rosa senza spine. 19. Oggi a me, domani a te. 20. Scopa nuova scopa bene.

[1] Many of the sentences from this point on contain words not given in the preceding vocabularies. See the statements on pp. 162 and 181.

6. *Translate into Italian:* 1. Whose ideas are those? They are not yours, I hope. 2. If you hadn't told it to me yourself, I shouldn't have believed it. 3. If you haven't the money, I'll lend it to you with pleasure. 4. I was afraid that you were [1] wrong, but according to my cousin's letter you are right. 5. How many times has he repeated it to you? 6. Whom are they calling? I thought that they were [1] all here. 7. He was studying there at the desk, and didn't even look at them when they came in. 8. Although there are not so many churches here, they are more interesting than those we visited yesterday. 9. Why didn't he let us go in? Probably because it was too early. 10. Who was it that telephoned to you? That gentleman to whom I telephoned this morning. He is going back tomorrow to Venice.

[1] Use the subjunctive.

LESSON 18. THE MODERN POLITE FORM OF DIRECT ADDRESS

Study **52.**

EXERCISE 18

1. *Translate in two ways* (*as third person feminine, and as used in direct address*): lei è qui, con lei, la chiamavano, chiamo lei, le parlerò, è certa, è restata, lei cantava, dopo di lei, la ringrazio, guardavano lei, le telefonerei, sarà fortunata, si è divertita.

2. *Translate in three ways* (*as third person masculine, as third person feminine, and as used in direct address*): era là, l' aiuterò, glielo mandai, si trova, se lo ripete, parli, mi parli, è gentile, il suo libro, studiava, l' incontrai, gliene ha parlato, si diverte, ceda, si spieghi, era giovane, i suoi occhiali.

3. *Translate in two ways* (*as third person, and as used in direct address*): sono qui, loro erano pronti, contro di loro, li chiamava, le incontrai, riceverò loro, parlerò loro, si trovano, se lo ripetono, parlino, mi parlino, sono certi, erano entrate, il loro treno.

4. *Replace these phrases by the corresponding phrases in modern polite usage, supposing one person to be addressed:* sarete qui, voi ci capite, secondo voi, vi troverò, cercavo voi, vi applaudivano, ve lo presto, vi siete ferito, ve lo ripeteste, guardate, sentitemi, il vostro ombrello.

5. *Replace the phrases in section* **4** *by the corresponding phrases in modern polite usage, supposing two men to be addressed.*

NOTE. — In the remainder of this exercise, and in all the following exercises, use only the modern polite form of direct address, and suppose the English ' you ' to be singular, unless there is some indication that it refers to more than one person.

6. *Translate into Italian:* you are working, *you* will sing, for you, I'm waiting for you, I will serve you, he will telephone to you, I was speaking to *you*, did he send it to you?, you were explaining yourself, did you repeat it to yourself?, stay, thank him, you are happy, you have returned, your brother.

7. *Translate the first five sentences in Ex.* **14,** *section* **6,** *and the first five in Ex.* **16,** *section* **6,** *supposing them to be used in direct address.*

8. *Translate into Italian the first five sentences in Ex.* **15,** *section* **3,** *and the first five in Ex.* **17,** *section* **6,** *using the modern polite form of direct address.*

LESSON 19. *ANDARE* AND *FARE*

Study **92** *through* 2 (**Fare**); *also* **48** (*a*), (*b*),(*e*), **54** (*h*), **56**(*b*), **78**(*d*).

EXERCISE 19

1. *Translate:* andò, andrete, vanno, andaste, va', era andato, ci andrei, vada, andavano, sono andati, vi andai, andavo, sarebbe andata, vattene, si va.

2. *Translate into Italian:* we went, you [1] go, they will go, you went there, he will go, he has gone there, they are going away, it goes, we should have gone, go, she went away, let them go.

[1] Remember the directions given in the NOTE on p.131.

3. *Translate:* faccia, faceste, fatto, facciamo, fecero, aveva fatto, faresti, fo, li fece, farà, lo facciano, si fa, è fatto, lo si fa, fateli entrare, la fa leggere,[1] le fa leggere la lettera, gliela fa leggere, me lo fece trovare.

[1] Translate this phrase in two ways.

4. *Translate into Italian:* I did, he will do, they are making, doing, they would make, make, you made, we have made, let them make, they will do it, we made them, they are made, I'll have him sing, I'll have it sung, I'll have him sing it.

5. *Study these sentences:* 1. Mi faccia il favore di chiamarlo subito. 2. Chi va piano va sano[1] e va lontano. 3. Facciamo una partita al biliardo? Oggi no, ho troppo da fare, io. 4. Se lo perde, glielo faranno cercare. 5. I suoi affari andrebbero meglio se non amasse tanto il dolce far niente. 6. Quando lui tornò da fare il soldato, lei

[1] *sano,* 'safely.' Predicate adjectives are often adverbial in force.

si era fatta sposa con un altro. 7. "Ah sì?" fece lui, "lasci fare a me." 8. Fa freddo: perchè non fanno un po' di fuoco qui? 9. Dopo faranno molte nuove conoscenze, che si chiameranno anche amicizie, ma le più vere saranno sempre le amicizie fatte in giovinezza. 10. Se n' andò in America, e subito si fece ricco, ma poi perdette ogni cosa, e se ne tornò povero povero[1] com' era andato.

[1] The repetition of a word serves to emphasize it.

6. *Translate into Italian:* 1. He goes to the city every day. 2. Go and see if they are here. 3. I had him make it so because the other one was made so. 4. If they had gone there yesterday, they would have found him there. 5. We had him carry it to the village. 6. If they do as he has done, they will do more honor to him than to themselves. 7. We make more of it than they, and ours is better than theirs. 8. He went away this morning, but he'll come back soon. 9. Let him go and find it and bring it to me here. 10. It's a pretty place: we go there every Sunday.

LESSON 20. *DARE* AND *STARE*

Study **92,** 3 *and* 4; *also* **54** (*c*), (*d*).

EXERCISE 20

1. *Translate:* diede, darete, dia, danno, dette, darai, deste, diamo, diedero, dai, hanno dato, me lo davano, glielo darebbe?, ce lo dia, diamogliene, ve ne daranno, se ne dà, l' aveva dato loro, dammene, gli si è dato.

2. *Translate into Italian:* I should give, I gave, you are giving, give, we have given, I was giving, they gave them to me, he gives himself to us, he gave them some, I had given it to her, will you give me some?, we should have given them to you.

3. *Translate:* stareste, stavano, stette, stia, steste, stanno, stettero, starebbe, state, sta', stemmo, stai, stiano, stiamo, starà, sto lavorando, stava parlando, stava per dirmelo.

4. *Translate into Italian:* he was standing, they would stand, I stood, let them stand, we stood, you are standing, stand, let us stand, he stood, they are calling, I was about to thank you.

5. *Study these sentences:* 1. Cos' hai in quella mano? Dammelo subito. 2. Come sta? Benissimo, grazie, e Lei? 3. Stava per domandargli perchè non se ne fosse andato. 4. Per il Natale gli si diedero dei libri italiani. 5. Chi dà presto, è come se desse due volte. 6. Stia attento: non si faccia male. 7. Daranno il voto a chi meglio li paga. 8. Poveretta! Sta sempre lì a cucire. 9. Prima faceva l' ingegnere, ma poi si diede allo studio della filosofia. 10. Tutti gli facevano degl' inchini profondi, e gli davano dell' illustrissimo.

6. *Translate into Italian:* 1. He gave you two of them, and I gave you three. 2. They have [1] come back, but they are standing outside. 3. If it's his, give it to him. 4. They were explaining it to him when we came in. 5. Here you are at last: I was about to go and call you. 6. How much would *you* have given him? Not a cent. 7. They are giving a dinner this evening for that English writer. 8. Yesterday he was a little better, but today he's worse. 9. I thank you, sir: your words have given me the courage to (*di*) continue. 10. Give them some [2] money, but don't let them come in.

[1] Translate by the proper form of *essere*.
[2] Use the partitive construction.

LESSON 21. ARTICLES

Study **10–16** *inclusive,* **45** *(a)–(e) inclusive.*

EXERCISE 21

1. *Review Exercise* **3**, *sections* **2, 3, 4.**

2. *Study these sentences:* 1. Nell' unità sta la forza. 2. Preferisce l' Ariosto allo Spenser e Dante allo Shakespeare. 3. Andammo in Inghilterra colla madre, e quando noi tornammo lei ci restò con una sua cugina. 4. Era orfano, ma un suo zio gli faceva da padre. 5. Aveva i capelli neri e folti; neri anche gli occhi; nero l' abito, neri

i guanti. 6. Il medico gli toccava il polso: la febbre montava. 7.
Si è fatto molto male; avrà a restare a casa una settimana almeno.
8. Gli uomini più grandi hanno quasi sempre le maniere semplici.
9. È un gran poeta; chi lo nega parla da sciocco. 10. Ha venduto
la casa e ogni cosa, ed è partito per gli Stati Uniti d' America.

3. *Translate into Italian:* 1. Habits make us what we are. 2. We
are still in France, but we hope to (*di*) go to Italy this summer.
3. Mr. Rossi loves books, and spends almost all his time in
his study; if he isn't well, it's his fault. 4. Poor Ghedini was a
friend of mine. 5. Last year Queen Elizabeth travelled through
France. 6. He took off his hat and made us a low bow. 7. Venice
is perhaps the most beautiful of the cities of Italy. 8. If he is an
Italian, let him be worthy of his fatherland. 9. He is still very
young, but he talks like a man. 10. Give him your handkerchief
quick; he has cut his hand.

LESSON 22. IRREGULAR VERBS OF THE SECOND CONJUGATION

Read **64–67**; *study* **92**, 6–10.

EXERCISE 22

1. *Translate:* saprò, seppe, sai, sapremmo, sanno, sapevo, ca-
dono, cadrò, caddi, caduto, cadde, cadrebbe, dobbiamo, dovetti,
devi, dovemmo, doverono, dovrete, sedei, siedono, sedendo, sedete,
sedette, sedeva, veda, vide, vedrai, visto, vedano, videro; l' avremo
saputo, vi cadde, me lo deve, vi sedeva?, ce lo vedemmo, lo seppero,
ci sarebbe caduto, glielo dobbiamo, ci sedetti, li vedrà.

2. *Translate into Italian:* we know, they knew, you had
known, know, they fell, I was falling, we shall fall, you fell, he
owes, we should owe, they owe, owing, he is sitting, they will sit,
you were sitting, seated, we should see, let him see, I saw, let us
see; did he know it?, they had fallen there, they owe it to her,
they are sitting there, did they see us?

3. *Study these sentences:* 1. Stavano insieme alla finestra a guardare la neve che cadeva lenta lenta. 2. Che buio! Non ci si vede[1] punto! 3. Il povero vecchio stava seduto al canto del camino. 4. Videro il loro bambino che giocava[2] colle pistole dello zio. 5. Non so se Lei sappia la triste notizia. 6. Si vedeva nelle sue maniere un non so che di nuovo e di strano. 7. Mi hanno dato tutto; non mi si deve più nulla. 8. Coi pensieri che gli giravano per la testa non sapeva più in che mondo si fosse. 9. Il poco che si sa, si sappia bene. 10. Non dimenticate i caduti per la patria.

[1] *Non ci si vede,* 'One can't see.' There are several verbs that may assume the idea of possibility in the present and past descriptive tenses.

[2] *che giocava,* 'playing.' An Italian relative clause is often equivalent to an English participle.

4. *Translate into Italian:* 1. Let's see where they are going. 2. He was standing there talking with his brother, when a brick fell on his head. 3. Did you see them speak to him? Do you know their names? 4. They will not know what we are doing. 5. See: they have given me some[1] gloves like yours. 6. I hope that tomorrow you will all know the lesson. 7. If I see him I'll give him the ten *lire* I owe him. 8. He had him sit down beside the desk. 9. Were they not standing there when you saw them? 10. He owed him everything, yet he went away leaving him alone and sick.

[1] Use the partitive construction.

LESSON 23. NOUNS

Study **22, 23, 24, 25.**

EXERCISE 23

1. *Review Exercise* **4,** *sections* **2** *and* **3.**

2. *Give the plural of each of these masculine nouns:* ago, amico, bacio, bosco, braccio, cantico, collega, dito, duca, equivoco, figlio, fuoco, ginocchio, guaio, luogo, miglio, monaco, nemico, obbligo, occhio, paio, patriarca, studio, turco, uovo.

3. *Give the plural of each of these feminine nouns:* biblioteca, coscia, fabbrica, faccia, frangia, fuga, giacca, lega, valanga, valigia.

4. *Give the masculine and feminine plural of each of these adjectives:* artistico, buio, carico, cieco, classico, doppio, fresco, grigio, largo, lungo, poco, proprio, simpatico, vago, vecchio.

5. *Study these sentences:* 1. La ricchezza dei contadini sta nelle braccia. 2. Tornarono tutti carichi di frutta e di confetti. 3. Si sentì tremare le ginocchia per la paura. 4. E i medici, non gli danno più speranza? 5. In quei villaggi ci sono moltissimi ciechi. 6. I suoi[1] lo credono un buon ragazzo; ma ha molti vizi e pochissime virtù. 7. Che c' è di nuovo? Gli operai hanno fatto sciopero. 8. Ha studiato il tedesco due anni, ed ora lo parla assai bene. 9. Il suo aspetto aveva qualche cosa di misterioso, quasi di divino. 10. Le loro facce e maniere hanno un non so che di semplice e di umano che fa vedere che la loro vita si fonda sul vero e non sul falso.

[1] *I suoi*, 'His family.' The masculine plural possessives are often used in this way.

6. *Translate into Italian:* 1. Yesterday morning they walked more than ten miles. 2. They hope that their old friends will arrive this evening. 3. We saw them with our own eyes. 4. The lakes are longer than they[1] are[1] broad. 5. He has finished his studies on the libraries of ancient times. 6. Give me two pairs of stockings. 7. They are very agreeable young men. 8. Her eyes were black as night, and her cheeks were white as snow. 9. He has lost two fingers of his right hand. 10. The monarchs of Milan were called dukes; those of Venice, doges; those of Rome, popes; and those of Naples, kings.

[1] Omit these words in translating.

LESSON 24. IRREGULAR VERBS OF THE SECOND CONJUGATION (continued)

Study **92,** 11–17.

EXERCISE 24

1. *Translate:* giacciono, giacque, giacendo, piacerei, piace, piacquero, taccia, taci, tacqui, suole, solito, solevano, dorrà, dolse, rimasero, rimanga, rimarreste, tiene, terrete, tenne, tenuti, tengano, teniamo; gli piace,[1] gli piaccio, le piacciono, vi piaceva?, piacque loro, gli duole,[1] vi rimangano, c' è rimasta, vi saranno rimasti, li teneva, teniamolo, l' aveva tenuto.

[1] The personal object of *piacere* or *dolere* is indirect.

2. *Translate into Italian:* he was lying, it lay, they please, you will please, they were silent, we shall be silent, they were wont, it grieves, remain, they remain, thou holdest, they would hold; it pleases me, I like it,[1] they please me, I like them, it pleased him, he liked it, she liked it, we liked it, they liked it, they have remained there, they are held, we should have held them.

[1] When 'like' has a noun or a pronoun as object, the sentence should be recast for translation into Italian by substituting 'please' for 'like,' and making the original object the subject and the original subject the object: 'I like it' = 'it pleases me.'

3. *Study these sentences:* 1. Gli piacerebbe molto se Lei glielo desse. 2. Arrivarono lunedì, e ci rimarranno almeno fino a domenica. 3. Non credo che quel posto gli piaccia:[1] non c' è niente da fare. 4. Ieri m' entrò una spina nel piede, e ancora mi duole. 5. Tengo per fermo che un tale dono non gli piacerà. 6. Faceva un gran freddo; ma si teneva vivo il fuoco, e si stava al caminetto. 7. È difficile piacergli, e lui non cerca mai di piacere a nessuno. 8. Ha tante buone qualità: peccato che non sappia tener la lingua. 9. Mi faccia il piacere di farmelo vedere. 10. La notte taceva: non un suono, non una voce; solo si sentiva, da lontano, il mormorio del fiume.

[1] *piaccia*, 'will please.' The present subjunctive often has a future tense-value.

4. *Translate into Italian:* 1. It fell and lay three days on the ground. 2. He was sitting in the room where his brother lay sick. 3. Have you seen my new coat? how do you like it? 4. If they keep still, we shall not know where they have been. 5. I have been studying too much; my eyes are paining me. 6. If you don't like this one, I will give you another. 7. It would grieve him very much if they should go[1] away now. 8. The village lies at the foot of the mountain, near the river. 9. Don't go now: stay to dinner, and then let's go to the theatre. 10. He kept us in doubt up to the last moment.

[1] 'should go': use the past subjunctive.

LESSON 25. AUGMENTATIVES, DIMINUTIVES, AND NUMERALS

Study **35–40** *inclusive.*

EXERCISE 25

1. *Pronounce and translate:* cinquantatrè, settantasei, novantadue, centodiciassette, dugentoquarantotto, quattrocentottantuno, seicentotrentanove, novecentosessantasette, milletrecentoventidue, millenovecentoquindici, tremilaquarantacinque.

2. *Read in Italian:* 31, 243, 854, 1265, 1492, 1621, 1775, 1915, 1998, 2001; Sisto IV, Innocenzo VIII, Alessandro VI, Pio III, Giulio II, Leone X, Adriano VI, Clemente VII, Pio IX, Leone XIII, Pio X, Benedetto XV, Giovanni XXIII, Giovanni Paolo II.

3. *Translate:* sono le tre, sono le cinque e dieci, sono le dieci e un quarto, sono le sei e mezzo, sono le nove meno venti, sono le otto meno un quarto, sono le due meno dodici.

4. *Translate into Italian:* it's four o'clock, it's 6:12, it's half past eight, it's 25 minutes of nine, it's six minutes of five; April 1, April 2, April 3, April 22.

5. *Translate in terms of American money:*[1] dieci centesimi, cinquanta centesimi, una lira e venti centesimi, trentun soldo, due lire e quaranta, cinque lire e mezzo, sette lire e cinquanta, venti lire, sessantadue lire e quarantacinque centesimi, mille lire.

[1] 2,000 *lira* = 1 *dollar.*

6. *Translate in terms of Italian money:* $.05, $.18, $.25, $.42, $1.00, $1.50, $6.38, $100.00.

7. *Study these sentences:* 1. La lettera fu datata "Roma, venerdì 15 febbraio 2001." 2. Lo fornì di una ventina di lire, troppe per chi le dava, troppo poche per chi le riceveva. 3. Il costo totale sarebbe di lire cinquantasei e centesimi settantacinque. 4. Lui allora aveva ventiquattro anni, e lei soltanto diciotto. 5. Erano in tutto quindici biglietti da dieci lire. 6. Nel quarantotto combattè a Milano contro gli Austriaci. 7. Ha pubblicato or ora un volume sulla pittura del

Trecento. 8. Vi andò nei primi giorni del 1612, e vi rimase fino a mezzo il 1614. 9. A che ora parte il treno? Alle quindici e mezzo, cioè alle tre e mezzo dopo mezzogiorno. 10. La raccolta più importante delle poesie italiane più antiche è il codice vaticano 3793.

8. *Translate into Italian:* 1. They woke me at five o'clock. It was dark and cold, and it was snowing hard. 2. The sonnet consists of 14 lines, and each line of 11 syllables. 3. The 15th century and the 16th are the two centuries of the Renaissance in Italy. 4. He made him repeat it five times. 5. The work of Manzoni falls in the first half of the 19th century. 6. I gave him 300,000 *lire*. and he bought two pairs of shoes. 7. Seven months have 31 days, four 30, and one 28 or 29. 8. Would you do me the favor to (*di*) lend me 10,000 *lire* or so until Monday? 9. From the tower one saw thousands [1] and thousands of persons crowded in the streets and the squares. 10. Victor Emmanuel II was the first king of the Third Italy.

[1] Use *migliaio.*

LESSON 26. IRREGULAR VERBS OF THE SECOND CONJUGATION (continued)

Study **92,** 18–22; *also* **79** (*b*) 1.

EXERCISE 26

1. *Translate:* varrò, valse, valgono, valemmo, valevano, valsero, vogliono, vuoi, vorrà, volevo, vuole, vorrei, paiamo, parvi, pari, parremmo, parvero, parrete, potei, possono, potendo, potete, potè, può, persuada, persuase, persuadevano, persuadiamo, persuaso, persuadi; lo varranno, l' hanno voluto, ci era parso, non avreste potuto, persuadeteli, non lo valeva, vorranno farlo?, gli parve, non si può, sono stati persuasi.

2. *Translate into Italian:* it would be worth, we are worth, it was worth, you were worth, they wished, I was wishing, we shall wish, you wished, it seems, we should seem, they seem, seeming, he can, they will be able, you were able, they can, we should persuade, let him persuade, I persuaded, let us persuade; will it be worth it?, did they wish it?, it seemed to us, we have not been able, haven't they persuaded him?

3. *Study these sentences:* 1. Rimanga se può, ma vada se ha da studiare. 2. Quanto crede che valgano quegli anelli? 3. È difficile, lo so, ma cosa vuole? faccia tutto quello che potrà. 4. Aveva fatto come pareva meglio a lui. 5. La chiesa sta più in alto: ci vuole un' ora per arrivarci. Oh allora non vale la pena. 6. Chi non può fare come vuole, faccia come può. 7. Non si può contentarlo: più ne ha e più ne vuole. 8. Due non basteranno: ce ne vogliono almeno quattro. 9. Se potesse farmi questo piacere Le sarei mille volte obbligato. 10. Volere è potere.

4. *Translate into Italian:* 1. We shall not be able to persuade him. 2. They seem large, but they cannot be good. 3. If you wish it, they will stay with you. 4. I should not have thought that they were worth[1] so much. 5. They owe me 20,000 *lire*, and they aren't willing to pay me. 6. I wanted to give it to you, but I couldn't. 7. My head aches so much that I can't study. 8. He's going away tomorrow, although he wants[1] to stay here. 9. I should like to speak to you about it; could you stay ten minutes or so? 10. It takes a brave man to (*a*) do a thing like that.

[1] Use the subjunctive.

LESSON 27. AUXILIARY VERBS

Study **54, 57.**

EXERCISE 27

1. *Translate:* devo parlare, dovevo parlare, dovei parlare, dovrò parlare, dovrei parlare, ho dovuto parlare, avevo dovuto parlare, avrò dovuto parlare, avrei dovuto parlare; posso parlare, potevo parlare, potei parlare, potrò parlare, potrei parlare, ho potuto parlare, avevo potuto parlare, avrò potuto parlare, avrei potuto parlare; voglio parlare, volevo parlare, volli parlare, vorrò parlare, vorrei parlare, ho voluto parlare, avevo voluto parlare, avrò voluto parlare, avrei voluto parlare; glielo avevano dovuto dare, non avremmo potuto persuaderlo, avreste voluto vederli?, non era potuto entrare, avrebbe dovuto finirlo, avevamo voluto comprarne; stiamo per andarcene, rimase tradito, va studiato così, lo fecero portare, bisognerebbe prestarglieli, hanno da cercarlo, non saprei spiegarlo, non potemmo a meno di non tacere.

2. *Translate into Italian:* they are to speak, we must speak, you were to speak, he had to speak, we shall have to speak, I ought to speak, he would have to speak, they have been obliged to speak, he must have spoken, she had had to speak, we shall have had to speak, he ought to have spoken, they were not able to speak, he may have spoken, they could have spoken, I should not have been able to speak, I might have spoken, will they be willing to speak?, he had been willing to speak.

3. *Study these sentences:* 1. Avendo tanto da fare in città, avreste dovuto partire col treno delle sette e mezzo. 2. Volle fare una visita a casa sua per vedere i suoi, che non aveva visti da tanto tempo. 3. A quel tempo non si poteva vedere tutto ciò che s' è veduto dopo. 4. Lasciano la scuola con l' odio per le cose di cui si sono dovuti occupare e per gli autori di cui hanno dovuto studiare le opere. 5. Non capisco come una cosa simile abbia potuto accadere. 6. Dopo aver fatto tutti gli sforzi possibili, si è dovuto capitolare. 7. Non sarebbe potuto arrivare a Firenze neanche la sera. 8. Ti chiamerò presto perchè dovrai andare alla stazione a piedi. 9. Aveva sperato che nella casa paterna avrebbe potuto godere almeno un po' d' affetto. 10. Molto sa chi poco sa, se tacer sa.

4. *Study these sentences:* 1. If I saw him, I should have to speak to him. 2. You ought to know when you will be able to bring it to us. 3. He would have had to keep still: he didn't know their names. 4. You must work if you want to please him. 5. They may find it, but I'm afraid that they have[1] left it in the city. 6. It grieves me, but I shall have to do it. 7. We ought to have kept still, but we couldn't help laughing. 8. He would like to know why they had to go away. 9. In what might I have the honor of serving you? 10. He always wanted to do what seemed best to him.

[1] Use the subjunctive.

LESSON 28. IRREGULAR VERBS OF THE THIRD CONJUGATION

Study **92** (*e*), (*f*), (*g*) (*on* *p.*92), 24–73 [*omitting verbs marked* Rare, *and forms in parentheses*].

EXERCISE 28

1. *Conjugate the present tenses of* affliggere, conoscere, crescere, *and* leggere.

2. *Translate:* accendendo, accese, afflitto, alludono, ardeva, arderà, risolvette, chiude, chiuderemo, conosciuto, conosca, conobbero, corriamo, correvano, corse, cresce, crescerà, cuoce, decida, decisi, difeso, diresse, dirigerò, discussero, distinti, divisero, esistito, esistono, esprimano, espresse, fitto, finga, fingiamo, frigge, fuso, invasero, leggano, lessero, mettiamo, misi.

3. *Translate into Italian:* I light, he alluded, I will shut, he knew, run, grown, cooking, they decided, let us divide, it exists, he will express, fried, they will invade, let him read, they put.

4. *Study these sentences:* 1. Gli espresse il suo rincrescimento per quel che si era fatto. 2. Gli si leggeva la gioia nel viso. 3. Ci mise davanti[1] un mucchio di carte. 4. Mi lasci parlare; non chiuda il cuore alla pietà. 5. Lo conobbi a Firenze l' anno scorso. 6. Il fondo del romanzo è storico, ma vi è mescolato il finto col vero. 7. Più li conosce e più gli cresce l' amicizia per loro. 8. Le opinioni si divisero: alcuni applaudirono la sua azione, altri la biasimarono. 9. Nel Cinquecento Francesi e Spagnoli corsero tutta l' Italia. 10. Distinguiamo nel suo carattere quel che vi è di sincero[2] e quel che vi è di falso.

[1] *Ci mise davanti*, 'He put before us.' When the logical object of an Italian preposition is an unemphatic personal pronoun, the use of a disjunctive pronoun is often avoided by putting a conjunctive pronoun before the verb and treating the preposition as an adverb.

[2] *quel che vi è di sincero*, 'its elements of sincerity.'

5. *Translate into Italian:* 1. It's the third time she has read that book. 2. Do you know my friend Mr. Ghedíni? 3. He went to the door, shut it, and put the key in his pocket. 4. I lighted the other

light and ran into the room.   5. Do you want fried eggs?   6. What
is she cooking now?   7. Do me the favor to (*di*) shut the door.   Have
those windows been shut?   8. Where did you put my hat?   I have
to go now, and I can't find it.   9. To whom was he alluding when he
spoke of his enemies?   10. The schools will be closed from June to
September.

LESSON 29. MOODS AND TENSES

Study **69–76** *inclusive.*

EXERCISE 29

1. *Study these sentences:* 1. Il lasciar le mura della città e il rivedere
la casa paterna nel piccolo villaggio furono sensazioni piene di gioia.
2. Vedendolo venire con quei libri in mano, n' era molto lieta, sperando
che glieli avrebbe regalati.   3. Partirono poco dopo il levar del sole,
e tornarono sul far della sera.   4. Non sapeva nè come fare nè dove
andare.   5. A continuare così si corre il pericolo di perdere tutto ciò
che si è guadagnato.   6. Credè di aver trovato quel che cercava da
tanto tempo.   7. Quando avrai gli anni che ho io, non sarai mica sì
pronto a giudicare gli altri.   8. Finita la lezione, tornarono a casa,
e trovarono il cugino che li aspettava.   9. Non ci avrebbe nulla [1] da
dare a un povero cieco?   10. Torno pian piano alla casa; picchio;
nessuno risponde; entro; e ci trovo — cosa crede?   11. Inutile
illudersi; non c' è più speranza.   12. L' esser simpatici non basta, no;
bisogna essere utili a qualche cosa.   13. Rimarrai fino alle cinque, non
è vero?   Non mi dire di no.   14. Quando arrivai a casa, mio padre
non c' era.   Mia madre si spaventò, perchè vedendomi così pallido
mi credette malato.   15. Augurata la buona notte al padrone, se
n' andò in fretta.   16. Lui gli vendè l' anima, e il diavolo gli promise
che per un certo tempo gli avrebbe ubbidito come a suo signore.   17.
Tornati che furono, domandarono subito da mangiare.   18. In quel
vagone è proibito fumare.   19. Appena mi vide, la sua espressione, da
irrequieta che era, [2] si fece minacciosa.   20. La strada che mena a
Sorrento è un succedersi continuo di punti di vista stupendi.

[1] *Non ci avrebbe nulla,* 'Haven't you anything?'   The use of the
past future gives the sentence an apologetic tone.

[2] *da irrequieta che era,* 'instead of anxious.'

2. *Translate into Italian:* 1. Do *you* prefer traveling to studying? 2. I'll have it given back at once. 3. Their manners may be crude, but they are sincere. 4. Gratitude is to be praised. 5. You know, doubtless,[1] that my brother has returned. 6. When you arrive in (*a*) Florence, you will find at the hotel a letter from (*di*) my agent. 7. Have you not heard him spoken of? 8. I have been here for two months, working[2] in the libraries. 9. Where are they? They are there outside, waiting for[3] you. 10. He ought to have spoken to you about it himself, instead of writing.

[1] Express this idea in the verb.
[2] Translate by *a* with the infinitive.
[3] Use a relative clause instead of a participle.

LESSON 30. IRREGULAR VERBS OF THE THIRD CONJUGATION (continued)

Study **92,** 75–124 [*omitting verbs marked* Rare *or* Poetical, *and forms in parentheses*].

EXERCISE 30

1. *Conjugate the present tenses of* muovere *and* sorgere.

2. *Translate:* mordono, mosse, moverà, nasce, nacquero, nascosto, nascondevo, negletto, offendendo, offesi, perso, perderebbe, pioveva, pioverà, prenda, preso, proteggono, protese, redenta, raso, rendevano, ridi, risero, risponda, risposi, rotti, ruppero, scendemmo, scorgiamo, scriva, scrissi, scosso, sorge, spargeva, sporgono, successe, teso, torce, torse, ucciderà, vince vinsero, volsi, volgerebbe.

3. *Translate into Italian:* they were moving, he was born, hide, we are losing, it is raining, let them take, he laughed, they answered, broken, write, he shook, they rise, she spent, it happens, it would kill, let him live, they turned.

4. *Study these sentences:* 1. Se te li presto, quando me li renderai? 2. La scodella gli cadde per terra e si ruppe in tre pezzi. 3. Soli quelli che gli vivono da presso sanno che lui è anche più buono che

Baptistry in front of Cathedral, Florence

Calcio (medievel football), Florence

grande. 4. Scriva un po' meglio; altrimenti non potranno leggere niente. 5. Successe una pausa, rotta finalmente da un grido di terrore. 6. Non si lasci vincere dall' ira. 7. Il codice fu scritto, pare, verso la fine del Trecento. 8. È successo quello che pur troppo non poteva non succedere. 9. L' Italia nacque come nascono tutte le nazioni nuove, dall' energia dei meno che porta al destino l' inerzia dei più. 10. Ben perduto è conosciuto.

5. *Translate into Italian:* 1. He put it on the table, but someone has moved it. 2. Let's stand under that tree while it rains. 3. If he had moved it, it would have fallen. 4. There the mountains rise from the waters of the lake. 5. Goldoni and Alfieri lived in the 18th century. 6. They are all running: what has [1] happened? 7. He shook his head, smiling, and turned [2] toward the door. 8. When I spoke to him about it, he laughed, and did not answer me. 9. In what year was Dante born? 10. They don't think he will live [3] if he remains here.

[1] Translate by the proper form of *essere*.

[2] Put the proper reflexive pronoun before the verb.

[3] Use the subjunctive.

LESSON 31. CONJUNCTIONS

Study **78**.

EXERCISE 31

1. *Give the meanings of these conjunctions:* a meno che non, acciochè, affinchè, anzi, avanti che, benchè, chè, dacchè, dato che, donde, dovunque, finchè, finchè non, mentre, neanche, ossia, perchè (*with indicative*), perchè (*with subjunctive*), per quanto, poichè, prima che, purchè, pure, qualunque, quasi, sebbene, se non che, siccome.

2. *Study these sentences:* 1. Seguitò a filare finchè il figlio del re non se ne fu andato. 2. L' avrebbe potuto fare, purchè l' avesse voluto. 3. Molti sono e i difetti e i pericoli di una tale decisione 4. I giorni passavano senza che il padre gliene parlasse. 5. Non l' avrebbe mai saputo, se non che le si spedì da Milano un giornale colla notizia. 6. Lo conoscevo nei giorni che era qui a visitare la nonna. 7. Non ci aiuta punto, anzi c' impedisce. 8. Le sue espressioni, per quanto fossero forti, non erano esagerate. 9. Mi dispiacque di non averla veduta prima che partisse. 10. Non voleva nemmeno vederlo, non che parlargli.

3. *Translate into Italian:* 1. They were sitting in the parlor while I was writing the letters. 2. Who is going there today? Either he or I. 3. They received them as if they were old friends. 4. He remained at the window until he heard them knock. 5. We will pardon him provided he will promise to (*di*) give it back to us at once. 6. I found it without difficulty, although he had hidden it with the greatest care. 7. When you see him, do me the favor to (*di*) give him these tickets. 8. I should like to speak to him before he goes. 9. Since they are worth what they cost, why don't you buy them? 10. I sent you [1] here in order that you should study, not in order that you should waste my money.

[1] Use the second person singular in translating this sentence.

LESSON 32. IRREGULAR VERBS OF THE THIRD
CONJUGATION (continued)

Study **92**, 127–133.

EXERCISE 32

1. *Translate:* bevano, bevve, berà, avrebbe bevuto, beviamo, bee, chiesto, chiesi, chiedete, chiederanno, chieda, chiedevano, condurrei, condotto, condussero, conduca, conduci, sono condotti, noceva, nuoce, nocque, ponga, posto, posi, poniamo, porrà, pone, traevano, trassero, traggono, trarremo, avevano tratto, tragga.

2. *Translate into Italian:* they would drink, he was drinking, I drank, let him drink, let us ask, he will have asked, they asked, we were asking, I conducted, let them conduct, he has conducted, I was conducting, it will harm, they harmed, we put, put, they are putting, they will put, he dragged, we should drag, I have dragged.

3. *Study these sentences:* 1. Quando avrà sei anni lo porremo a scuola. 2. Se bevesse un po' di quel vino, gli farebbe bene. 3. Il fumare troppo gli ha nociuto gravemente. 4. Non le sa negare quel che gli chiede.[1] 5. Soffrì lunghi anni di una malattia di cuore che finalmente lo trasse alla morte. 6. Ho sete: dammi da bere. 7. Vorrei chiederle una vacanza di pochi giorni, finchè mi rimetta un po' in salute. 8. Finì col darsi per vinto, e col concedere tutto quanto gli era richiesto. 9. Questo mi ha indotto a riconoscere in lui l' autore delle mie disgrazie. 10. Tutte le strade conducono a Roma.

[1] The personal object of *chiedere* is indirect.

4. *Translate into Italian:* 1. Drink a little water. 2. They are putting it in the other corner of the room. 3. Clouds of smoke were rising, and they were dragging everything out of the house. 4. I put it there because I found it there: don't move it. 5. Go and ask him why he didn't read what I wrote. 6. If you stay to dinner, we'll take [1] you to the theatre this evening. 7. The house was placed so that one could see between the hills as far as the river. 8. If you had asked me for [2] it, I should have given it to you. 9. Then he drew his sword and took [3] his place at the head of his company. 10. He put his hands on my shoulders and asked me if I had been a good boy.

[1] Use *menare*.   [2] *Chiedere* means ' to ask for.'   [3] Use *prendere*.

LESSON 33. THE SUBJUNCTIVE

Study **77** *through* (*f*).

EXERCISE 33

1. *Study these sentences:* 1. Senta: potrebbe prestarmi per qualche giorno una ventina di lire? 2. Bisognava che ne trovassero un altro perfettamente simile a quello che si era perduto. 3. Ci faccia sapere quale difficoltà ci sia. 4. È il poeta più classico e nondimeno il più moderno che abbia l' Italia. 5. Quanto male ci ha fatto! Non l' avessimo mai visto! 6. Se avesse uno che si prendesse cura di lui, anche lui potrebbe far meglio. 7. Legga, scriva, non sia mai ozioso, non chieda mai a nessuno, non speri che nel suo lavoro. 8. Non vi è più alcuno che creda alle loro storie. 9. Ti sia sempre nella mente che il compiacersi dei mali degli altri è crudeltà. 10. Se vuole andare, se ne vada; per me, ci avrei piacere. 11. Era un' idea di cui parlava in ogni conversazione che riguardasse il suo avvenire. 12. Fossi tu qui con me! Pur troppo bisogna ora che tu rimanga in città. 13. Badi di non parlarmi più così; e basti l' avviso per questa volta 14. Si mostrò pronto a tutto ciò che potesse piacere ai superiori. 15. Domandò alla serva se si potesse parlare al padrone. 16. Divisero la città in sei parti, ed elessero dodici cittadini che la governassero. 17. Nessuno se ne meravigli: era da aspettarsi. 18. Benchè non vi sia niente che abbia l' aria di essere esagerato, tutto il libro è una terribile accusa. 19. Se ci va spesso, è perchè ci si mangia bene. 20. Parrebbe impossibile a chi non lo conoscesse per quell' uomo che è.

2. *Translate into Italian:* 1. If *he* were here, perhaps he would be able to give us a little light. 2. He asked me if I were really a count. 3. This is the first and only pleasure I have had since I have been here. 4. It would be enough to (*per*) convince one who had not sworn to remain in the dark. 5. They wanted to give her a name that should recall her aunt's affection. 6. Russia is the only country in (*di*) Europe that he hasn't visited. 7. They are things that happen often, although they seem impossible. 8. Did they ask you if you had read his last novel? 9. Wherever I go, that scene is ever before my eyes. 10. They had placed a guard at the only door by which he could have escaped.

LESSON 34. IRREGULAR VERBS OF THE THIRD CONJUGATION (continued)

Study **92,** 134–148.

EXERCISE 34

1. *Translate:* coglie, colse, coglieremo, scelga, scelto, sceglievi, sciogliemmo, sciogliendo, avrebbe sciolto, tolgono, torrà, torrei, giungete, giunsero, sono giunti, piangi, pianse, piangerò, pinge, pingano, pingeranno, spegne, spense, spegneva, spinga, aveva spinto, spinsero, stretto, stringono, stringemmo.

2. *Translate into Italian:* they gather, we gathered, I was choosing, let them choose, we have taken, I shall take, you are weeping, I wept, they extinguish, we shall extinguish, you were pushing, I had pushed, we are bound, bind.

3. *Study these sentences:* 1. Il sole che calava tingeva di rosso le acque del lago. 2. La Cappella Sistina fu dipinta da Michelangelo tra il 1508 e il 1512. 3. Gli afferrò la destra e gliela strinse con forza, ma al ritirare la mano la vide tinta di sangue. 4. Tutti quelli con cui era stretto d' amicizia se n' andarono, lasciandolo solo solo. 5. Non si sapeva se riderne o piangerne; infatti alcuni piansero, sorridendo però fra le lagrime. 6. Se si potessero parlare una volta, le difficoltà sarebbero subito sciolte. 7. Erano giunti a un tal punto che bisognava o vincere o perder ogni cosa. 8. Stava inginocchioni colle mani giunte in atto di preghiera. 9. Gli tolse di mano il denaro senza nemmeno ringraziarlo. 10. L' imperatore, poeta lui stesso, protesse i poeti e li accolse e onorò nella sua corte.

4. *Translate into Italian:* 1. Among all the employees they chose him as the most industrious. 2. Then they looked at each other, and began to weep. 3. Go and gather some[1] flowers for the vases in the parlor. 4. When we arrived, the sacristan was putting out the lights. 5. Take[2] those papers from the table and put them on the desk. 6. In ancient times cities were surrounded by walls and ditches. 7. He pushed me into (*a*) this business, and now he ought to help me. 8. They were crying like children; she was going from one to the other, trying to (*di*) comfort them. 9. We found ourselves compelled to (*a*) ask him for it. 10. He might have surrendered: he chose to (*di*) die.

[1] Use the partitive construction.   [2] Use *togliere*.

LESSON 35. PREPOSITIONS

Study **79.**

EXERCISE 35

1. *Give the meaning of these prepositions:* accanto a, al di là di, attorno a, circa, contro, dentro di, dietro, dirimpetto a, dopo, eccetto, fin da, fino a, fuori di, innanzi, intorno a, lungo, oltre, quanto a, rispetto a, secondo, sino a, sotto, su, tra, tranne.

2. *Study these sentences:* 1. Se vuol rimanere con noi, ha da fare quel che voglio io. 2. Ora le ha comprato una macchina da cucire. 3. Ce lo giurò per quanto aveva di più caro. 4. Da allora in poi visse da buon cristiano. 5. Lo so per certo che oggi non gli hanno dato da mangiare. 6. Al di là del fiume si vedevano delle vecchie torri medioevali. 7. Ci si ammalavano a centinaia per giorno. 8. C' era una volta un bel fanciullo dai capelli biondi e dagli occhi azzurri, che aveva fra i dieci e i dodici anni. 9. Lui, poveretto, stava zitto a guardarmi, ed io gli parlai con un tono da fargli coraggio. 10. Alla porta della chiesa c' era una vecchia che accattava da chi entrava; il ragazzo andò da lei, e le diede metà del suo pane.

3. *Translate into Italian:* 1. They want to have (*fare*) lunch before the others. 2. You can't persuade him to vote against the government. 3. We'll be at your house in an hour and a half. 4. They will arrive on (*con*) the 5.20 train. 5. He went to France in 1995, and remained there for three or four years. 6. Go tell[1] them they'll have to do without me. 7. His arrival was greeted by all with an exclamation of surprise. 8. I begged my father to take[2] me to the city to see my cousins. 9. They have been living in Venice for six months. 10. You ought to do something for him instead of letting him suffer so.

[1] Use *dire*, the personal object of which is indirect.
[2] Use *menare*.

LESSON 36. IRREGULAR VERBS OF THE FOURTH CONJUGATION

Study **92,** 149–163.

EXERCISE 36

1. *Translate:* aprono, aprì, sono aperti, copra, coperse, coprite, offrimmo, offrirà, offersi, soffrii, hanno sofferto, soffrirei, costruivano, digerisce, esaurito, è stato sepolto, cucivo, empiono, empì, empiere, muoia, morranno, è morto, segui, seguì, seguirei, sparve, spariscono, sparirà.

2. *Translate into Italian:* we opened, they would open, cover, I covered, let us offer, he has offered, he is suffering, you will suffer, she was sewing, he died, I shall die, following, let us follow, it would disappear, they disappeared.

3. *Study these sentences:* 1. Se la tua patria avrà bisogno di te, offrile te stesso. 2. Le finestre dello studio si aprono all' est. 3. Possa tu godere quant' io ho sofferto e soffro. 4. Tutti i figli le erano morti, l' uno dopo l' altro, ed era rimasta sola sola al mondo. 5. Gli apparve in sogno un fantasma che lo minacciava di morte. 6. Lui proseguiva il lavoro senza badare a ciò che facevano gli altri. 7. Di questo si tratterà nel capitolo seguente. 8. Ha la sposa ricca, ma morrebbe piuttosto che chiederle un soldo. 9. Compiuti gli studi, fece un lungo viaggio per l' Europa. 10. Muor giovane colui che al cielo è caro.

4. *Translate into Italian:* 1. If the window isn't open, do me the favor to open it. 2. He died last night at half past eleven. 3. Those are old customs that now are disappearing. 4. Let's offer them to her, and if she doesn't want them we'll keep them for ourselves. 5. The king is dead: long[1] live the king! 6. She covered her face with her hands and wept. 7. You have written a song that will not die. 8. I opened the window and called them, but they didn't hear me. 9. If I suffered as they have suffered, I should die. 10. They are building a theatre on the site of those old shops.

[1] Omit this word in translating.

LESSON 37.   THE SUBJUNCTIVE (continued)

Study **77** (*g*), (*h*), (*i*).

EXERCISE 37

1. *Study these sentences:*[1] 1. Pare che se ne siano scordati affatto. 2. Badi che non gli facciano male! 3. Se le dispiace che lo facciano gli altri, non lo faccia lei stesso. 4. Mi rincresce che Lei abbia dovuto partire senza vederli. 5. Non permise però che finisse così. 6. Cosa

[1] In several of these sentences the *che* clause should be replaced, in translation, by an infinitive construction.

pensi tu che ci sia da fare? 7. Non sapeva che s' era proibito che i forestieri visitassero la fortezza? 8. Non potrai venire domani? Avrei bisogno che tu mi aiutassi. 9. Il ponte par che segni il punto in cui il fiume entra nel lago. 10. Non si può non sospettare che l' abbiano saputo. 11. Pareva ci fossero degli spiriti invisibili. 12. Teme che gli si possa togliere quel che ha guadagnato. 13. Voglia il cielo che non venga un giorno in cui si penta di non avermi ascoltato. 14. Lascino ch' io gli parli ancora una volta prima che se ne vada! 15. Chi vuoi che le compri, delle scarpe così? 16. Ho letto quelle pagine col più vivo interesse, e vorrei che le potessero legger tutti. 17. Se vuole che gli si porti rispetto, deve imparare a rispettare gli altri. 18. L' ho sentito negare che la vita per sè stessa sia desiderabile. 19. Pagare e poi pagare, perchè i nostri soldati vadano a morire nell' Africa, non si può pretendere che piaccia al popolo italiano. 20. Non possiamo permettere che certi punti del Mediterraneo siano presi ed occupati da coloro che un giorno potrebbero esserci nemici.

2. *Translate into Italian:* 1. I am surprised that you do not understand it. 2. I know they wanted me to stay[1] until tomorrow. 3. It seemed to us that they were afraid that someone would recognize them. 4. He begged them to give[1] him a little bread. 5. It may be believed that he has earned in this way more than 200,000 *lire*. 6. He was ashamed that they should think that he had not been content. 7. Yesterday I heard that he was a little better. 8. Doesn't it seem to you that he is asking too much? 9. He ordered them all to be[1] silent. 10. I hope he'll give you all you want.

[1] Use a *che* clause, turning the preceding personal pronoun into a subject.

LESSON 38. IRREGULAR VERBS OF THE FOURTH
CONJUGATION (continued)

Study **92,** 164–168.

EXERCISE 38

1. *Translate:* dissero, diceva, è stato detto, di', dicano, diresti, sali, salga, salite, salivano, salgo, salirà, vieni, verrà, venne, sono venuti, venga, verrei, udirono, ode, udiranno, esca, usciamo.

2. *Translate into Italian:* you say, he said, say, they are ascending, I ascended, let us ascend, they came, I shall come, she has come, they hear, hearing, we had heard, he is going out, they went out, I should go out.

3. *Study these sentences:* 1. Quando uscii di camera, mia madre, già alzata, mi aspettava per dirmi addio. 2. Che cosa vuol dire questa parola? 3. Ci dice che sono venuti tutti, e che rimarranno fino alle dieci. 4. I prezzi delle carni sono già saliti assai. 5. Morì benedicendo i figli e i figli de' figli suoi. 6. Rifiutò nondimeno l'aiuto che gli veniva offerto. 7. Erano sempre severi con lui, senza mai dirne il perchè. 8. Poi le venne in mente che aveva promesso di restituirglieli il giorno dopo. 9. I fatti che siamo venuti narrando bastano a dimostrare la falsità dell'accusa. 10. Dimmi con chi pratichi e ti dirò chi sei.

4. *Translate into Italian:* 1. They come and they disappear. Where do they all go? Tell me, do they all die? 2. I'm afraid they won't come if it rains. 3. If it's he, call him, and tell him I should like to speak to him. 4. He is much better now; he goes out almost every day. 5. Let them tell him to come at once. 6. They told me that he had arrived Monday. 7. They came; I heard them open the door; they went up; and then they disappeared. I went out, but they had gone away. 8. Did they tell you when they would come? 9. If he had told you that, what would you have done? 10. I came, I saw, I conquered.

LESSON 39. ADVERBS AND INDEFINITE PRONOUNS

Study **80–91** *inclusive.*

EXERCISE 39

1. *Give the meanings of these indefinite pronouns and adjectives:* alcuno, altri, altrui, ambedue, certo, chi, chicchessia, ciascheduno, ciascuno, meno, nessuno, nulla, ognuno, parecchi, per quanto, qualchecosa, qualcuno, qualunque, si, un tale.

2. *Study these sentences:* 1. Sentì qualcheduno che piangeva lì dentro. 2. Se fossi Lei, gli scriverei un' altra volta, benchè non Le abbia mai risposto. 3. Sentiva un gran desiderio di fare qualcosa di strano e di terribile. 4. L' uno e l' altro me n' hanno dato parola. 5. Ci andremo insieme, non è vero? Non mi dica di no. 6. Cosa fai lì? O che vuoi bruciar la casa? 7. Ed ecco che le apparì sulla soglia un non so che di bianco. 8. L' ha cambiato tutto, ed ora sì che mi piace! 9. Non si va in quel luogo se non per vedere la fontana. 10. Questo mondo è fatto a scale, chi le scende e chi le sale.

3. *Translate into Italian:* 1. Do you go there often now? What? Yes, every eight or ten days. 2. I shall be there too, day after to-morrow, and I shall stay the whole week. 3. We saw certain things there that we didn't like at all. 4. I should never have believed that they would both leave me. 5. Take care that no one sees you start. 6. Each of you ought to give him something. 7. One must respect the rights of others. 8. One can't say, though, that such a work isn't worth anything. 9. I have but two, but if you want one of them, here it is. 10. He must have known them well; he has lived there for several years.

LESSON 40. REVIEW

EXERCISE 40

1. *Give the plural of each of the following combinations:* l' animale grigio, il mio braccio, del caffè nuovo, nell' estasi (*fem.*), poca facoltà, dalla tua famiglia, la mano bianca, l' operaio eroico, l' origine mistica, quel paio, il gran palco, col vecchio porco, la radice profonda, l' ultima riga, al bel rogo, lo scherzo comico, sullo scoglio pittoresco, il buon sindaco, il telegramma lungo, il suo zio.

2. *Translate:* lo apra, l' avremmo, me lo chiesero, li coglie, condottovi, ve lo conobbe, glielo devono, ce lo dia, ditele, lui li ha divisi, eccotelo, n' esce, glielo fece portare, vi foste, ci pianse, lo lessi loro, l' aveva mosso, muoiano loro, vi nacque, offertoglielo, vi sarebbe parso, dovreste piangerne, lo potemmo vedere, me lo rese, li ruppero, si vorrebbe sapere, le scrissi, avrebbe dovuto seguirli, ci steste, l' avranno stretto, lei tacque, lo tenga lei, li trae, ci vanno, erano venuti, ci videro, ci ha vissuto.

3. *Translate into Italian:* will you be there?, *they* chose it, we had come, he was dying there, give it to him, will they go there?, he has been killed, do you know it?, do you know him?, they would have lost it, they ought to have opened it, he could not persuade him, it pleased him, I put it there, they made me read it, *we* shall remain there, it seemed to them, they have seen us, tell it to *me*, they wish it.

4. *Study these sentences:* 1. Mi rispose di sì,[1] e che ci avrebbe molto piacere. 2. Lui piangeva piangeva, e gli altri stavano zitti a guardarlo. 3. Sedevano attorno alla tavola, impazienti che si servisse la colazione. 4. Morto, le parve assai più grande e buono che non le fosse mai parso vivo. 5. Finalmente riuscì a farselo restituire. 6. Gli abitanti si rifugiavano su per i monti, portandovi quel che avevan di meglio.[2] 7. Nel succedersi degli avvenimenti in mezzo ai quali veniva innalzato al soglio, parve manifestarsi la mano della Provvidenza. 8. Prevedeva di doversene tornare a casa, di lì a pochi giorni, povero com' era venuto. 9. Che molti di quei temi esistessero nella poesia più antica, ci pare pienamente dimostrato. 10. Se li perdo, che sarà di me? 11. Le stava davanti, quasi aspettasse che gli dicesse d' andarsene. 12. Queste poche pagine poste in principio serviranno di introduzione a tutto il libro. 13. Decise di sentire tranquillamente ciò che allo zio piacesse d' aggiungere. 14. Si trasse dal dito l' anello magico, e se lo mise in bocca. 15. Adesso le spiegherò, meglio ch' io non facessi allora, che cosa vogliamo fare. 16. Non posso non farlo, nè vorrei, anche potendo, non farlo. 17. Una società che si formi così deve finire con l' esser composta di ribelli. 18. Parleremo prima di lui, non perchè lui sia il più antico, ma perchè è il più importante. 19. Non si erano mai accorti delle occhiate di ammirazione con cui lui li guardava. 20. Alcuni contadini, credendo che cercasse dei tesori, e persuasi che avesse già qualche cosa di prezioso in tasca, gli si avvicinarono per accertarsene.

[1] *di sì,* 'that he would.'

[2] *quel che avevan di meglio,* 'the best of their belongings.'

5. *Translate into Italian:* 1. He told me that he had desired it for many years. 2. I should not have believed that you had spoken of it to him. 3. If I'm not mistaken, we shall be there in a few minutes. 4. I am surprised that they haven't called you yet. 5. I know him only by (*di*) sight; I have seen him several times in the Public Gardens. 6. The prisoner has [1] escaped and has hidden himself in the wood; the farmers are protecting him. 7. I was sure of it, although her face did not betray any surprise. 8. Did they tell you when they would come to your house? 9. We could have given it to you, if we had known that you wanted it. 10. It isn't impossible that he has seen it, but I don't believe so.

[1] Translate by the proper form of *essere*.

LESSON 41. OLD AND POETIC FORMS

Study section **3** (*f*) *on p.* 7, *the second footnote on p.* 11, *the second footnote on p.* 17, *section* **44** (*a*), *the first footnote on p.* 38, *section* **48** (*e*), *the footnote on p.* 42 , *section* **63** (*d*), *section* **68,** *the forms given in section* **92** *in parentheses and footnotes, the verbs numbered* 23 *and* 169, *and those among nos.* 24–125 *that are marked* Rare *or* Poetical; *also the verbs* gire *and* ire *given on p.* 102.

EXERCISE 41

1. *Give the modern prose equivalents of:* lo giorno, i capei, tai re, ne [1] parla, mel dice, nol credo, sen va, ameria, parleria, parlaro, parlerebbono, parloe, parle, parlar, compro,[2] sentio, fenno, feste, face, diero, ave, avea, avieno, aggia, arà, ei, caggiano, dee, denno, il veggo, volsi, puote, ponno, poria, enno, suto, sete, fora, foro, fia, chieggo, corre, torre, piagne, vegna.

[1] Do not regard this *ne* as meaning 'of it.'
[2] Do not regard this form as present indicative.

2. *Study these lines:*
1. Or fia ch' ei vegna solo?   Ahi, meglio fora!
2. Udrassi allor chi puote il ver narrare.
3. Morte emmi il gire, e il rimaner m' è morte.
4. Stavvi sempre — nol sai? — cui starvi lice.
5. Tormeli credi?   Chi dietti tal forza?

Temple of Condord, Agrigento, Sicily

Scaliger's Castle, Sirmione

6. La patria amar; lieti per lei moriro.
7. Il veggio, o parmi, coi fratei venire.
8. Qual fuggitivo non vorria mostrarmi.
9. "O felici costor!" pareane dire.
10. "Lasciar ti debbo" poi sen gia cantando.

ADDITIONAL EXERCISES IN PRONUNCIATION

A

Acacia, accecare, acciaio, acquaiuolo, aggiungere, ahi, allegro, amicizia, archibugio, artiglieria, bicchiere, biglietto, Boccaccio, Boiardo, bugia, buio, buoi, canzone, Carducci, cascaggini, Castiglione, cavalleria, Cellini, cencio, centottantotto, cerchio, Checchina, chiacchiere, chiaroscuro, Chioggia, cicatrice, ciglio, cinquecento, Civitavecchia, cogliere, coraggio, corridoio, costituzionale, crescendo, cugino, cuocere, dolcezza, doppio, dunque, echeggiare, faccione, fasciare, fazzoletto, fiocchi, fischio, floscio, Fogazzaro, Francesco, fruscìo, fuorchè, gaio, ghiaccio, ghiaia, Ghirlandaio, giaciglio, ginocchio, gioia, Giorgio, Girgenti, giudizio, grigio, guai, guerra, Guido Guinizelli, hai, hanno, ho, ignobile, incognito, inginocchiatoio, inscioglibile, iridescenza, Italia, laggiù, larghezza, lenzuolo, letteratura, liscio, luccichìo, Machiavelli, menzogna, merciaio, Michelangelo Buonarroti, minchioneria, negozio, Niccolò, noialtri, occhiacci, oceano, orecchio, ossia, Pagliacci, Palermo, pazienza, Petrarca, piazza, pieghevolezza, Pintoricchio, Poliziano, Pollaiuolo, Pozzuoli, può, quacquero, quaggiù, quegli, ricchezza, richiamiamo, risuscitare, ruota, Sacchetti, sbercio, scegliere, schermisce, scherzo, schiamazzo, sciagurato, sciogliere, sciupacchiare, scricchiolìo, sdraiato, sdrucciolo, Sforza, sgherro, Sicilia, singhiozzo, slanciano, squarciagola, stizzisce, sudicio, tazza, treccia, tribù, uggia, uguale, uovo, usciamo, vecchio, viaggio,

B

Un mio amico raccontava una scena curiosa alla quale era stato presente in casa di un giudice di pace in Milano, molti anni fa. Lo aveva trovato tra due litiganti, uno dei quali perorava caldamente la sua causa; e quando costui ebbe finito, il giudice gli disse: "Avete ragione."

"Ma, signor giudice," disse subito l' altro, "lei mi deve sentire anche me, prima di decidere."

"È troppo giusto,"[1] rispose il giudice, "dite pur su,[2] che v' ascolto attentamente."

Allora quello si mise con tanto più impegno a far valere la sua causa, e ci riuscì così bene che il giudice gli disse: "Avete ragione anche voi."

C' era lì accanto[3] un suo bambino di sette o otto anni, il quale, giocando pian piano con non so qual balocco, non aveva lasciato di stare anche attento alla discussione, e a quel punto, alzando un visino stupefatto, esclamò: "Ma babbo, non può essere che abbiano ragione tutt' e due."

"Hai ragione anche tu," gli disse il giudice.

MANZONI.

[1] *È troppo giusto*, 'That's only fair.'
[2] *dite pur su*, 'go ahead.'
[3] *accanto*, 'in the room with them.'

C

Che sia il Pincio nell' ora che sul ponente color d'arancio si dipinge la gigantesca ombra di San Pietro e del Vaticano, non c' è lingua che possa dire. È un incanto, un' estasi, un sogno, è un confuso viavai d' immensi pensieri, è un tumulto di memorie grandiose e di speranze arcane, in cui la mente si perde, come in un mare senza confini. Guardando il Gianicolo e Monte Mario, che stanno in faccia, par di vedere nel fondo dell' angusta vallata passar silenziosi i secoli fra le nebbie della sera, e un brivido corre per le ossa, come se da quel fondo si rizzassero taciturni e cupi gli spettri dei grandi, che resero temuta e sacra alle genti questa terra fatale. Questo piccolo spazio, che lo sguardo abbraccia senza fatica, è il punto più storico di tutto il mondo. Tutta la civiltà antica s' è condensata fra questi colli, e di qui, risalendo il Tevere, s' è distesa a conquistar la maggior parte della terra conosciuta. Di qui mossero gli eserciti invasori, qui ne furono celebrati i trionfi, di qui si propagarono le leggi e la lingua che fecero di gran parte dello sterminato impero un popolo solo. Quando poi i vinti si ribellarono, la non vinta regina soggiogò colle speranze di un' altra vita tutti coloro che ricusavano il suo dominio in questa; e in nome di Cristo risollevò l' impero caduto. Poichè le furono strappate di mano le armi, regnò disarmata: ricuperò con un altro vessillo la corona perduta, nè fu meno grande e potente di prima. E l' emblema di questa storia, nodo dei tempi anteriori e dei successivi, è là sotto gli occhi: un obelisco egiziano, portato in Roma dagl' imperatori romani e sormontato dalla croce, compendia la storia di tutta la civiltà.

GABELLI.

NOTE ON READING ITALIAN VERSE

In reading Italian verse the verbal stress is the same as in prose. There is no such artificial shifting of the stress as in Latin scansion.

Two adjacent vowels in the same word are usually to be pronounced as belonging to the same syllable, the voice gliding quickly from the first vowel to the second. They are however to be pronounced as belonging to separate syllables (1) when the first is *a*, *e*, or *o* and the second is stressed; (2) when the first of the two vowels is the last stressed vowel of the line; (3) in some other cases (there is one instance in Exercise E, line 4: *trionfale*).

Two vowels standing one at the end of a word and the other at the beginning of the next word and not separated by a mark of punctuation are usually to be pronounced, also, as belonging to the same syllable. (There are no exceptions in these exercises. Exceptions occur when the first of the two vowels is stressed or is immediately preceded by a stressed vowel, and in some other cases.) If the two vowels are different, the voice glides quickly from the first to the second; if they are identical, they are pronounced as a single long vowel.

Two adjacent vowels separated by a mark of pronunciation are to be pronounced as belonging to separate syllables; though as a matter of technical versification they are arbitrarily reckoned as belonging to the same syllable, unless they are of one of the types referred to as exceptional.

D

Lungo la strada vedi su la siepe
ridere a mazzi le vermiglie bacche:
nei campi arati tornano al presepe
tarde le vacche.

Vien per la strada un povero che il lento
passo tra foglie stridule trascina:
nei campi intuona una fanciulla al vento:
Fiore di spina! . . .

PASCOLI.

Line 1. *su la:* the prepositions which normally contract with a following definite article are in verse often uncontracted.

4. *tarde* is a predicate adjective used with adverbial force: 'slowly.' *intuona.*

8. *Fiore di spina:* these are the first words of a peasant song.

E

Lievi e bianche a la plaga occidentale
Van le nubi: a le vie ride e su 'l foro
Umido il cielo, ed a l' uman lavoro
Saluta il sol, benigno, trionfale.

Leva in roseo fulgor la cattedrale
Le mille guglie bianche e i santi d' oro,
Osannando irraggiata: intorno, il coro
Bruno de' falchi agita i gridi e l' ale.

Tal, poi ch' amor co 'l dolce riso via
Rase le nubi che gravarmi tanto,
Si rileva nel sol l' anima mia,

> E molteplice a lei sorride il santo
> Ideal de la vita: è un' armonia
> Ogni pensiero, ed ogni senso un canto.
>
> CARDUCCI.

Line 2. *'l* is a form of *il* often used in verse.

10. *Rase* is a past absolute used with the force of a present perfect: 'has swept.' — *gravarmi:* see section **68** (*d*).

Sorrento, Campania

Italian–English Vocabulary

This vocabulary contains all Italian words appearing in exercise sections involving translation from the Italian and all words appearing in Exercises B–E on pp. 158–161, with the following exceptions: articles, cardinal and ordinal numerals, possessive and personal pronouns, and words occurring only in the following exercise sections: Ex. 28 sect. 2 Ex. 30 sect. 2, Ex. 31 sect. 1, Ex. 34 sect. 1, Ex. 35 sect. 1, Ex. 36 sect. 1, Ex. 39 sect. 1. The meanings of all words occurring in these sections are given in the portions of the Grammar assigned for the lessons in question. The irregular verb forms occurring in Exercises B–E (except the forms of *avere* and *essere*) are separately entered here.

The position of the secondary stress is indicated only in words in which it falls upon an open e or o.

Nouns ending in o are masculine and those ending in a are feminine, unless indication to the contrary is given.

A

a, to, toward, at, in, on, upon, for, by, of; **a fare,** doing, if one does; **al fare,** on doing, when one does.

abbracciare, to embrace.

abitante, *m.*, inhabitant.

abito, coat.

accadere, to happen.

accanto, — **a,** beside.

accattare, to beg.

accertarsi, to make certain.

accogliere, to welcome.

accorgersi di, to notice.

accusa, accusation.

acqua, water.

addio, good-by.

adesso, now.

affare, *m.*, affair.

affatto, entirely.

afferrare, to seize.

affetto, affection.

Africa, Africa.

aggiungere, to add.

agitare, to agitate, wave.

ah, ah; **ah sì?,** is that so?

ahi, ah.

aiutare, to help.

aiuto, help.

ala, wing.

albero, tree.

alcuno, some; *pron.*, anyone.

alloggiare, to lodge.

allora, then; **da — in poi,** thereafter.

almeno, at least.

alto, high, tall; **in —,** high up.

altrimenti, otherwise.

altro, other; **l' uno e l' —,** both.

alzare, to raise; **alzato,** up.

amare, to love, be fond of.

America, America.

amicizia, friendship.

amico, friend.

ammalarsi, to fall sick.

ammirazione, *f.*, admiration.

amore, *m.*, love.

anche, also, too, even, at the same time.

ancora, still, yet, again, even, more.

andare, to go; **andarsene,** to go off *or* away; **va fatto così,** it must be done so.

anello, ring.

angusto, narrow.

anima, soul.

anno, year; **di due anni,** two years old; **avere due anni,** to be two years old.

anteriore, former.

antico, ancient, old.

anzi, even, rather, on the contrary.

apparire, to appear.

appena, scarcely, as soon as.

applaudire, to applaud.

aprire, aprirsi, to open.

arancio, orange.

arare, to plough.

arcano, secret.

aria, air; **aver l' —,** to seem.

Ariosto, Ariosto.

armi, *f. pl.,* arms.

armonia, harmony.

arrivare, to arrive, get; **— a,** to reach.

ascoltare, to listen, listen to.

aspettare, to wait, wait for, expect.

aspetto, aspect, appearance.

assai, enough, very, considerably, much.

assente, absent.

attentamente, attentively.

attento, attentive, careful.

atto, act, attitude.

attorno, — a, around.

augurare, to wish.

aurora, dawn.

austriaco, Austrian.

automobile, *m.,* automobile.

autore, *m.,* author.

autunno, autumn.

avanti, forward, come in.

avere, to have, possess, hold; **ho da,** I have to, I must. *Other idioms in which* **avere** *appears are registered only under the other words concerned.*

avvenimento, event.

avvenire, to happen; *n. m.,* future.

avvertire, to warn.

avvicinarsi a, to approach.

avviso, warning.

avvocato, lawyer.

azione, *f.,* action.

azzurro, blue.

B

babbo, papa.

bacca, berry.

badare, to notice, take care, pay attention.

balocco, toy.

bambino, child, small boy.

bastare, to be enough, suffice.

battaglia, battle.

battere, to beat, strike.

baule, *m.,* trunk.

bello, beautiful, fair, handsome, pretty, fine.

benchè, although.

bene, well; *n. m.,* good thing, happiness; **far —,** to do good.

benedire, to bless.

benigno, benign.

benissimo, very well.

bere, to drink.

bianco, white.

biasimare, to blame, condemn.

bicchiere, *m.,* glass.

biglietto, ticket, bill.

biliardo, billiards.

biondo, blond, golden.

bisognare, to be necessary.
bisogno, need; **aver — di,** to need.
bocca, mouth.
bottone, *m.*, button.
braccio, arm.
brivido, shudder.
bruciare, to burn.
bruno, brown, dark.
buio, dark; *n.*, darkness.
buono, good.

C

cadere, to fall.
caffè, *m.*, coffee.
calare, to sink, set.
caldamente, warmly, eagerly.
caldo, hot, warm.
cambiare, to change.
camera, room.
caminetto, fireplace.
camino, chimney.
campo, field.
cantare, to sing.
canto (1), song.
canto (2), corner.
capello, hair.
capire, to understand.
capitolare, to capitulate, surrender.
capitolo, chapter.
cappella, chapel.
cappello, hat.
carattere, *m.*, character.
carico, laden.
carne, *f.*, meat.
caro, dear.
carta, paper.
casa, house, home.
cattedrale, *f.*, cathedral.
cattivo, bad.
causa, cause, case.

cedere, to yield.
celebrare, to celebrate.
centesimo, centime.
centinaio, hundred.
centro, centre.
cercare, to seek, search, look for, try.
certo, certain; **per —,** for a certainty.
che, *conj.*, that, because, and, than; **fatto — ebbe,** when he had made; **ecco —,** suddenly; **non —,** to say nothing of; **se non —,** if . . . not, but; **non . . . —,** only; **poi —,** when; **sì — è buono,** it's very good indeed; **o —,** *used without translatable force to introduce a question.*
che, *pron.*, what, what a, who, which, that, when; **— cosa,** what; **ciò —, quello —,** what, that; **un non so — di buono,** something good, a certain goodness.
chi, who, he who, one who, if anyone; **— . . . —,** some . . . others; **di —,** whose.
chiamare, to call; **come si chiama?,** what is the name of?
chiaro, clear, bright.
chiave, *f.*, key.
chiedere, to ask.
chiesa, church.
chiudere, to close, shut.
ci, here, there, in it; *often pleonastic.*
cieco, blind; *n.*, blind man.
cielo, sky, heaven.
ciò, that; **— che,** what, that.
cioè, that is.

città, city.
cittadino, citizen.
civiltà, civilization.
classico, classic.
co 'l, *poetic,* = **col.**
codice, *m.,* manuscript.
cogliere, to gather.
colazione, *f.,* lunch.
colle, *m.,* hill.
colore, *m.,* color; — **d' arancio,** orange-colored.
coloro, those.
colui, he.
combattere, to fight.
come, how, as, like.
cominciare, to begin.
compagnia, company.
compendiare, to sum up.
compiacersi, to take pleasure.
compire, to complete, finish.
complimento, compliment.
comporre, to compose.
comprare, to buy.
con, with, by, in, on, to.
concedere, to concede, grant.
condensare, to condense, concentrate.
condurre, to lead.
confetti, *m. pl.,* candy.
confine, *m.,* limit.
confondere, to confuse.
conoscenza, acquaintance.
conoscere, to know, make the acquaintance of, recognize.
conquistare, to conquer.
consiglio, counsel.
contadino, peasant.
contentare, to content, satisfy.
continuare, to continue.
continuo, continual.
contro, — **di,** against.

conversazione, *f.,* conversation.
coraggio, courage; **da far** —, encouraging.
coro, choir.
corona, crown.
coronare, to crown.
correre, to run, overrun.
corte, *f.,* court.
cortesia, courtesy.
corto, short.
cosa, thing, what; **che** —, what; **ha qualche** — **di buono,** there is something good about it.
così, so, such.
costare, to cost.
costo, cost.
costoro, they.
costui, he.
credere, to believe, think.
crescere, to grow, increase.
cristiano, Christian.
Cristo, Christ.
croce, *f.,* cross.
crudeltà, cruelty.
cucire, to sew; **macchina da** —, sewing-machine.
cugina, cousin.
cugino, cousin.
cui, whom, which, to which, he to whom.
cuore, *m.,* heart.
cupo, gloomy.
cura, care.
curioso, curious.

D

da, from, by, for, with, to, of, as, like, such as to; **da lontano,** in the distance; **da presso,** near; **da mangiare,** something *or* anything to eat.

Dante, *m.*, Dante.

dare, to give, devote; — **del,** to call; **darsi per vinto,** to give in.

datare, to date.

davanti, — **a,** before, in front of.

decidere, to decide.

decisione, *f.*, decision.

denaro, money.

dentro, within, in.

desiderabile, desirable.

desiderare, to desire.

desiderio, desire.

destino, destiny.

destra, right hand, right.

deve, *3rd sing. pres. ind. of* **dovere.**

di, of, about, with, from, by, in, to, than, as; **dare del,** to call; **dire di sì,** to say 'yes'; **al di là di,** beyond; **del pane,** some bread.

diavolo, devil.

dietro, — **a,** behind.

difetto, defect.

difficile, difficult.

difficoltà, difficulty, trouble.

dimenticare, to forget.

dimostrare, to demonstrate, prove.

dipingere, to paint.

dire, to say, tell; — **di sì,** to say 'yes'; **voler —,** to mean.

disarmato, unarmed.

discussione, *f.*, discussion.

disgrazia, misfortune.

dispiacere, to displease; **mi dispiace,** I'm sorry, I don't like.

disse, *3rd sing. past abs. of* **dire.**

distendere, to distend; *refl.*, to reach out.

disteso, *pp. of* **distendere.**

distinguere, to distinguish.

dite, *2d pl. imv. of* **dire.**

dito, finger.

divertire, to divert, amuse.

dividere, to divide.

divino, divine.

dolce, sweet.

dolere, to pain.

domandare, to ask, ask for.

domani, tomorrow.

domenica, Sunday.

dominio, dominion.

donna, woman.

dono, gift.

dopo, after, afterward, since.

dormire, to sleep.

dove, where.

dovere, to owe, be obliged; **devo,** I am to, I have to, I must; **dovrei,** I ought to.

duro, hard.

E

e, and, both; **le due e dieci,** ten minutes past two; **più . . . e più,** the more . . . the more.

ecco, here is, there is; — **che,** suddenly.

ed, and.

egiziano, Egyptian.

eh, eh.

eleggere, to elect.

emblema, *m.*, emblem.

energia, energy.

entrare, to enter, go in, get in, come in.

esagerare, to exaggerate.

esame, *m.*, examination.

esclamare, to exclaim.

esercito, army.

esistere, to exist.

espressione, *f.*, expression, remark.

esprimere, to express.

essere, to be, become; *refl.*, to be.

est, *m.*, east.
estasi, *f.*, ecstasy.
età, age.
Europa, Europe.

F

facchino, porter.
faccia, face; di —, in —, opposite.
facile, easy.
falco, falcon.
falsità, falseness.
falso, false.
fame, *f.*, hunger.
fanciulla, girl.
fanciullo, boy, child.
fantasma, *m.*, phantom.
fare, to do, make, have, let, take,
    say, be, act, serve as; *refl.*, to
    become, get; lascia — a me,
    leave it to me; dolce — niente,
    sweet idleness; sul — di, toward;
    fa, ago. *Other idioms in which*
    fare *appears are registered only*
    under the other words concerned.
fatale, fateful.
fatica, fatigue, difficulty.
fatto, fact.
favore, *m.*, favor.
febbraio, February.
febbre, *f.*, fever.
fecero, *3rd pl. past abs. of* fare.
felice, happy.
ferire, to wound.
fermo, firm, certain.
ferro, iron.
figlio, son.
filare, to spin.
filosofia, philosophy.
finalmente, finally, at last.
finchè, as long as, until; — . . .
    non, until.

fine, *f.*, end.
finestra, window.
fingere, to feign; finto, fictitious.
finire, to finish, end; — coll' an-
    dare, finally to go.
fino a, until.
fiore, *m.*, flower.
fiorino, florin, *an obsolete*
    coin
Firenze, *f.*, Florence.
fiume, *m.*, river.
foglia, leaf.
folto, thick.
fondare, to found.
fondo, depth, trough, hollow, basis.
fontana, fountain.
forestiere, *m.*, foreigner, stranger.
formare, to form.
fornire, to furnish; — di, to give.
foro, forum, market place.
forse, perhaps.
forte, strong.
fortezza, fort.
fortunato, fortunate.
forza, force, strength; con —, hard.
fotografia, photograph.
fra, between, among, amid.
    through.
francese, French.
frasca, bush.
frase, *f.*, sentence.
fratello, brother.
freddo, cold; fare —, to be cold.
fretta, haste.
frutto, fruit.
fuggire, to flee.
fuggitivo, fugitive.
fulgore, *m.*, glow.
fumare, to smoke.
fuoco, fire.
fuorchè, except.

G

galleria, gallery.
garantire, to guarantee.
gente, *f.*, people, nation.
gentile, gentle, polite, kind.
già, already.
giacere, to lie.
giallo, yellow.
Gianicolo, Janiculum.
giardino, garden.
gigantesco, gigantic.
ginocchio, knee.
giocare, to play.
gioia, joy.
giornale, *m.*, journal, newspaper.
giorno, day; **per —,** daily.
giovane, young; *n. m.*, young man.
Giovanni, *m.*, John.
giovine, young.
giovinezza, youth.
girare, to whirl.
gire, *poetical,* to go; **girsene,** to go away.
gita, trip, excursion.
giudicare, to judge.
giudice, *m.*, judge, justice.
giungere, to join, clasp; **— a,** to reach.
giurare, to swear.
giusto, just, fair.
godere, to enjoy.
governare, to govern.
grande, great, large, big; *n. m.*, great man; **fare un — freddo,** to be very cold.
grandioso, grand.
gravare, to weigh down, oppress.
gravemente, gravely, seriously.
grazia, favor; *pl.,* thanks.
grido, cry.
guadagnare, to earn, gain, win.
guanto, glove.
guardare, to look, look at, watch
guglia, pinnacle.

I

idea, idea.
ideale, *m.*, ideal.
ieri, yesterday.
illudere, to deceive.
illustrissimo, excellency.
immenso, immense.
imparare, to learn.
impaziente, impatient.
impedire, to hinder.
impegno, pledge, earnestness.
imperatore, *m.*, emperor.
impero, empire.
importante, important.
impossibile, impossible.
in, in, at, to; **da allora in poi,** thereafter.
incanto, enchantment.
inchino, bow.
incontrare, to meet.
indorare, to gild.
indurre, to induce, lead.
inerzia, inertia.
infatti, in fact.
ingegnere, *m.*, engineer.
Inghilterra, England.
inginocchioni, kneeling.
innalzare, to raise.
insegnare, to teach.
insieme, together.
interessante, interesting.
interesse, *m.*, interest.
intonare, to intone, start singing.
intorno, round about.
introduzione, *f.*, introduction.
inutile, useless.

Major Church of San Giorgia, Venice

Vallombrosa, Tuscany

invasore, *m.*, invader; *adj.*, invading.
invece, instead.
inverno, winter.
invisibile, invisible.
ira, anger.
irraggiato, radiant.
irrequieto, anxious.
Italia, Italy.
italiano, Italian.

L

là, there; al di là di, beyond.
lago, lake.
lagrima, tear.
lasciare, to leave, let, fail; lascia fare a me, leave it to me.
latte, *m.*, milk.
lavorare, to work.
lavoro, labor, work.
legge, *f.*, law.
leggere, to read.
lento, slow, quiet, gentle.
lettera, letter.
levare, to raise, rise.
lezione, *f.*, lesson.
lì, there; di lì a, within.
libertà, liberty, freedom.
libro, book.
licere, *poetical*, to be permitted.
lieto, glad.
lieve, light.
lingua, tongue, language.
lira, lira, an Italian coin.
litigante, *m.*, litigant.
lontano, distant, far; da —, in the distance.
lume, *m.*, light.
lunedì, Monday.

lungo, *adj.*, long.
lungo, *prep.*, along.
luogo, place.

M

ma, but.
macchina, machine.
madre, *f.*, mother.
maggiore, greater.
magico, magic.
mai, never, ever; non . . . —, never.
malato, sick.
malattia, sickness, trouble.
male, badly, ill; *n. m.*, harm, ill; far —, to hurt.
mandare, to send.
mangiare, to eat.
maniera, manner.
manifestare, to manifest.
mano, *f.*, hand.
mare, *m.*, sea.
Maria, Mary.
Mario, *proper name*.
matita, pencil.
mattina, morning.
mazzo, cluster.
medico, doctor.
medioevale, mediaeval.
Mediterraneo, Mediterranean.
meglio, better, best.
mela, apple.
memoria, memory.
menare, to lead, take.
meno, less; le due — dieci, ten minutes of two; non potere a — di non, not to be able to help; i —, the minority.
mente, *f.*, mind; venire in —, to occur.
mentre, while.

meravigliare, to surprise.

mercato, market.

mescolare, to mingle.

mese, *m.,* month.

metà, half.

mettere, to put, set; *refl.,* to begin.

mezzo, half; **in — a,** amid; **fino a —,** until the middle of; **le due e —,** half past two.

mezzogiorno, noon; **dopo —,** P. M.

mica: non . . . —, not.

Michelangelo, Michelangelo.

migliore, better, best.

Milano, *f.,* Milan.

minacciare, to threaten.

minaccioso, threatening.

mise, *3rd sing. past abs. of* **mettere.**

misterioso, mysterious.

moderno, modern.

moglie, *f.,* wife.

molteplice, manifold.

moltissimo, very much, a great deal of.

molto, much, very much; *adv.,* much, very; **far — male,** to hurt badly.

momento, moment.

mondo, world; **non sapere in che — si sia,** not to know where one is, to be completely bewildered.

montare, to mount, go up.

monte, *m.,* mountain, mount.

morire, to die.

mormorio, murmur.

morte, *f.,* death.

mossero, *3rd pl. past abs. of* **muovere.**

mostrare, to show; *refl.,* to appear.

mucchio, pile.

muovere, to move, start.

muro, wall.

N

Napoli, *f.,* Naples.

narrare, to narrate, tell.

nascere, to be born *or* formed.

Natale, *m.,* Christmas.

nazione, *f.,* nation.

ne, thence; **andarsene,** to -go off *or* away.

nè, nor, neither; **non . . . nè . . . nè,** neither . . . nor.

neanche, non . . . —, not even.

nebbia, mist.

necessario, necessary.

negare, to deny, refuse.

nemico, enemy.

nemmeno, non . . . —, not even.

nero, black.

nessuno, no one; **non . . . —,** not anyone.

neve, *f.,* snow.

nido, nest.

niente, non . . . —, nothing, not anything; **dolce far —,** sweet idleness.

no, no, not.

nodo, knot, link.

nome, *m.,* name.

non, not, no; **— . . . che, — . . . se —,** only; **— che,** to say nothing of; **se —,** except; **se — che,** if . . . not, but; **più . . . che —,** more than; **— potere —,** not to be able to avoid *or* fail; **— potere a meno di —,** not to be able to help; **un — so che di buono,** something good, a certain goodness; **— so quale,** some . . . or other.

nondimeno, nevertheless.
nonna, grandmother.
notizia, notice, news.
notte, *f.*, night.
nube, *f.*, cloud.
nulla, non . . . —, nothing.
numero, number.
nuocere, to hurt.
nuovo, new; che c' è di —?, what's the news?

O

o, *conj.*, or, either.
o, *interj.*, O; o che, *used without translatable force to introduce a question.*
obbligare, to oblige.
obelisco, obelisk.
occasione, *f.*, occasion.
occhiali, *m. pl.*, glasses.
occhiata, glance.
occhio, eye.
occidentale, western.
occupare, to occupy.
odio, hatred.
offrire, to offer.
oggi, today.
ogni, every.
oh, oh.
ombra, shadow.
ombrello, umbrella.
onorare, to honor.
onore, *m.*, honor.
opera, work.
operaio, workman.
opinione, *f.*, opinion.
ora, *adv.*, now; or —, just.
ora, *n.*, hour, time.
orfano, orphan.
oro, gold.

osso, bone.
ozioso, idle.

P

pace, *f.*, peace.
padre, *m.*, father.
padrone, *m.*, master.
pagare, to pay.
pagina, page.
palazzo, palace.
pallido, pale.
pane, *m.*, bread.
paniere, *m.*, basket.
parere, to seem, appear.
parlare, to speak.
parola, word.
parte, *f.*, part.
partire, to depart, leave; — di, to leave.
partita, match, game.
passare, to pass.
passo, step.
paterno, of one's parents.
patria, fatherland.
paura, fear.
pausa, pause.
pazienza, patience.
peccato, sin; *interj.*, too bad.
pena, trouble.
penna, pen.
pensare, to think.
pensiero, thought.
pentirsi, to repent.
per, for, through, along, in, on, as, as for; — quanto sia buono, good as it is; stare —, to be about to.
pera, pear.
perchè, why, because, in order that; *n. m.*, reason.
perdere, to lose.

perfettamente, perfectly, exactly.
pericolo, danger.
permettere, to permit, allow.
però, however, though.
perorare, to plead.
persuadere, to persuade, convince.
pesce, *m.*, fish.
pezzo, piece.
piacere, to please; *n. m.*, pleasure, favor; **aver —,** to be glad; **mi piace,** I like.
piangere, to weep, cry, weep for.
piano, smooth, slow; *adv.*, softly, quietly.
picchiare, to knock.
piccolo, little, small.
piede, *m.*, foot; **a piedi,** on foot.
pienamente, fully.
pieno, full.
pietà, pity.
Pietro, Peter.
pigliare, to take, catch.
Pincio, Pincian Hill.
pistola, pistol.
pittore, *m.*, painter.
pittura, painting.
più, more, most, longer, again; **— ...e —,** the more . . . the more; **non . . . —,** not, no, not any; **i —,** the majority.
piuttosto, rather.
plaga, sky.
po', *abbreviated form of* **poco.**
pochissimo, very little.
poco, little, a little.
poesia, poetry, poem.
poeta, *m.*, poet.
poi, then; **da allora in —,** thereafter; **— che,** when.
poichè, after.
polso, pulse.

ponente, *m.*, west.
ponte, *m.*, bridge.
popolo, people.
porre, to put, place, send.
porta, door.
portare, to carry, bring, take, show.
possa, *3rd sing. pres. subj. of* **potere.**
possibile, possible.
posto, place.
potente, powerful.
potere, to be able; **posso,** I can, I may; **non — non,** not to be able to avoid *or* fail; **non — a meno di non,** not to be able to help.
poveretta, poor woman.
poveretto, poor fellow.
povero, poor; *n.*, poor man.
pranzo, dinner.
praticare, to practice, associate.
preferire, to prefer.
preghiera, prayer, entreaty.
premere, to press.
prendere, prendersi, to take.
presentare, to present.
presente, present.
presepe, *m.*, stable.
presso, da —, near.
prestare, to lend.
presto, quickly, soon, early.
pretendere, to expect.
prevedere, to foresee.
prezioso, valuable.
prezzo, price.
prima, first, before; **— di, -— che,** before.
principio, beginning.
profondo, deep, low.
proibire, to forbid.

promettere, to promise.
pronto, ready, quick.
propagare, to spread abroad.
proseguire, to continue.
proteggere, to protect, patronize.
provvidenza, providence.
pubblicare, to publish.
punto, point; *adv.*, at all.
può, *3rd sing. pres. ind. of* **potere.**
purchè, provided that, if only.
pure, yet, just; — **troppo,** unfortunately.

Q

quadro, picture.
qualche, some, a few; **ha — cosa di buono,** there is something good about it.
qualcheduno, someone.
qualcosa, something.
quale, which, what, as; **il —,** who, which; **non so —,** some . . . or other.
qualità, quality.
quando, when.
quanto, how much, as much, as much as, all that, that, as; **per — sia buono,** good as it is.
quarto, quarter.
quasi, almost, as if.
quello, that, that one, the one, the, he; — **che,** what, that.
questo, this, this one.
qui, here; **di —,** hence.

R

raccolta, collection.
raccontare, to narrate, tell, tell about.
radere, to shave, sweep.
ragazza, girl.

ragazzo, boy.
ragione, *f.*, reason; **aver —,** to be right.
rase, *3rd sing. past abs. of* **radere.**
re, *m.*, king.
regalare, to give.
regina, queen.
regnare, to reign.
rendere, to render, give back, make.
resero, *3rd pl. past abs. of* **rendere.**
restare, to stay.
restituire, to give back.
ribellarsi, to rebel.
ribelle, *m.*, rebel.
ricchezza, riches, wealth.
ricco, rich.
ricevere, to receive, get.
richiedere, to ask.
riconoscere, to recognize.
ricuperare, to recover, regain.
ricusare, to refuse, deny.
ridere, to laugh.
rifiutare, to refuse.
rifugiarsi, to take refuge.
riguardare, to look again, regard, concern.
rilevare, to raise again; *refl.*, to rise again.
rimanere, to remain, be left, be.
rimettere, to replace; *refl.*, to gain.
rincrescere, to displease; **mi rincresce,** I'm sorry.
rincrescimento, regret.
ringraziare, to thank.
ripetere, to repeat.
risalire, to go up.
riso, smile.
risollevare, to raise again.
rispettare, to respect.

rispetto, respect.

rispondere, to answer, reply.

rispose, *3rd sing. past abs. of* **rispondere.**

ritardo, delay; **in —,** late.

ritirare, to draw back.

riuscire, to go out again, succeed.

rivedere, to see again.

rizzare, to raise; *refl.*, to rise.

Roma, Rome.

romano, Roman.

romanzo, novel.

rompere, to break.

rosa, rose.

roseo, rosy.

rosso, red.

rotondo, round.

S

sacro, sacred.

salire, to go up.

salotto, parlor.

salutare, — a, to greet.

salute, *f.*, health.

sangue, *m.*, blood.

sano, sane, safe.

santo, holy; saint.

sapere, to know, find out, know how, be able; **far —,** to tell; **non — in che mondo si sia,** not to know where one is, to be completely bewildered; **un non so che di buono,** something good, a certain goodness; **non so quale,** some . . . or other.

scala, stair.

scarpa, shoe.

scena, scene.

scendere, to go down.

sciocco, fool; **da —,** foolishly.

sciogliere, to untie, remove.

sciopero, strike; **fare —,** to strike.

scodella, bowl.

scopa, broom.

scopare, to sweep.

scordarsi di, to forget.

scorso, last.

scrivania, desk.

scrivere, to write.

scuola, school.

scuro, dark.

se, if, whether; **se non,** except; **se non che,** if . . . not, but; **non . . . se non,** only.

secolo, century.

secondo, according to.

sedere, to sit; **seduto,** sitting.

seggiola, chair.

segnare, to mark.

seguente, following.

seguire, to follow.

seguitare, to follow; **— a,** to keep on.

semplice, simple.

sempre, always.

senno, wisdom.

sensazione, *f.*, sensation.

senso, sense.

sentire, to feel, hear, listen, listen to; **sentite,** I say, tell me.

senza, — che, without.

sera, evening.

serva, servant.

servire, to serve.

servitore, *m.*, servant.

sete, *f.*, thirst; **aver —,** to be thirsty.

settimana, week.

severo, severe.

sforzo, effort.

sguardo, glance.

sì, yes, so; **ah sì?**, is that so?; **sì che è buono**, it's very good indeed.

siepe, *f.*, hedge.

signora, lady.

signore, *m.*, lord, gentleman, master, Mr.

silenzioso, silent, still.

simile, similar, like, such.

simpatico, sympathetic, agreeable.

sincero, sincere.

Sistina, Sistine.

so, *1st sing. pres. ind. of* sapere.

società, society.

soffrire, to suffer.

soggiogare, to subjugate.

soglia, threshold.

soglio, throne.

sogno, dream.

soldato, soldier.

soldo, penny, cent.

sole, *m.*, sun, sunlight.

solere, to be wont.

solo, alone, single, only.

soltanto, only.

sorella, sister.

sormontare, to surmount.

Sorrento, Sorrento.

sorridere, to smile.

sospettare, to suspect.

sotto, beneath.

spagnolo, Spanish; *n.*, Spaniard.

spaventare, to frighten.

spazio, space.

spedale, *m.*, hospital.

spedire, to send.

speranza, hope.

sperare, to hope.

spesso, often.

spettro, spectre, ghost.

spiegare, to explain.

spina, thorn.

spirito, spirit.

sposa, wife.

sposo, bridegroom; *adj.*, engaged

stamane, this morning.

stanno, *3rd pl. pres. ind. of* **stare**

stanotte, last night.

stanza, room.

stare, to stand, be, stay, sit; — **per**, to be about to.

stasera, this evening.

stato, state.

stazione, *f.*, station.

sterminato, boundless.

stesso, same, self.

stoffa, stuff, goods.

storia, history, story.

storico, historic, historical.

strada, street, road.

strano, strange.

strappare, to snatch, tear.

stretto, narrow.

stridulo, harsh, rustling.

stringere, to bind, press.

studente, *m.*, student.

studiare, to study.

studio, study.

stupefatto, astonished.

stupendo, fine.

su, up, on, upon.

subito, at once; — **che**, as soon as.

succedere, to succeed, follow, happen; **succedersi**, *n. m.*, succession.

successivo, succeeding.

suono, sound.

superiore, superior.

T

tacere, to be silent *or* still.

taciturno, taciturn, silent.

tale, such, so.

tanto, so much, as, so; — **più,** all the more.

tardi, late.

tardo, slow.

tasca, pocket.

tavola, table.

teatro, theatre.

tedesco, German.

telefonare, to telephone.

tema, *m.,* theme.

temere, to fear, be afraid.

tempo, time, weather; **tanto —,** so long.

tenere, to hold; — **per fermo,** to be certain; — **vivo,** to keep up.

terra, earth, ground, land, world.

terribile, terrible.

terrore, *m.,* terror.

tesoro, treasure.

testa, head.

Tevere, *m.,* Tiber.

tingere, to tinge, stain.

toccare, to touch, feel.

togliere, to take; — **a,** to take from.

tono, tone.

tornare, to return, go back, come back; **tornarsene,** to come home.

torre, *f.,* tower.

torto, wrong; **aver —,** to be wrong.

totale, total.

tra, between, through.

tranquillamente, calmly.

trarre, to draw, bring, take.

trascinare, to drag.

trattare, to treat.

tremare, to tremble.

treno, train.

trionfale, triumphal

trionfo, triumph.

triste, sad.

troppo, too, too much, very; **pur —,** unfortunately.

trovare, to find.

tumulto, tumult.

tutto, all, everything; — **il,** the whole; **tutti e due,** both.

U

ubbidire, to obey.

uccello, bird.

udire, to hear.

ultimo, last, latest.

umano, human, of man, kindly.

umido, wet.

unire, to unite.

unità, unity, union.

università, university.

uno, one, some, someone; **l' — e l' altro,** both.

uomo, man.

uscio, doorway, door.

uscire, to go out; — **di,** to leave.

utile, useful, good.

V

vacanza, vacation.

vacca, cow.

vagone, *m.,* car.

valere, to be worth; **far —,** to prove.

valigia, valise, bag.

vallata, valley.

van, *3rd pl. pres. ind. of* **andare.**

vaticano, Vatican.

vecchia, old woman.

vecchio, old; *n.,* old man.

vedere, to see; **far —,** to show.

vendere, to sell.

venerdì, Friday.

Venezia, Venice.

venire, to come, be; — **in mente,** to occur.

ventina: **una — di,** twenty or so.

vento, wind.

verde, green.

vermiglio, vermilion, red.

vero, true; **non è —?,** *a request for assent, to be translated, according to the context, as* am I not?, was he not? *etc.*

verso, toward.

vessillo, banner.

vestito, dress.

vi, there, to it, in it.

via, way, street; *adv.,* away.

viaggio, journey.

viavai, *m.,* coming and going, surging.

vien, *3rd sing. pres. ind. of* **veníre.**

villa, villa.

villaggio, village.

vincere, to win, vanquish, conquer, overcome; **darsi per vinto,** to give in.

vino, wine.

vinto, *pp. of* **vincere.**

virtù, *f.,* virtue.

visino, little face.

visita, visit.

visitare, to visit.

viso, face.

vista, sight, view.

vita, life.

vivere, to live.

vivo, alive, keen; **tener —,** to keep up.

vizio, vice.

voce, *f.,* voice.

volere, to will, be willing, wish, want, like, intend, decide, grant, think; — **dire,** to mean; **ci vuole,** it takes; **cosa vuole?,** never mind.

volta, time; **una —,** once, once upon a time; **un' altra —,** again.

volume, *m.,* volume.

voto, vote.

Z

zio, uncle.

zitto, silent.

English–Italian Vocabulary

This vocabulary contains all English words appearing in exercise sections involving translation into Italian, except articles, cardinal and ordinal numerals, and possessive and personal pronouns.

Italian nouns ending in o are masculine and those ending in a are feminine, unless indication to the contrary is given.

Irregular Italian verbs are marked with a star.

A

able: be —, potere.*

about, (= *approximately*) circa; (= *around*) intorno a; **— it,** ne; **be — to,** stare * per.

according to, secondo.

ache, dolere.*

affection, affetto.

afraid: be —, temere.

after, dopo; **day — tomorrow,** doman l' altro.

again, ancora.

against, contro; (*before a disjunctive pronoun*) contro di.

agent, fattore, *m.*

agreeable, simpatico.

all, tutto; **not . . . at —,** non . . . punto.

allude, alludere.*

almost, quasi.

alone, solo.

already, già.

although, benchè.

always, sempre.

among, fra.

amuse, divertire.

ancient, antico.

and, e; **go —,** andare * a.

another, un altro.

answer, rispondere.*

any, *adj.,* alcuno; **not . . . —,** non . . . nessuno; *pron.,* ne.

anything, qualche cosa; **not . . . —,** non . . . niente.

applaud, applaudire.

apple, mela.

April, aprile, *m.*

arrival, arrivo.

arrive, arrivare.

as, come, tanto, quanto: *see* **32; as soon as,** subito che; **as far as,** fino a.

ascend, salire.*

ashamed: be —, vergognarsi.

ask, (*lesson* **15**) domandare; (*lesson* **32** *and later lessons*) chiedere *; **— for,** chiedere.*

at, a; **at last,** finalmente; **at least,** almeno; **at once,** subito; **at his house,** da lui; **not . . . at all,** non . . . punto; **look at,** guardare.

aunt, zia.

automobile, automobile, *m.*

autumn, autunno.

away, via; **go —,** andarsene.*

B

back, dietro; **come** *or* **go —,** tornare; **give —,** restituire.

bad, cattivo.

bag, valigia.

basket, paniere, *m.*

be, essere *; (of health)* stare *; I am to,* devo.* *Other idioms with* **be** *are registered only under the other words concerned.*

beat, battere.

beautiful, bello.

because, perchè.

before, *adv.,* prima; *conj.,* prima che; *prep., (of time)* prima di; *(of place)* davanti.

beg, pregare.

begin, cominciare.

behind, dietro; *(before a disjunctive pronoun)* dietro a.

believe, credere.

beside, accanto a.

best, *adj.,* migliore; *adv.,* meglio.

betray, tradire.

better, *adj.,* migliore; *adv.,* meglio.

between, tra.

big, grande.

bind, stringere.*

black, nero.

book, libro.

born: be —, nascere.*

both, tutti e due.

bow, inchino.

boy, ragazzo.

brave, coraggioso.

bread, pane, *m.*

break, rompere.*

brick, mattone, *m.*

bring, portare.

broad, largo.

brother, fratello.

build, costruire.*

business, affare, *m.*

but, ma; *(= only)* non . . . che.

button, bottone, *m.*

buy, comprare.

by, da; *(in special cases)* di, per.

C

call, chiamare.

can: I —, posso.*

care, cura; **take —,** badare.

carry, portare.

cent, soldo.

centre, centro.

century, secolo; *see* **39** (*c*).

certain, certo.

cheek, guancia.

child, fanciullo.

choose, scegliere.*

church, chiesa.

city, città.

close, chiudere.*

cloud, nuvola.

coat, abito.

coffee, caffè, *m.*

cold, freddo.

color, colore, *m.*

come, venire*; **— back,** tornare, **— in,** entrare.

comfort, confortare.

company, compagnia.

compel, costringere.*

conduct, condurre.*

conquer, vincere.*

consist, constare.*

content, contento.

continue, continuare.

convince, convincere.*

cook, cuocere.*

corner, canto.

cost, costare.
count, conte, *m.*
country, paese, *m.*
courage, coraggio.
cousin, cugino.
cover, coprire.*
crowd, affollare.
crude, crudo.
cry, piangere.*
custom, costume, *m.*
cut, tagliare.

D

dark, scuro; (*lessons* **25** *and* **33**) buio.
day, giorno; — **after tomorrow,** doman l' altro.
decide, decidere.*
depart, partire.
desire, *n.*, desiderio.
desire, *vb.*, desiderare.
desk, scrivania.
die, morire.*
difficult, difficile.
difficulty, difficoltà.
dinner, pranzo.
disappear, sparire.*
ditch, fossa.
divide, dividere.*
do, fare.* *For* do *as auxiliary, see* **54** (*g*).
doge, doge, *m.*, *duke of Venice.*
door, porta.
doubt, dubbio.
down, giù; sit —, sedere.*
drag, trarre.*
draw, trarre.*
dress, vestito.
drink, bere.*
duke, duca, *m.*

E

each, *adj.*, ogni; *pron.*, ognuno; — other: *see* **47**, 2 *and* **51** (*f*).
early, presto.
earn, guadagnare.
easy, facile.
eat, mangiare.
egg, uovo.
either, o.
Emmanuel, Emanuele, *m.*
employee, impiegato.
end, finire.
enemy, nemico.
English, inglese.
enjoy, godere.
enough, abbastanza; **be** —, bastare.
enter, entrare.
entreaty, preghiera.
escape, scappare.
Europe, Europa.
even, ancora; **not** . . . —, non . . . nemmeno.
evening, sera; this —, stasera.
ever, sempre.
every, ogni.
everything, tutto.
examination, esame, *m.*
exclamation, esclamazione, *f.*
exist, esistere.*
explain, spiegare.
express, esprimere.*
extinguish, spegnere.*
eye, occhio.

F

face, faccia.
fall, cadere.*
far, lontano; as — as, fino a.
father, padre, *m.*

Florence

Portofino

fatherland, patria.
fault, colpa.
favor, favore, *m.*
fear, temere.
feel, sentire.
few, a —, pochi.
fight, combattere.
finally, finalmente.
find, trovare.
fine, bello.
finger, dito.
finish, finire.
first, *adv.*, prima.
flee, fuggire.
Florence, Firenze, *f.*
flower, fiore, *m.*
follow, seguire.*
foot, piede, *m.*
for, per; — two years, due anni,
  da due anni: *see* 79 (*e*); ask —,
  chiedere *; look —, cercare;
  wait —, aspettare.
foreigner, forestiere, *m.*
France, Francia.
French, francese.
friend, amico.
from, da; (*in special cases*) di.
fry, friggere.*
full, pieno.

G

gallery, galleria.
garden, giardino.
gather, cogliere.*
gentleman, signore, *m.*
get, ricevere.
girl, ragazza.
give, dare *; — back, restituire.
glasses, occhiali, *m. pl.*
glove, guanto.
go, andare *; go away, andar-

sene *; go back, tornare; go
  in, entrare; go out, uscire *;
  go up, salire.*
good, buono.
goods, stoffa.
government, governo.
gratitude, gratitudine, *f.*
great, grande.
greet, salutare.
grieve, dolere.*
ground, terra.
grow, crescere.*
guarantee, garantire.
guard, guardia.

H

habit, abitudine, *f.*
half, *n.*, metà; *adj.*, mezzo; —
  past two, le due e mezzo.
hand, mano, *f.*; right —, destra.
handkerchief, fazzoletto.
handsome, bello.
happen, succedere.*
happy, felice.
hard, *adv.*, forte.
harm, nuocere.*
hat, cappello.
have, avere *; (*causative*) fare *;
  (*expressing obligation*) dovere.*
  For have *as auxiliary, see* 54, 3.
head, testa.
health, salute, *f.*
hear, sentire; (*lesson* 38) udire.*
help, aiutare; not to be able to —,
  non potere * a meno di non.
here, qui, ci: *see* 84; — is, ecco.
hide, nascondere.*
high, alto.
hill, colle, *m.*
hold, tenere.*
home, casa.

honor, onore, *m.*
hope, sperare.
hotel, albergo.
hour, ora.
house, casa; **at his —,** da lui.
how, come; **— much,** quanto.

I

idea, idea.
if, se.
impossible, impossibile.
in, in; (*with the name of a city*) a; (= *within*) fra; (*in special cases*) di; **come** *or* **go in,** entráre; **in order that,** perchè; **in this way,** così.
industrious, industrioso.
instead, invece.
interesting, interessante.
into, in; (*in special cases*) a.
invade, invadere.*
Italian, italiano.
Italy, Italia.

J

John, Giovanni, *m.*
June, giugno.

K

keep, tenere *; **— still,** tacere.*
key, chiave, *f.*
kill, uccidere.*
king, re, *m.*
knock, picchiare.
know, sapere *; (= *be acquainted with*) conoscere.*

L

lady, signora.
lake, lago.
large, grande.

last, ultimo; **at —,** finalmente; **— night,** stanotte; **— year,** l' anno scorso.
late, in ritardo.
latest, ultimo.
laugh, ridere.*
lawyer, avvocato.
lead, menare.
leaf, foglia.
least: at —, almeno.
leave, (*intransitive*) partire; (*transitive*) lasciare.
lend, prestare.
lesson, lezione, *f.*
let, lasciare. *For* **let** *as auxiliary, see the note on p. 115.*
letter, lettera.
library, biblioteca.
lie, giacere.*
life, vita.
light, *n.,* lume, *m.*
light, *vb.,* accendere.*
like, *prep.,* come; **— a man,** da uomo.
like, *vb.,* (*with an infinitive*) volere *; **I like it,** mi piace.*
line, linea.
little, piccolo; **a —** (= *some*), un po' di; (= *somewhat*), un po'.
live, vivere.*
long, lungo.
look, — at, guardare; **— for,** cercare.
lose, perdere.
love, amare.
low, profondo.
lunch, colazione, *f.*

M

make, fare.*
man, uomo; **young —,** giovane, *m.*

manner, maniera.
market, mercato.
Mary, Maria.
may: I —, posso.*
Milan, Milano, *f.*
mile, miglio.
minute, minuto; ten minutes past two, le due e dieci; ten minutes of two, le due meno dieci.
mistaken: be —, sbagliarsi.
moment, momento.
monarch, monarca, *m.*
Monday, lunedì.
money, denaro.
month, mese, *m.*
more, più.
morning, mattina; this —, stamane.
most, più.
mother, madre, *f.*
mountain, montagna.
move, muovere.*
Mr., signor.
much, molto; how —, quánto; so —, tanto; too —, trôppo; very —, molto.
must: I —, devo.*

N

name, nome, *m.*
Naples, Napoli, *f.*
near, vicino a.
necessary, necessario; be —, bisognare.
never, mai.
new, nuovo.
newspaper, giornale, *m.*
night, notte, *f.*; last —, stanotte.
no, no; — one, nessuno.
noon, mezzogiorno.

not, non.
novel, romanzo.
now, ora.

O

obliged: be —, dovere.*
o'clock: two —, le due.
of, di; of it, of him, of them, ne; ten minutes of two, le due meno dieci.
off, via; take —, levare.
offer, offrire.*
often, spesso.
old, vecchio.
on, su; (*in special cases*) con.
once, una volta; at —, subito.
one, uno; (*as indefinite subject*) si; no —, nessuno; other —, altro; that —, the —, quello; this —, questo; — who, chi.
only, *adj.*, solo; *adv.*, soltanto.
open, *adj.*, aperto.
open, *vb.*, aprire.*
or, o; ten or so: *see* **40.**
order, *n.*, ordine, *m.*; in — that, perchè.
order, *vb.*, comandare.
other, — one, altro; each —: *see* **47,** 2 *and* **51** (*f*).
ought: I —, dovrei.
out, fuori; go —, uscire *; put —, spegnere.*
outside, di fuori.
owe, dovere.*
own, proprio.

P

pain, dolere.*
pair, paio.

paper, carta.
pardon, perdonare.
parlor, salotto.
past, passato; **half — two,** le due e mezzo.
patience, pazienza.
pay, pagare.
peasant, contadino.
pen, penna.
pencil, matita.
perfectly, perfettamente.
perhaps, forse.
person, persona.
persuade, persuadere.*
photograph, fotografia.
picture, quadro.
place, *n.*, posto.
place, *vb.*, porre.*
please, piacere.*
pleasure, piacere, *m.*
pocket, tasca.
poem, poesia.
polite, gentile.
poor, povero.
pope, papa, *m.*
porter, facchino.
praise, lodare.
prefer, preferire.
present, presentare.
press, premere.
pretty, bello.
prisoner, prigioniero.
probably, probabilmente.
promise, promettere.*
protect, proteggere.*
provided, purchè.
public, pubblico.
push, spingere.*
put, (*lessons* **28** *and* **30**) mettere *; (*lessons* **32** *and* **34**) porre *; **— out,** spegnere.*

Q

queen, regina.
quick, subito.

R

rain, piovere.*
read, leggere.*
ready, pronto.
really, veramente.
recall, ricordare.
receive, ricevere.
recognize, conoscere.*
red, rosso.
remain, rimanere.*
Renaissance, Rinascimento.
repeat, ripetere.
respect, rispettare.
return, tornare.
right, diritto; **— hand,** destra; **be —,** aver * ragione.
rise, sorgere.*
river, fiume, *m.*
Rome, Roma.
room, stanza.
rose, rosa.
round, rotondo.
run, correre.*
Russia, Russia.

S

sacristan, sagrestano.
say, dire.*
scene, scena.
school, scuola.
search, cercare.
seated, seduto.
see, vedere.*
seek, cercare.
seem, parere.*

self, stesso.
send, mandare.
sentence, frase, *f.*
September, settembre, *m.*
servant, servitore, *m.*
serve, servire.
several, parecchi.
sew, cucire.*
shake, scuotere.*
shoe, scarpa.
shop, bottega.
short, corto.
shoulder, spalla.
show, mostrare.
shut, chiudere.*
sick, malato.
sight, vista.
silent, silenzioso; be —, tacere.*
since, (*causal*) poichè; (*temporal*) dacchè.
sincere, sincero.
sing, cantare.
sir, signore, *m.*
sister, sorella.
sit, — down, sedere.*
site, sito.
sleep, dormire.
small, piccolo.
smile, sorridere.*
smoke, fumo.
snow, *n.*, neve, *f.*
snow, *vb.*, nevicare.
so, così; so much, tanto; I think so, lo credo; ten or so: see 40.
some, alcuno, qualche, ne: see 89.
someone, qualcuno.
something, qualche cosa.
song, canto.
sonnet, sonetto.
soon, presto; as — as, subito che.
speak, parlare.

spend, (*of money*) spendere *; (*of time*) passare.
square, piazza.
stand, stare.*
start, partire.
station, stazione, *f.*
stay, (*lesson 15*) restare; (*lesson 24 and later lessons*) rimanere.*
still, *adj.*, quieto; keep —, tacere.*
still, *adv.*, ancora.
stocking, calza.
street, via.
student, studente, *m.*
study, *n.*, studio.
study, *vb.*, studiare.
such a, un tale.
suffer, soffrire.*
summer, estate, *f.*
sun, sole, *m.*
Sunday, domenica.
sure, sicuro.
surprise, *n.*, sorpresa.
surprise, *vb.*, sorprendere *; be surprised, meravigliarsi.
surrender, rendersi.*
surround, cingere.*
swear, giurare.
sword, spada.
syllable, sillaba.

T

table, tavola.
take, prendere*;   (= *take away*) togliere *; (= *accompany, lead*) menare; — care, badare; — off, levare; it takes, ci vuole.*
talk, parlare.
tall, alto.
telephone, telefonare.
tell, (*lessons 13–17*) raccontare; (*lessons 35–40*) dire.*

than, che, di: *see* **33.**
thank, ringraziare.
that, *conj.,* che; **in order** —, perchè.
that, *pron.,* quello, ciò, che: *see* **42** *and* **44;** — **one,** quello.
theatre, teatro.
then, poi.
there, là, vi, ci: *see* **84;** — **is:** *see note on p. 109.*
thing, cosa.
think, (= *meditate*) pensare; (= *suppose*) credere.
this, questo; — **one,** questo; **in** — **way,** così; — **morning,** stamane; — **evening,** stasera.
though, però.
thousand, migliaio.
through, per.
ticket, biglietto.
time, tempo, volta: *see note on p. 119.*
to, a; (*before the name of a country*) in; (*in special cases*) da, di, per; **according to,** secondo; **be about to,** stare * per. *For* **to** *before an infinitive, see* **79** (*b*); *for* **to** *with an unemphatic personal pronoun, see* **47–50.**
today, oggi.
tomorrow, domani; **day after** —, doman l' altro.
too, — **much,** troppo; **he** —, anche lui.
toward, verso.
tower, torre, *f.*
train, treno.
travel, viaggiare.
tree, albero.
true, vero.
trunk, baule, *m.*

try, cercare.
turn, (*intransitive*) volgersi*; (*transitive*) volgere.*

U

umbrella, ombrello.
under, sotto.
understand, capire.
until, *conj.,* finchè non; *prep.* fino a.
up, su; **up to,** fino a; **go up,** salire.*

V

vase, vaso.
Venice, Venezia.
very, — **much,** molto.
Victor, Vittorio.
view, vista.
villa, villa.
village, villaggio.
visit, visitare.
vote, votare.

W

wait, — **for,** aspettare.
wake, svegliare.
walk, camminare.
wall, muro.
want, volere.*
warm, caldo.
waste, sprecare.
watch, guardare.
water, acqua.
way, via; **in this** —, così.
weather, tempo.
week, settimana.
weep, piangere.*
well, bene.
what, *interj.,* come.

what, *pron.*, quello che, che, che cosa: *see* **42–44.**

when, quando.

where, dove.

wherever, dovunque.

which, che, quale: *see* **43** *and* **44.**

while, mentre.

white, bianco.

who, chi, che: *see* **43** *and* **44; one** —, chi; **whom,** cui.

whole, intero; **the** —, tutto il.

whose, di chi.

why, perchè.

wife, moglie, *f.*

willing: be —, volere.*

wind, vento.

window, finestra.

winter, inverno.

wish, volere.*

with, con.

without, senza; (*before a disjunctive pronoun*) senza di.

woman, donna.

wont: be —, solere.*

wood, bosco.

word, parola.

work, *n.*, lavoro; (*literary work*) opera.

work, *vb.*, lavorare.

worse, peggio.

worth: be —, valere.*

worthy, degno.

write, scrivere.*

writer, scrittore, *m.*

wrong: be —, aver* torto.

Y

year, anno.

yellow, giallo.

yes, sì.

yesterday, ieri.

yet, ancora; (= *nevertheless*) eppure.

yield, cedere.

young, giovane.

The Venice canals

Villa along Lake Como

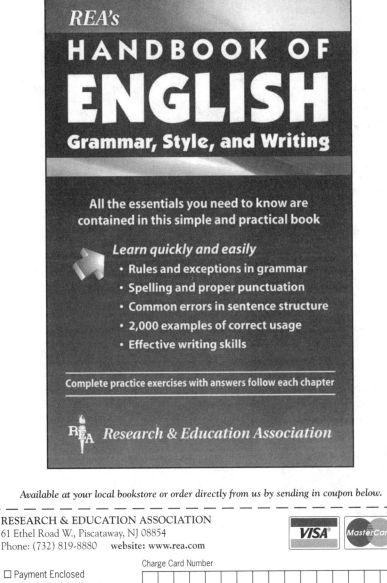

REA's
HANDBOOK OF
ENGLISH
Grammar, Style, and Writing

All the essentials you need to know are contained in this simple and practical book

Learn quickly and easily
- Rules and exceptions in grammar
- Spelling and proper punctuation
- Common errors in sentence structure
- 2,000 examples of correct usage
- Effective writing skills

Complete practice exercises with answers follow each chapter

Research & Education Association

Available at your local bookstore or order directly from us by sending in coupon below.

RESEARCH & EDUCATION ASSOCIATION
61 Ethel Road W., Piscataway, NJ 08854
Phone: (732) 819-8880   website: www.rea.com

VISA **MasterCard**

☐ Payment Enclosed
☐ Visa   ☐ MasterCard

Charge Card Number

Expiration Date: _____ / _____
Mo.   Yr.

Please ship REA's **"Handbook of English"** @ $21.95 plus $4.00 for shipping.

Name _____

Address _____

City _____ State _____ Zip _____

Super Review® Language Books

- ☑ **French**
- ☑ **French Verbs**
- ☑ **Greek** (Classical/Ancient)
- ☑ **Italian**
- ☑ **Japanese for Beginners** (With CD)
- ☑ **Japanese Grammar** (With CD)
- ☑ **Japanese Verbs**
- ☑ **Latin**
- ☑ **Spanish**
- ☑ **Spanish Verbs**

- The material is presented in student-friendly form that makes it easy to follow and understand

- Individual topics can be easily located

- Provide excellent preparation for midterms, finals and in-between quizzes

 Visit our website at: www.rea.com

 **Research & Education Association**
61 Ethel Road West • Piscataway, NJ 08854
Phone: (732) 819-8880 • FAX: (732) 819-8808